How Race Is Made

how
race
is
made

SLAVERY,
SEGREGATION,
AND THE
SENSES
MARK M. SMITH

made

THE UNIVERSITY OF NORTH CAROLINA PRESS Chapel Hill

Set in Quadraat type by Keystone Typesetting Inc.
Manufactured in the United States of America

This book was published with the assistance of the
Fred W. Morrison Fund for Southern Studies of the
University of North Carolina Press.

The paper in this book meets the guidelines for permanence
and durability of the Committee on Production Guidelines for
Book Longevity of the Council on Library Resources.

Library of Congress Cataloging-in-Publication Data
Smith, Mark M. (Mark Michael), 1968–
How race is made : slavery, segregation, and the senses / by
Mark M. Smith.
    p. cm.
Includes bibliographical references and index.
ISBN-13: 978-0-8078-3002-4 (cloth : alk. paper)
ISBN-10: 0-8078-3002-X (cloth : alk. paper)
1. Racism—Southern States—History. 2. Southern States—
Race relations—History. 3. African Americans—Segregation.
4. African Americans—History—1877–1964. 5. Senses and
sensation—Southern States—History. 6. Stereotype
(Psychology)—Southern States—History. I. Title.
E185.61.S648 2006
305.896′073075—dc22   2005022833

10 09 08 07 06   5 4 3 2 1

For

Tony Kushner,

Eugene Genovese,

Robert Weir, and

Bennett Smith

CONTENTS

Introduction: Making Sense of Race 1

1 Learning to Make Sense 11

2 Fooling Senses, Calming Crisis 29

3 Senses Reconstructed, Nonsense Redeemed 48

4 Finding Homer Plessy, Fixing Race 66

5 The Black Mind of the South 96

6 The *Brown* Concertina 115

Notes 141

Acknowledgments 191

Index 195

ILLUSTRATIONS

2.1. "Stowage of the British Slave Ship 'Brookes'" 31

2.2. "Gordon" the slave 45

5.1. Two young "black" men in South Carolina in 1957 105

6.1. "The Negro, The Ape" 129

6.2. "The Kiss of Death" 133

6.3. "Youth Movements" 134

Introduction
Making Sense of Race

Several years ago I had a chance conversation in a loud church hall at a small wedding on one of those implausibly hot southern summer evenings. I had not been there long when I bumped into Frank. Frank knows my wife from high school, and we see him occasionally when mutual friends marry or get engaged. Slim, white, and tall, he patted me on the back and asked how I was doing. Frank is in his thirties, smart, southern, with a robust sense of humor. I like him. He asked about my "new book." I smiled, suspecting I was about to learn something. My wife's friends are a constant source of information about the South, always willing to share stories, ribald and refined, with her strange husband—an Englishman who studies southern history, no less.

I told him that I was working on an ambitious history of slavery and segregation. I did not elaborate, said nothing about my work on senses and race, on how southern whites and blacks thought they saw, heard, smelled, touched, and tasted one another.

"I've a story for you," Frank offered. He lingered. "Now it isn't polite."

I stepped in closer, listening hard, trying to parry the noise of the wedding band. Frank always had good stories.

"My grandmother, real southern," he said, accent thick with Carolina purl. I nodded.

"Well, one day, years ago, probably in the twenties, she left her house on some errands. She returned, walked in, and discovered her house had been broken into." He paused.

"Know what she said?" He knew how to tell a story—as I said, a southerner. I shook my head.

"I smell nigger."

The historical record confirmed what I had just heard above the hubbub: white southerners believed they did not need their eyes alone to authenticate racial identity, presumed inferiority, and, in this instance, criminality. By this point in my research I had read enough letters, journals, and newspaper accounts to know that what Frank had just told me, while rarely uttered in polite company in modern America, was common fare in the antebellum and segregated South (and, for that matter, the North of the same eras). Whites' noses and ears, their senses generally, could be used to detect blackness—or so they claimed.

There was not a great deal of logic to this claim. In fact, that was the point of sensing race: nonvisual senses often indexed viscera and emotion more than thought and reason. As Havelock Ellis argued in his controversial *Studies in the Psychology of Sex* (1903): "Personal odors do not, as vision does, give us information that is very largely intellectual." Rather, "they make an appeal that is mainly of an intimate, emotional, imaginative character."[1] The association between the senses and emotion, between race-thinking and gut-feeling, was, in many ways, a central theme of southern history. It is also an analytical centerpiece of this book.

LOSING SIGHT, FINDING RACE

Modern discussions of "race" and racial identity are hostage to the eye. With few exceptions, popular writing as well as many academic works— even the most theoretically sophisticated ones—tend to treat race as an exclusively visual phenomenon, so much so that the panacea for modern ills is, by some lights, a color-blind society. Even though we know that "race" is a construct, an invented category that defies scientific verification, we still understand that construction as a largely visual enterprise. "Color" is always seen. But the preference for "seeing" race is as much a social construction as "race" itself. This tendency is so pervasive that many historians seem largely unaware that when they search for "perspective" or try to "focus" on the problems of race and racism in U.S. history, they unnecessarily stunt understanding.[2]

There are certain physiological explanations for our ocularcentrism. After all, we are largely visual creatures, our eyes enabling us to accumulate information rapidly and at distances greater than the reach of our other senses unaided. But it is also worth noting that the way we look, the relative emphasis we place on seeing as opposed, say, to hearing, changes over time and place. While we readily appreciate the importance of the ways we look and are looked at, what we see and choose not to see, there are other ways of understanding, ways that are far more visceral than the cool, rationalizing gaze of an eye always searching for Enlightenment perspective and balance (itself a product of the Age of Reason). We seem to have lost sight of other ways to understand beyond vision and, in the process, have quietly endorsed the long-standing Western tendency to denigrate the nonvisual, "lower" senses.[3]

As a growing literature on the anthropology of the senses suggests, there is no compelling reason for historians to fixate on what was seen rather than heard, smelled, tasted, and touched; nor is there any compelling reason to treat the senses as unchanging "natural" endowments. While some "fundamental characteristics seem to exist, which no amount of cultural mediation can radically alter," it does seem clear that to understand the function of the senses is essentially a historical enterprise.[4]

What if we begin to restore the other senses—hearing, smell, touch, taste—to our understanding of the ideology of "race" and racial identity in southern history? Such a restoration does not amount to a wholesale dismissal of seeing race. Plainly, seeing remains—and always has been— extraordinarily important for locating racial identity. But remembering that race was mediated and articulated in ways in addition to seeing helps profile ordinarily hidden dimensions of racial thought and racism —at base, the belief in "race"—and tells us a good deal about the nature and workings of antebellum southern slavery, the rise of formal segregation in the late-nineteenth-century South, the meaning of the segregationists' reaction to the 1954 Brown v. Board of Education decision, and the nature and significance of African American behavior in the face of white racism. My project is ambitious, certainly, not least because so little work has been done on the subject. Although sensory history has made great strides of late, historians of the senses have been surprisingly quiet on the topic of race. Sustained scholarly treatments of the sensory aspects of race and racism do not exist, and so any initial effort to chart the topic is necessarily speculative and skeletal.[5]

Taking seriously the sensory history of race and racism helps us appreciate just how unthinkingly race is made, how racism is learned, and how the ideology of race and racism have arisen historically. Limited to just seeing race, we expect people to behave rationally, coolly, in a calculating, stable manner. After all, Enlightenment eyes tend to strive for focus, balance, perspective, considered insight. Without denying the emotional content of particular sights, a wide range of research suggests that some of the other senses in particular historical contexts and circumstances appeal more to the gut than to the mind. Once we begin to understand that people sensed their worlds—heard sounds they did not want to hear (we are without ear lids, after all), had to smell smells they did not want to smell, used the putatively premodern, proximate, nonvisual senses to invent "modern" racial stereotypes—we begin to understand the historically conditioned, visceral, emotional aspect of racial construction and racism.[6]

I offer this book, then, as an exploratory essay. The research is here, and I do aim to persuade, of course, but in addition I want to stimulate thinking not just about the way "race" is understood but also about the role of the senses in structuring historical meaning.

POINTS OF SENSING; THE PLAN OF THE WORK

At its simplest, this is a broad, two-hundred-year story about how many southern whites manufactured sensory stereotypes about black people and how black people in turn challenged those assumptions. The book begins in the late eighteenth century and ends in the late 1950s. A central argument is that the sensory construction of race held important benefits for whites. Not only did the invention and subsequent application of the stereotypes help justify slavery and segregation, but the senses also allowed white southerners not to have to think about race. I do not deny that there was a vibrant life of the mind in the South at any point in time. There is simply too much work to suggest otherwise. But I do agree with W. J. Cash's famous if now unfashionable 1941 estimation that when it came to race, white southerners demonstrated "an inclination to act from feeling rather than from thought." I argue that the senses facilitated the rule of feeling and made men and women unthinkingly comfortable with their racial worlds. Sensory stereotypes about black people shellacked the white southern mind, holding reason hostage. The sensory underpinnings of slavery and especially of segregation took on a visceral quality that relieved most white southerners of the discomfort of thinking, levied no tax on the mind, and allowed white conceits about blackness to go unchecked.[7]

Sensing race proved handy for other reasons. White southerners (northerners too) used more than just sight to validate, betray, and affirm racial identity. The need to sense race beyond vision began in the colonial period when a racially mixed population increased to the point where sight alone could not always reliably authenticate race. As a result, slaveholders, with pseudoscientific backing from Europe and the North, began toying with other ways to supposedly detect racial identity—by smelling, touching, listening, and tasting, as well as by looking.

By the antebellum period, the idea that there were nonvisual sensory markers of racial identity was de rigueur. The way slaveholders sensed their black slaves was deeply implicated in their paternalist ethos. Yes, slaveholders said, blacks smell, sound, look, feel, even taste different (and often inferior), but we live with them and work with them and love them regardless. The slaveholders also cast blackness in sensory terms both to justify and to explain exploitation. As everyone knew, slaves had very thick but supple skin, well suited to picking cotton. The very labor to which slaves were consigned and the rationing of sensate niceties— good food, refined music, delicate clothes—served to create and then reaffirm stereotypes. Slaveholders invented and then acknowledged the sensory difference of blacks and based a part of their paternal largesse on the indulgence of that difference. Slavery was never really about physical segregation because the paternalist web linking master and slave mandated close, often intimate association that required each group to see, hear, smell, touch, and taste the other on a daily basis. Love and hate regulated southern slavery, and at the center of that perverse intersection stood an intimate, uneven, sensory exchange between the races.

Sensory racial stereotypes served another important function in the antebellum period. Several historians have argued that, beginning principally in the 1850s, racial identity—and, hence, race-based slavery—was becoming increasingly problematic for southern slaveholders. A rapidly increasing mixed-race population (courtesy of the slaveholders themselves) produced slaves who looked white, thus muddying the logic of racial slavery to such an extent that southern slaveholding society, so the argument goes, edged toward crisis precisely because racial identity could no longer be verified. There is a good deal of nonsense in this argument—matters to which I shall later return—but for now it is worth wondering why the belief in "race" proved so enduring if the idea of "race" was so unstable? The reason that some historians believe in the increasing instability of race in the 1850s is because they *view* race, literally. Certainly, over time it became more difficult to ascertain "true" racial identity by the eye alone, as some slaves became whiter in the late antebellum period. But once we grant that southern whites believed they could detect racial identity using senses in addition to the eye, it becomes clear that the so-called racial crisis of the antebellum period was, from the slaveholders' perspective, no such thing.

With the end of the peculiar institution in 1865, the old arguments about sensory otherness took on deeper, more visceral meaning. The intellectual components and iterations of the proslavery defense were barely detectable in the postbellum segregationist screed that relied on gut and feeling and raw emotion, not the mind, to make its case. No longer required, as they saw it, to "support" blacks, southern whites strove to separate the races, their paternalism evaporating with the end of the Civil War and their way of life. The late nineteenth century saw the legal consolidation of this desire to establish separate spaces for black and white, and even in the driest legal document we find senses playing pivotal roles in segregating streetcars, restaurants, theaters, and all manner of public accommodations well into the twentieth century.

Intellectual hiccupping and contradictions abounded, at once animating southern society and forcing awkward, perverse compromises. Whites maintained close ties with blacks throughout the twentieth century in the segregated South. Even as segregationists claimed black difference and sensory offensiveness, even as they publicly reviled black scent, mocked the sound (more often, noise) of blackness, and proclaimed the terrible dangers of coming into contact with black skin, they also experienced blackness with rude appetite and appalling eagerness. White tongues tasted food prepared by black hands; white noses smelled black maids who washed white clothes and tidied white houses; white bodies inhaled, touched, and tasted black wet nurses; whites reveled in the beauty of black singing; and, clandestinely, white men experienced the intimacy of black women while publicly proclaiming the utter necessity of protecting white womanhood from the touch and taste of black men. The sensory justifications of segregation, in fact, would have lost legitimacy if there had been a complete separation of the races. After all, blacks labored for whites and of necessity engaged in sensory exchange. It was only through day-to-day familiarity with the sensory dimensions of blackness, as whites invented and styled them, that they could maintain the fiction of sensory inferiority. The reality of segregation was far more complicated and contingent than its rhetoric. Whites often suspended rules simply because the effective functioning of southern society mandated such suspension: black hands, for example, had to cook white food. Rules were also suspended because the suspension itself, far from challenging the core of the segregated social order, worked to augment white authority. Whites were sufficiently powerful to suspend their own protocols, powerful enough to ignore their own hypocrisy, strong enough to offer occasional reminders of who was who. Sometimes relaxed, sometimes taut, rules were rules less because of their consistency and more because of the race of their authors.

But there were other, quite pressing reasons to sense race under seg-
regation at century's end. Put simply, many whites worried that black- ness was in danger of becoming whiteness. The number of visually ambiguous "black" people increased (the great age of "passing" was 1880–1925), and sight became ever less reliable as an authenticator of racial identity. Ascertaining racial identity was even more important under segregation than under slavery because race had to be authenti- cated on a daily basis between strangers in a modernizing, geographi- cally fluid South. The basis of segregation, a system that argued for the utter, intrinsic, static, and meaningful difference between black and white, was a product of a late-nineteenth-century, largely Western ques- tioning of vision, in which Western elites generally, southern segrega- tionists included, found they could no longer rely solely on their modern eyes to verify all sorts of truths, racial ones included. Segregationists faced this visual tremor with aplomb. The problems with seeing gave further authority to nonvisual sensory stereotypes, such that smell- ing, tasting, feeling, and hearing race were now more important—and, whites liked to believe, more reliable—than ever. They acknowledged the visual instability of race by increasing their reliance on the one-drop rule, which, if anything, confirmed the argument that race could not, in fact, be seen. And instead of fretting about the invisibility of race, segre- gationists invoked the other senses as authenticators. Becoming visually whiter did not necessarily entail a dilution of the other sensory charac- teristics. Mulattoes, as one observer claimed in 1918, might look white and have "the skin coloration of the white man," but they would retain "the body odor of the Negro." Blackness, whites had to believe, was always vulnerable to sensory detection.[8]

Was there a material basis to the claims made by southern whites? Did black people really have an innate, identifiable scent? While, by their own account, black people smelled distinctive because of diet, the use of particular perfumes and hair products, and their predominance in man- ual, sweaty labor, whites of all classes reconstituted these historically contingent differences as biologically governed or coded blackness as culturally determined, static, and natural. Certainly, matters of class complicated the picture, but white segregationists—and even white lib- erals and some elite blacks—maintained that class dynamics were always secondary to race. The belief that blacks as a group smelled, that they sounded a particular way, that their skin felt different (usually thick and sometimes coarse—that's why they were manual laborers, or "hands"), and that there was much to be feared from touching and tasting blackness—all these sensory constructions muted class distinctions under southern segregation in the first half of the twentieth century. Although southern elites acknowledged that poor southern whites—mill hands and "rednecks"—might well smell different, might well have rougher skin, might well sound inferior, they did not sound, smell, or feel like blacks.[9] Poor and unrefined though they were, their white skin rescued them. Exceptions abounded, of course, and deep loyalties and cherished friendships exempted some blacks from the charge of sensory inferiority. Yet exceptions only proved the rule, and the sensorial dimensions of blackness were prerogatives to be applied and suspended as whites saw fit.

Poor and working-class whites under segregation endorsed the thinking of those higher in social rank because, in reality, their rough skin also rasped, their bodies also smelled, and they too could sound loud and noisy. But by racializing what was in effect a class distinction, lower-class whites elevated themselves. They exalted the manliness and scented nobility of the "sweat of their labor" while telling blacks who performed manual work that their sweat stank. Poor and laboring whites achieved this level of false consciousness on a daily basis because they had every incentive to do so.

This book is hardly unmindful of the African American experience. I examine the ways that black slaves used the senses—materially and ideologically—to thwart slaveholders and I pay attention to blacks' partial and strategic application of sensory stereotypes to other black people. I also make the point that southern black sensory stereotypes of whiteness were far milder and less systematic than those deployed by whites, principally because they did not possess the power to make the stereotypes politically and socially meaningful. For African Americans to argue for an innate sensory dimension to whiteness would be to endorse the logic of their oppressors. Instead, black people challenged segregationist sensory stereotypes in other, more fundamental ways. Among their most powerful arguments was a materialist, common-sensical critique, one that effectively exposed the constructed nature of race while profiling the grinding reality of racism. Yes, they said, we might well smell, but if you did the work we have to do and lived in the conditions we live in, then you would smell too. In this respect, as both slaves and freedpeople, African Americans employed a style and language of critique favored by nineteenth-century materialists and one that white liberals found essential to their campaign against segregation during the Civil Rights Movement.

Understanding the sensory history of race allows us to understand how and why the clumped notions of "black" and "white," of binary notions of racial identity, gained such social currency. Of course, it is historically misleading to speak of the "black experience" or of the "white experience." The gradations and the variety of views and experiences within such a large region over such a long period of time were considerable. Interracial unionism, interracial ties, the activities of white "liberals" in fostering interracialism, class divisions within the black and white communities, instances where gender seemed more important than race—all are topics now at last getting their due from historians.[10] And yet it is important to remember that contemporaries, particularly whites of all classes, racialized the senses in a deliberate effort to impose and maintain the artificial binary between "black" and "white." Whatever the instances of complication, nuance, and subtlety—and there were many—historians still face a South that divided along the fundamental lines of something people called "black" and "white." The senses were central to the creation of that clumsy world even as it was belied by everyday contingencies, compromises, and complications.

This book is also a primer of sorts, a call to think about the many ways in which race has been made. To effectively counter racism, we need to understand, precisely and more fully, the nature, origins, and sources of the creation of racial imagery, how race is made, and the mechanisms by which those images—so damaging and so powerful that they can make unthinking creatures of rational people—are reproduced. One way, as W. E. B. Du Bois argued, is to rewrite those stereotypes. Indeed. But doing so requires an understanding that race is made in ways in addition to vision.[11]

Here, we would do well to ponder Paul Gilroy's work, particularly his *Against Race*, a powerful meditation on the need to renounce race-thinking and venture beyond the color line. Gilroy explores the subtleties of racism, and he is painfully aware of the role played by the senses in helping perpetuate race-thinking, in shaping histories and memories of race and its meaning. His recognition of the importance of the senses urges us to embrace the idea that if we are to really venture beyond race-thinking, we need to understand how race and racism in all their sensory forms are constructed, peddled, and marketed. Without understanding the role of the senses in race-thinking, we will remain doomed to live within the bounds of the color line, a place replete with banal calls for absolute racial identity, chilling forms of extremism, and "raciology's brutal reasonings." What Gilroy says of modern race-thinking, that the "essentialist theories of racial difference that are currently so popular" are best understood "as symptoms of a loss of certainty around 'race,'" is an observation equally applicable to aspects of race-thinking—more properly, "race-feeling"—in southern history. It was no accident that the most vicious sensory stereotypes whites applied to blacks occurred when certainty in the identification of race was evaporating. As Gilroy says, "The human sensorium has had to be educated to the appreciation of racial differences," and to understand the extent of that education, historians need to consider the role of the senses in shaping race and race-thinking.[12] Part and parcel of thinking beyond race entails coming to terms with the historical construction of race in all its forms and in all its senses.

Learning to Make Sense

Englishmen first encountered Africans through their eyes in a context that stressed the reliability of vision to ascertain truth.[1] English travelers saw West Africans before they sensed them in any other way. Robert Baker described first encounters in 1562 and 1563:

> And entering in [a river], we see
>   a number of black soules,
> Whose likelinesse seem'd men to be,
>   but all as blacke as coles.

This point—though not its historical importance—has been made before by historians. "Negroes looked different" to English eyes; the "most arresting characteristic of the newly discovered African was his color," followed closely by dress and other visual markings. That Englishmen saw Africans with their eyes focused on blackness—their vision generating and reflecting cultural associations of blackness with filth, dirt, evil, and degeneracy—was quite natural given the context and the suddenness of contact.[2]

It is impossible to say how quickly other ways of sensing became important. Early sensory stereotypes concerning the smell, sound, and skin of Africans were a product of curiosity and newness and proved remarkably enduring, helping to lay the basis for the making of race in the eighteenth and nineteenth centuries. The construction of sensory inferiority enabled elite whites to depict black slaves as both human and animalistic. The sources for this projection were at once religious, pseudoscientific, and classical, and they were important not just to whites' understandings of racial superiority but also to their surveillance of a restless slave population. Drawing implicitly on Aristotle, who argued that "lower forms" mediated their existence through the rudimentary senses of smell, sound, and touch, colonial and antebellum racists stressed the inferiority of black slaves, who, they maintained, not only emitted distinctive odors and possessed unusual skins but also were hostage to primitive, passionate outbursts. These "inferiors" had a propensity to make noise and react strongly to nonvisual stimuli. According to elite whites, then, not only was blackness sensorily distinctive, but blacks themselves sensed differently, relying more on the putatively lower senses of smell, sound, and touch, and less on the rational, refined, Enlightened perspective of the eye.[3] Indeed, the very forms of slave resistance, which often depended on heightened sensitivity to their surroundings, confirmed in white minds that blacks sensed differently.

COLONIAL STORIES

We have no reliable way of knowing when, exactly, whites first constructed sensory stereotypes that created "black" people. White and black had been mixing in Africa and Europe long before Columbus lucked his way across the Atlantic, and sensory awareness of race probably predated the Columbian encounter with the New World. What we can say with some assuredness, though, is that sensory stereotypes were applied by whites to Africans with growing frequency during the eighteenth century and that the meaning of these stereotypes lingered into the antebellum period, when they were used to anchor slaveholding southern paternalism.[4]

For the most part, eighteenth-century whites liked the way they looked. "Of all the colours by which mankind is diversified, it is easy to perceive, that ours is . . . the most beautiful to the eye," judged Irish novelist, playwright, and poet Oliver Goldsmith in his popular 1774 study, *History of the Earth*. The reasons were both aesthetic and religious: "The fair complexion . . . has a transparent covering to the soul" through which one can see "all the variations of the passions." Not so with darker skin through which soul and passions are not "so visible." Although whiteness was the original color of man, Goldsmith did not argue for innate black characteristics. The "varieties of climate, of nourishment, and custom, are sufficient to produce every change," he ventured, stressing that "we have all sprung from one common parent." But making whiteness the standard necessarily made blackness deformed and degenerative, and it remained unclear if the "condition" was reversible. It would, Goldsmith maintained, take "centuries" to effect the change.[5]

But if blacks looked less appealing than whites, they looked better, too. According to Charles White, English surgeon, member of the Royal Society, author of the 1799 *An Account of the Regular Gradation in Man* (read in "important quarters" in America), while they lacked the visual aesthetic of dress and decency—hence their gaudiness and nakedness—some "Negroes" were blessed with an "acuteness of sight." White marveled at reports of "the extraordinary distance" at which they see "very minute objects." The "optic nerves" were "uncommonly large in the African." A similar duality applied to black sound and aurality. White cited various authorities on "the indolent Hottentots" comparing the "sound of their voices" to indolent "sighing," their language to the "clucking of a turkey." But sounding less than agreeable did not mean poor hearing. Africans could hear horses, "the noise of an enemy," and "a flock of sheep" at great distances. Olfactory stereotypes also had two meanings: that Africans smelled rank did not necessarily mean that their sense of smell was inferior. To White it was "observable that Negroes have wider nostrils than Europeans. . . . They find the subtilty of the sense of smell very useful in their military expeditions; for by it they perceive, at a distance, the smoke of a fire, or the smell of a camp." But Africans were not as sensitive as, say, "dogs," which "possess this sense in the greatest perfection."[6]

If "Negroes" had noses almost as sensitive as those possessed by animals, how they smelled to white nostrils helped anchor black inferiority. Stereotypes concerning black scent percolated so deeply into colonial society that they crop up in even the driest documents. Official speculations on the possible success of silk cultivation in Georgia sent to London in the 1750s, for example, included warming reassurances that "gathering of the Mulberry Leaves, and supplying the Worms with them whilst they are feeding . . . can be done even by a Negro Girl, if she is carefull; For upon Trial, it appears, there is not the least Ground for the Apprehension some People have had, that the Smell from the Negro would be offensive to the Worms." While worms seemed oblivious, whites were not. To J. F. D. Smyth's British nose and ears, the slave South in the 1780s was a place whose flowers "regale[d] the smell with odoriferous perfumes" but where "Negroes" gave off a "rank offensive smell . . . extremely disagreeable and disgustful to Europeans."

The stereotype had wide purchase throughout the colonies and was by no means limited to the South. As one Philadelphia resident with a retinue of black domestic servants wrote in 1769, "The negroes . . . stink damnably."[7]

Not all blacks smelled the same. Charles White considered "The RANK SMELL . . . much stronger in some tribes or nations than others." Sweating, though, was not the cause: "The negroes sweat much less than Europeans," probably "owing to the thickness of their skins." Other observers, such as the Jamaica historian Bryan Edwards, also believed that there were differences within African groups, differences not just in skin tone but also in skin scent. The "Mandingoes," he said, "are in a great degree, exempt from that strong and fetid odor, which exhales from the skin of most" Africans, and Oliver Goldsmith reckoned "those of Mosambique [to] . . . have no ill smell whatsoever." But these were mere variations on a common scale, for to whatever degree African groups were separated from one another, many whites came to believe that Africans per se were a kind unto themselves. For example, the Scottish philosopher Lord Kames argued that Africans generally could be both seen and smelled. "The black colour of Negroes, thick lips, flat nose, crisped woolly hair, and rank smell, distinguish them from every other race of men," he wrote in the 1770s. These traits had little to do with climate or environment because the "Abyssinians[,] . . . their complexion a brown olive, features well proportioned," enjoyed the same climate as those in "Negroland." No, pondered Kames, from the beginning of time, men had been created as different races.[8]

The notion that black smell was innate and not indicative of a lack of hygiene found further credence when black scent was compared to red smell (or, rather, the way whites chose to represent the odors). Naturalist Mark Catesby's 1754 examination of "the Indians of Carolina and Florida" confirmed the racial dimensions of aroma. "They are naturally a very sweet People, their Bodies emitting nothing of that Rankness that is so remarkable in Negres [sic], and as in traveling I have sometimes necessitated to sleep with them, I never perceived any ill Smell" even though "their Cabbins [sic] are never paved nor swept, and kept with the utmost Neglect and Slovenliness." Indeed, Indians' innate sweetness of odor was sufficient to overcome the stench usually produced by unkempt living, so much so that Indians were superior to poor whites in this regard.[9]

In his 1774 History of Jamaica, Edward Long made no bones about the nature of black scent. For him the way blacks smelled was an olfactory confirmation of innate difference and affirmation of the hierarchy in the human species, in which "Negroes" were "a different species of the same GENUS." Climate effected no change in color, maintained Long, a man whose works were read and commented on in both Britain and the United States. Black looks and skin remained unchanged whatever the environment. So did their scent—"their bestial or fetid smell, which they all have in a greater or less degree." The precise cause of the variation or "degree" Long declined to explain, but he was certain that Angolans had the greatest stench while "those of Senegal . . . have the least of this noxious odour." To his credit, whereas most observers felt comfortable merely stating that Africans stank, Long offered extended commentary on the nature and origins of the smell. Long believed that dancing, and physical activity in general, exacerbated black scent; it was "a complica- tion of stinks, [rather] than any one in particular, and so rank and powerful, as totally to overcome those who have any delicacy in the frame of their nostrils." That blacks themselves seemed unaffected by their own scent spoke volumes about their lack of "delicacy," although, of course, such an absence did not mean they could not smell other scents, often at some distance, as Charles White argued. Long also noted that "the Blacks of Afric assign a ridiculous cause for the smell peculiar to the goat," an explanation that involved a story of an angry goddess who presented the goats "with a box of a very fetid mixture, with which they immediately fell to bedaubing themselves. The stench of it was communicated to their posterity; and, to this day, they remain ignorant of the trick put upon them, but value themselves on possessing the genuine perfume; and so are anxious to preserve it undiminished, that they very carefully avoid rain, and every thing that might possibly impair the delicious odour." For Long, blacks were the goats, but he could not take the analogy too far since the African explanation for smell was not innate but contextual, with smell smeared on, not teased out of, the body. Therefore, Long ventured, "this rancid exhalation, for which so many of the Negroes are remarkable, does not seem to proceed from uncleanliness, nor the quality of their diet." It was a necessary argument because, theoretically, clean blacks with different diets could smell sweet. To Long, the reek was innate. Out of "science," Long retreated to anecdote. "I remember a lady, whose waiting-maid, a young Negro girl, had it [the odor] to a very disagreeable excess." Because she was a favorite servant "her mistress took great pains, and the girl herself spared none, to get rid of it. With this view, she constantly bathed her body twice a day, and abstained wholly from salt-fish, and all sorts of rank food. But the attempt was similar to washing the Black-a-moor white; and, after a long course of endeavours to no purpose, her mistress found there was no remedy but to change her for another attendant," someone "somewhat less odoriferous."[10]

And so colonial slaveholders, and Atlantic elites generally, were told what they already thought they knew. Without their commenting on how whites smelled, it was clear that to them blacks smelled different and inferior. Whether or not slavery was blacks' natural condition, whether or not their color and attendant physical characteristics were ordained by God and by genes, or whether blacks could, many years hence, escape their blackness, were, of course, questions of incalculable import to eighteenth-century thinkers. But, for the moment, it was enough to know that blacks were different. They sensed different and sensed differently—in both instances, like animals. Thus even though Thomas Jefferson believed that blacks' moral sense was equal to that possessed by whites, their physical and intellectual differences were, for the most part, natural, innate, and ineluctable. Jefferson's "proof" resided as much in his day-to-day experience with slaves as it did in his considered reason. "They secrete less by the kidneys, and more by the glands of the skin, which gives them a very strong and disagreeable odour," he offered in *Notes on the State of Virginia*.[11]

Given the importance whites attached to skin in signifying color and shaping smell, it is hardly surprising that black skin itself was subject to sensory scrutiny, less to affirm visual stereotypes of color than to deepen associations between blackness, inferiority, and slavery. Stereotypes about touch (the haptic) were very important indeed for helping justify black slavery.

But first things first: why was black skin, well, black? Dr. John Mitchell of Urbana, Virginia, offered an account in the *Philosophical Transactions* of the Royal Society in 1744, a widely read source in eighteenth-century Anglo-America. Mitchell's explanation drew on Newtonian optics, and he made the relatively unusual claim that because white was a product of all colors and black none, he "aligned all peoples on a single spectrum," emphasizing "the fundamental sameness of men of the most diverse appearances." Mitchell's thinking went like this: on examination, skin in the case of blacks "will appear much thicker and tougher . . . than in white People." Cut it, and it feels "more tough and thick." Why? Because "a black Body retains more Heat than a white one, or any other Colour, it will be very plain, that their skins must be thicker or denser" or "more cartilaginous or callous, to award [sic] off this Violence of the Sun's Beams." Sticking firmly to his environmentalist argument, Mitchell explained that in summer sweat gave black skin a greasy feel, whereas in the dry winter months, it became "more coarse, hard, and rigid." All in all, it was this "Thickness and Density of the Skins of Negroes" that was "the grand Cause of their Colour." Neither was white skin the "natural" color. Thanks to climate, it had deviated from natural "tawny." Habits of living also accounted for the thickness and, ergo, the color of skin, "as wee see in Smiths, &c. constantly used to handle hot and hard Things, who have the Skin of their Hands become so thick and hard or cartilaginous by it, as to be able in time to handle even hot Iron." So it was with Africans and the effect of environment. Not only was black skin suited to hard labor, its "rank Smell" was closely linked to disease: "The perspirable Matter of black or tawny People is more subtil and volatile in its Nature; and more acrid, penetrating, and offensive, in its Effects; . . . more apt to degenerate to a contagious *Miasma*, than the milder *Effluvia* of Whites." If Mitchell was right—that environment conditioned skin color, thickness, and smell—could the coloration and its associated aspects be reversed, perhaps "by removing them [Negroes] from their intemperate scorching Regions"? Well, hedged Mitchell, "it must be observed, that there is a great Difference in the different Ways of changing Colours to one another: Thus Dyers can very easily dye white Cloth black, but cannot so easily discharge that Black, and bring it to its first Colour." The very process of emblackment made chances of reversal unlikely: "And thus, altho' the Skins of white, or even swarthy People, are easily affected by the greater Power of the Sun's Beams than what they have been used to, and thereby become black; yet they are thereby rendered so thick and hard, or tough and callous, as not to be so easily affected, or readily wrought upon, to render them again of their original swarthy or pale Colour, by any of those Causes, as the Absence of the Sun, Coldness of the Climate, or Ways of Life in it." Once black, there was little chance of going back, even in this environmentalist explanation.[12]

Some progressive late-eighteenth-century thinkers endorsed such reasoning. After reading Dr. Benjamin Rush's thoughts on the origins of the races, one wonders whether this staunch antislaveryite did more harm than good when it came to initiating serious discussion about abolishing slavery. In his 1792 address to the American Philosophical Society—published seven years later—Rush argued that the "Negro" was black because his environment, taken to include diet, customs, and diseases, had led to a high incidence of leprosy. Blackness of the skin was due to leprosy, and, in turn, the disease caused the "skin" to become "black, thick and greasy." The skin itself—not innately, mind you, but just because of the leprosy—"exhale[s] perpetually a peculiar and disagreeable smell, which I can compare to nothing but the smell of a mortified limb." "This smell," Rush maintained, "continues with a small modification in the native African to this day." So, thick black skin and its accompanying scent, argued Rush, was a product of leprosy. But there was more, and it was to prove important for those who defended slavery on the basis that the African was ideally suited to manual labor and fit to endure ferocious punishment. "The leprosy," argued Rush, quite innocent of the implications of his argument, "induces a morbid sensibility in the nerves. In countries where the disease prevails, it is common to say that a person devoid of sensibility, has no more feeling than a leper. This insensibility belongs in a peculiar manner to the Negroes." Witness the findings of other "experts," counseled Rush: "They bear surgical operations much better than white people, and what would be a cause of insupportable pain to a white man, a Negro would almost disregard." None of his arguments, of course, had any basis in scientific fact, and we should not doubt that Rush believed he was making a case for ending slavery. Yes, locating leprosy as the cause of blackness did mean that a "cure" was possible, and it also meant that blackness was not innate, which held out the prospect of ending racial slavery. Yet in choosing to explain blackness in this way, by seizing on the ancillary questions of skin, tactility, and smell, Rush inadvertently helped perpetuate the notion that blacks were irretrievably different and inferior.[13]

Haptic racial stereotypes projected black skin as thick and insensitive. "The Negroes, in general," offered Oliver Goldsmith, "are of a black colour, with a smooth soft skin . . . the strength of which gives a roughness to the feel" of white hands. Skin, argued Charles White, "is well known to be thicker in the African than the Europeans, and," he concluded, "still thicker in monkeys." White's assessment of black skin was linked, quite seamlessly, to his characterization of Africans as having little "sense of feeling." Blacks' "thicker and harder" skin, especially on their feet, ventured White, served "to defend them from injury." He went further, relating black touch to sensory refinement: "The thicker" the skin, "the duller must be the sense of touch. It is no wonder then, that Negroes have not that lively and delicate sense of touch that the whites have." Black slaves were clumsy creatures, their skin wholly suited to the demands of outdoor manual labor and tough enough to take an especially hard beating.[14]

Europeans also thought blacks had no aesthetic capacity, not least because blacks seemed incapable of tasting quality. White suggested the point when he argued that "Negroes have stronger powers of MASTICA-TION than Europeans." Blacks' physical—and, by extension, cultural—ability to taste was numb, an ordinarily refined sense overwhelmed by brute animal-like jaws.[15]

These sensory stereotypes did little to inhibit physical contact between the races. In fact, they probably offered whites powerful rationalizations for sexual exploitation. Sensory associations helped animalize blacks, who would not feel anything anyway, what with their poor sense of touch. Moreover, if twentieth-century studies are to be credited, what was perceived as black smell functioned to both repulse and allure. Regardless, interracial sexual trysts were abundant. South Carolina, for example, embraced mulattoes and in the process defended interracial sex and happily confessed to a tolerance of sensory intimacy between the races. In the mid-eighteenth century few slaveholders and whites believed an interracial "kiss" was shocking. Indeed, the level of what was later termed "miscegenation" was high in the colonial period, with the first significant mixing of blacks and whites coming in the late seventeenth century, principally in the Chesapeake. The first mulattoes were a product of planters' exploiting slave women and of liaisons between poor whites and slaves. Although seventeenth-century authorities in Virginia and Maryland punished miscegenation and even though eighteenth-century America generally attempted to curb both mixing and marriage of white servants with black slaves, interracial liaisons were not uncommon.[16]

By the end of the eighteenth century, events conspired to make Virginians in particular think hard—and act curiously—on the question of what constituted black and white, slave and free. Courtesy of economics and the ideological impulses of the American Revolution, no few Upper South masters emancipated their slaves, and the burgeoning free black population began to look less mulatto and more "black." As a result, legislatures attempted to establish a firmer line distinguishing between the rights of whites and the privileges of free blacks. Part and parcel of this process involved defining "blackness." Virginia offered its version in 1785: one was black if one had a black parent or grandparent. The effect muddied the relationship between the eye and race to the extent that race was not always easily seen. Under such circumstances, it is hardly surprising that nonvisual ways of identifying race were touted by the likes of Charles White and Oliver Goldsmith. Such "methods"—more properly, "beliefs"—became increasingly important to the day-to-day operation of antebellum southern slaveholding society and, in the longer run, to segregation.[17]

ANTEBELLUM ECHOES

People in the eighteenth- and nineteenth-century South experienced sights, smells, and sounds that were both apart from and integral to notions of racial identity. Complaints about the stench from refuse, animals, and human waste in cities, for example, were common. But the way the senses functioned on a daily basis provided antebellum white southerners with an idiom and lexicon for ways to mark otherness, difference, and inferiority. Sensory impressions were understood by antebellum southerners from a young age to indicate binary values: good or bad, healthy or unhealthy. George F. Holmes's *The Southern Pictorial Third Reader: For Schools and Families*, published in New York just after the Civil War, explained the physiological and, to some extent, the psychological and behavioral functioning of all the senses. It was especially attentive to the role played by smell. "The sense of smell is useful in helping us to know or judge of the nature of things" because "in this way we may often know if they are good or bad, and if proper for food or not."[18]

In fact, antebellum children's books—frequently published in the North but also read in the South—dealt with the senses in some detail and taught children the physiological and cultural functioning of the senses, which in turn could help justify a given social order. Animals were often depicted as having acute senses. "Man uses his hands, feet, tongue, and lips for feeling: Monkeys do the same," although with greater sensitivity. All senses were the product of the nerves ("By their means, we feel, see, hear, smell, and taste"), and nerves were conduits of pleasure and pain. The senses—or, rather, sensory impressions—also indexed society and helped differentiate between types of people. People with deadened senses were those who worked with their hands. "Habit will, however, render them almost insensible; blacksmiths and others, who are always handling very hard substances, and lifting hammers, can for a short time even bear fire without feeling it." Although the "senses of hearing, smelling, and sight are strengthened by exercise out of doors," one had to be careful about how the senses were used. "The *hearing* is rendered dull by violent and sudden noises," and "*taste* is injured by the constant use of pungent food, and by indulging in spices." Senses had to be protected, lest they suffer permanent damage: "If these are persevered in, the tongue and palate are made insensible to any thing less stimulating, and a simple diet becomes tasteless."[19]

While children's books established binaries around the senses, southern slaveholding paternalism was at once more subtle and just as clumsy. For antebellum southern slaveholders, paternalism mediated sensory intimacies and revulsions. Paternalism did not mean that slavery was kind or that slaveholders were not racist, exploitative, and sometimes unapologetically cruel. Although public pronouncements to the paternalist effect were essential to preserving the southern racial and social hierarchy, southern whites also freely indulged in the possession and enjoyment of the sensory dimensions of black otherness, as scholarship on interracial sexual encounters under slavery clearly shows. The ways of constructing blackness, however, were not contradictory to southern whites, for the demarcation of blacks as different and inferior allowed whites to maintain the rhetoric of otherness while also experiencing that difference.[20]

The paternalist impulse toward kindness and cruelty, the web that tethered master to slave and slave to master, and how this complex relationship impinged on and was articulated through the senses can be seen in a variety of ways, but perhaps most helpfully through the lens of a single family. Charleston's Mary Pringle, wife of William Bull Pringle (a planter with more than three hundred slaves in the 1850s), for example, found familiar black hands clasping hers following the death of her son in 1859. According to Rebecca, her daughter, the servants greeted Mary with "quiet silence" as she entered the yard and with "the deepest pity and feeling shook her hand. Some enquired about her health, but most of them shook her hand without saying a word." "I wished an abolitionist could have witnessed the behavior," wrote Rebecca. In such instances, the slaveowners welcomed tender touches not because they connoted equality (obviously absurd) but because they believed the gesture sincere, a happy affirmation of their own cherished view of the slave-master relationship. But just as the Pringles courted touch on occasion, the imperatives of slavery, and the fact that their loving and loyal servants were sometimes less than loyal or loving, meant that they had to police slaves' senses in numbingly cruel ways. Mary Pringle's 1834 household inventory included two "gagging irons," devices that were locked over slaves' heads to prevent use of the mouth and tongue—especially handy for silencing talk or preventing eating or drinking of the family's food while it was being prepared. Similarly, Pringle family members laughed at the livery and uniforms they made their slaves wear, making it almost impossible for some slaves to avoid the charge of having gaudy taste, which, infuriatingly, was not theirs to begin with.[21]

Beyond the Pringles, white understanding and use of black senses served to deepen stereotypes. White patricians tended to cast black musical expression as rousing, emotional, but unrefined. William D. Valentine, a North Carolina lawyer, claimed in 1837 that the "negro has a genius for music," one sent "through the heart," and powerful enough even to affect whites ("I have often felt it," nodded Valentine). Powerful musical production was not, however, the same as refined musical consumption. Want rousing emotionalism? Go to a black church, advised Valentine, but "a service proper for an intelligent and refined auditory is not so well adapted to the negroes."[22]

Christianity, slaveholders believed, had helped black senses evolve. Foreigners agreed. The Swedish writer Fredrika Bremer, who traveled extensively in the United States from 1849 to 1851, believed that "there is a vast, vast difference between the screeching improvisation of the Negroes in Cuba, and the inspired and inspiring preaching of the Savior, . . . which I heard extemporized in South Carolina, Georgia, Maryland, and Louisiana." The former, "low and sensual," suggested the "intoxication of the senses" and compared unfavorably with "that spiritual intoxication in song and prayer, and religious joy, which is seen and heard at the religious festivals of the Negro people here." Slaveholders, too, heard what Bremer heard, and congratulated themselves on having "improved" their slaves and saved souls along the way.[23]

Fundamentally, though, antebellum slavery was about the consistent and efficient exploitation of labor. The demands of the plantation casually and daily affirmed eighteenth-century racialized sensory stereotypes. Planters summoned slaves as they summoned animals. Some thought dogs and blacks understood whistles by means of sharp ears, although slaves, as humans, earned a slightly different tone than dogs.

"I was . . . busy one morning after breakfast," recalled a former slave, "when I was summoned by the shrill call of my master's whistle to the office. I may mention that whistle. It was an unique object, massive and of solid gold, and as an heirloom for generations in the family it had its legend. It was double throated, sounding two distinct notes, the one shrill and keen he used for his dogs, the other more musically sonorous he used for calling his Negroes."[24]

Most southern slaves labored in the field under wretchedly hard conditions, and the very nature of their work, its very physicality, gave currency to stereotypes concerning black touch. Slaveholders argued that black skin was well suited to plantation labor. While nimble enough to pick cotton, black hands were coarse, clumsy, and awkward, and a good, light hoe was wasted on them. The solution was to give slaves heavy, hardy ones. In this sense, slaveholders turned black resistance— hoe breaking—into an affirmation of the haptic stereotype. Similarly, the belief in a numbed black touch probably led slaveholders to buy "very coarse" cloth from which to make clothes, to assign "heavy brogans . . . made of horse hide," which were "stiff as board," to have the women fashion dresses out of the same coarse material men used for pants, and to have them go barefoot in summer.[25]

And, of course, tough skin had to be punished especially hard, just to ensure that pain was felt. Hard whippings achieved this in part, but there were other ways, too. Recalled a former slave: "My husban' said a family named Gullendin was mighty hard on their niggers. He said ole Missus Gullendin, she'd take a needle and stick it through one of the nigger women's lower lips and pin it to the bosom of her dress, and the woman would go 'round all day with her head drew thataway and slobberin'. There was knots on the nigger's lip where the needle had been stuck in it." Black skin was insensible to some white eyes.[26]

There was also the association between blacks' skin, especially "thick lips," and their lack of taste. Of course, white and black could be seen working fields together, "drinking from the same gourd—the darky always after his master—eating from the same rude table, and sharing the same bed," with evenings sometimes capped off with singing and dancing. But such instances of paternalist largesse—sharing good food—did not necessarily mean that blacks tasted with the same refinement as whites. It "was hard to teach them to eat cooked meat," recalled one southerner. "They wanted it raw and bloody." Such a stereotype fed key elements of the southern social order. Delicious food should be tasted by lips and tongues able to appreciate it; black lips tasting good food smacked too much of equality. "Turkeys are too good for niggers!" and so too was fish, according to one South Carolina "slave-driver." Why waste tasty food on dull tongues?[27]

Slaveholders loved to have it both ways: black sensory inferiority was indeed innate, but the master or mistress could refine things a little. Slaveholders' need for labor led them to affirm if not their power to erase black scent then at least their ability to minimize it. Paul, an Alabama field hand of mulatto stock, recalled standing in a lineup, praying to be selected by his master and mistress as their next house servant. The "master carelessly flashed his glance up and down the line." Paul was chosen, much to his happiness, convinced his "tidy and cleanly habit" had something to do with the selection. "You need not to trouble about clothes," said the mistress. "We will have new clothes made for you at home." Some efforts at detoxification were required for Paul to enter the space of the house and work in close physical proximity to whites: "Have your old clothes burned. We can not allow the smell of the plantation to invade the house," she said, at once qualifying the notion that black smell was innate (she tagged the smell of the "planta-tion," not the man) and conferring on herself the ability to mask the stench of outside work. Such a task tested even the most powerful. After all, the strength of the odor—"absolutely capable of being *weighed* and *seen* as well as *tasted* and *smelt*"—not only carried disease but also impreg-nated "the walls and under the floors of negro cabins . . . with foul smells, which continued in them long after they were exposed to winds and rains." The notion that black space was identifiable by a tenacious, unyielding odor lasted long after slavery ended.[28]

The touch of black hands on white skin—and white hands on black—was especially important to paternalism, presumably because of the level of intimacy involved in the tactile. Postbellum men recalled with sweet nostalgia how, as children on the plantation, they had been "car-ried to the house in a negro's arms." Young slaves, boys and girls, were allowed to touch their mistresses. "I and my brother," recalled one woman, "used to scratch and rub her feet for her." "The truly Southern man acknowledges the principle of humanity in his servant," ventured one writer for the *Southern Literary Messenger* in 1854, explaining that the slaveholder "feels no degradation in the touch of the negro's hand," unless, of course, it was the touch of a black man on a white woman.[29]

Although female slaves were especially vulnerable—but not always helplessly so—to the master's literal touch, bondmen too had their problems. Consider the case of Paul once he entered the household as a domestic servant. He recalled the intimate advances of a house guest, a "lively young lady," Miss Noltrieb. Miss Noltrieb delighted in Paul's handsome features, her hungry look betraying an unabashed desire to touch: "Look at his legs, how trim and well-rounded and straight! Negro that he is, I don't think I ever saw so handsome a leg before. It makes one almost want to squeeze it."[30]

Slaves well understood that on occasion whites could suspend ordinary rules of physical separation, the suspension itself reaffirming the same authority that cast blacks as different and inferior. Paul's hands, evidently sufficiently smooth, were recruited to massage the fatigue from white skin, kneading "the fat but somewhat flaccid calves and knees of the lady"; the hands' "mesmeric touch" induced a "thrill" even as slaveholders held dear the notion that black skin—tough, malleable, rough—was best suited to manual labor of a less delicate nature. In southern slaveholding society, there was enough room for exceptions, principally because they proved the rule and reflected the awesome power of largesse.[31]

For antebellum southern slavery to work, racial categories had to be kept in line, which meant that the way blacks smelled, sounded, and sensed generally could not be too similar to the way that whites, especially poor whites, smelled, sounded, and sensed generally. Slavery mandated such close contact that the races could learn to mimic one another, sometimes to worrying effect. Some white men had occasionally to sound black if they were to maintain control on plantations. In the process, such men contributed to the perpetual game played by black and white southerners of fooling the senses to gain authority or, sometimes, just a decent meal. John Andrew Jackson recalled that his former "slave-driver," "owing to his having been brought up among Negroes, . . . was perfectly familiar with their peculiarities of dialect." Such knowledge and mimetic ability proved handy if he suspected that the plantation slaves had obtained fish and meat illicitly. "He would sneak to the nigger houses in the dead of night," explained Jackson, "and say, in their peculiar manner, 'brudder, ope't' door; I want to 'peak to you for a minnit.' This would deceive the Negroes, and they would open the door." Such mimicry was perfectly acceptable because it in no way suggested permanency. But even in the act of sounding black, white drivers and overseers likely feared the possibility of blacks' sounding white, mouthing their way into white society if their skin was light enough.[32]

Yet the existence of poor and nonslaveholding whites in the Old South presented something of a challenge to slaveholders, not least because the material conditions experienced by poor whites often approximated those endured by black slaves: their houses were similar, their work was equally sweaty, their diet was not unalike, and the chances that they would smell similar were quite high. Moreover, slaveholders, like most elites in the nineteenth century, also tended to view the relationship between body and smell through the lens of labor. In short, if one worked physically and did not bathe often enough, then one, quite reasonably, smelled. But the racial imperatives of southern slave society meant that elites rarely attributed sensory stereotypes to nonelite whites. Yes, in their depictions of violence among poor whites, they suggested that poor whites had no respect for the couriers of the senses. Such men gouged eyes and cut skin and sounded like animals as they did so. But there is no evidence that slaveholders and elites considered such behavior innate.[33]

Perhaps the nearest we come to sensory stereotypes of nonslaveholding southern whites is found in northern abolitionist literature. James Gilmore's *Down in Tennessee* (1864) described very poor southerners, "mean whites," as having "dull heavy eyes" and "coarse carroty hair," a poor white version of the black stereotype. In terms of their aural character, "they often [spent] weeks at camp-meetings, shouting" and "groaning." He also hinted that they smelled. They lived in houses resembling a "swine-sty or dog kennel" and had "a mortal antipathy to water." Nonslaveholding yeoman types fared a little better. Their eyes were more alert—they had "keen restless eyes," which with enough education might gain perspective and focus. But their skin was also "rough dark." They were, of necessity, hard men, for slavery meant that material wealth was denied them. Without luxuries, without access to the "velvet-cushioned cars" used by the "Northern working-man," their skin was likely to remain raspy-tough. Gilmore was not at all clear as to whether these traits were environmental or innate, not least because, as an outsider without much at stake in southern racial solidarity, he did not have to think carefully about such matters.[34]

Regardless of the contradictions of southern slaveholding society, planters, not without some justification, thought themselves models of consistency compared to bourgeois Yankees. In his *Social Relations in Our*

Southern States, D. R. Hundley stressed that while "Republicans . . . turn[ed] up their nose at the 'vulgar herd,'" southern slaveholders, "democratic in their instincts," evinced a certain rough equality and physical intimacy with their slaves, wearing "homespun every day and work[ing] side by side with their slaves." But Hundley went further, latching onto the exemplary role of southern yeomen as a way to expose the hypocrisy of northern liberals. "Senator Seward himself could not demand any greater show of equality, than what is often exhibited by the Yeomen of the South in the treatment of their negroes," puffed Hundley, "and we think it would cure even him of his rabid mania on the subject of the ultimate extinction of the peculiar institution, could he be brought into personal contact with some of the free and easy specimens of poor down-trodden Africans we have had the luck to fall in with now and then in the Slave States." Indeed, after such close contact, "if he did not carry with him to his grave a very unflattering remembrance of this loutish, lazy, lousy, and foul-scented black 'brothers' [sic], then he is not the dainty gentleman we have been accustomed to consider him." Republicans' cries against slavery, smirked Hundley, might well change because "the people of the Free States are possessed of olfactories like the rest of mankind, and individually entertain a very wholesome dread of coming personally in contact with" slaves, which explained why most northerners shunned such contact with free blacks in the North, the occasional "din[ing] with them sleep[ing] with them" and a few instances of "a big buck African . . . familiarly slap[ping] a white man on the back" notwithstanding.[35]

Some supporters of slavery considered nonsouthern senses so politicized that they doubted that abolitionists, whatever their nationality, really sensed as southern whites did. Although they heard with the same anatomical ears, saw with the same eyes, smelled with the same noses, what and how they chose to hear, see, smell was shaped by their social, economic, and political background. In his 1860 review of Charles Mackay's highly critical book on southern slavery, South Carolina's William J. Grayson suggested the political conditioning of the senses. Whereas Grayson understood the "slave mart in New Orleans" to be "clear and comfortable," filled with slaves "cheerful and anxious to be sold; like hired men, they seek to be employed," Mackay, "the sensitive traveler" who had "just arrived with lungs and sensibilities undisturbed, from the boothies and hovels of English laborers, . . . where the stench is intolerable to strangers," found the mart simply appalling. From

Grayson's perspective, Mackay's experience with the English working class had dulled his senses, preventing him from appreciating the
"comfortable" nature of the mart. More pointedly, Mackay's senses
were not to be trusted, suggested Grayson, because they were shaped by
his political views. After all, exclaimed Grayson, Mackay even doubted
"that a peculiar odor exhales from the Negro." Grayson could not
fathom this "traveler's nose." Then again, Grayson did not have to.
As long as he believed in his ability to sense race, all was right with
his world.[36]

2 | Fooling Senses, Calming Crisis

Always important to antebellum slaveholding paternalism generally, sensory stereotypes proved critical in the 1850s. In response to growing northern criticism, slave resistance, and visual changes within southern society, slaveholders and proslavery ideologues started to talk about race and the senses more publicly and more often and, sometimes, more urgently. Although some historians argue that the increasing presence of visually white slaves in the 1850s posed a serious problem to slaveholders, masters liked to think they managed to stabilize race by appealing to all the senses, at least rhetorically. For the slaveholders, the "crisis" of the 1850s was more of a gloss on an old trend inherent to their chosen society. Responding to it did not involve a qualitatively new defense of bondage; it demanded a clear, emphatic statement on the relationship between race and the senses. In addition to shoring up teetering racial categories intellectually, southern slaveholders had to deal with slaves who used the senses to resist bondage and a growing chorus of northern voices of complaint. As it turned out, northerners were easier to combat than slaves, at least before 1861.[1]

COMMON SENSE

Southern slaves used their senses pragmatically. In contrast to the essentialist construction of blackness championed by colonial and antebellum whites, little evidence suggests that black southerners perceived whiteness in the same way. Slaves' understanding of the world was shaped, first, by the fundamental belief that racial identity was more fungible and plastic than many whites were willing to admit and, second, by the notion that their senses could be used to resist bondage.

Slaves dwelled less on the sensory meaning of whiteness, preferring instead to fool slaveholders' senses and resist bondage.

What little evidence there is suggests that although enslaved Africans regarded white "complexions," skin, "sound," and hair as alien and different, there is little indication that these images became enduring stereotypes. There is even less evidence suggesting that African Americans considered them innate to whites. Take, for example, Olaudah Equiano's "interesting" narrative of the late eighteenth century in which he counters white sensory stereotypes while avoiding the temptation of applying ethnological stereotypes to whites. Near the beginning of his account, he takes care to show his white audience that images of filthy, smelling Africans are highly exaggerated and misleading. "Before we taste food," he notes, stressing habits of cleanliness, "we always wash our hands." "Indeed," he presses, "our cleanliness on all occasions is extreme." "Our principal luxury is in perfumes," particularly an "odoriferous wood of delicious fragrance." He then gives his audience an olfactory standard by which to judge African odor: "It resembles musk in strength, but is more delicious in scent, and is not unlike the smell of a rose." The fragrance is then impregnated into black bodies: beaten into powder, the wood is mixed with palm oil "with which both men and women perfume themselves."[2]

Equiano was equally careful to contextualize white senses. While he remarked on the difference of white "complexions," their strange sounds and language, their "horrible looks, red faces, and loose hair," and their "savage . . . manner," none of this was innate. Whites did not stink, but what they did reeked, for their slaving vessels emitted a "stench." These "loathsome smells," coupled with "fearful noises," "shrieks of the women, and the groans of the dying" suggested only a lack of refinement, not a genetic predisposition on the part of white men. Europeans, suggested Equiano, plainly harbored a radical contempt for the range of African senses. Just looking at schematics of the appallingly close, sardined quarters of the slave ships suggests he was not far off the mark. (See illustration 2.1.) Is it possible, even dimly, to imagine something of the smell, noise, taste, and feel of the sensory worlds contained by those decks? In that contempt for black bodies and black senses, slave traders revealed much about the power of greed to deaden sentiment and sensory appreciation. The nearest Equiano came to turning sensory stereotypes around was in England: although he was "astonished at the wisdom of the white people," he was "amazed" at

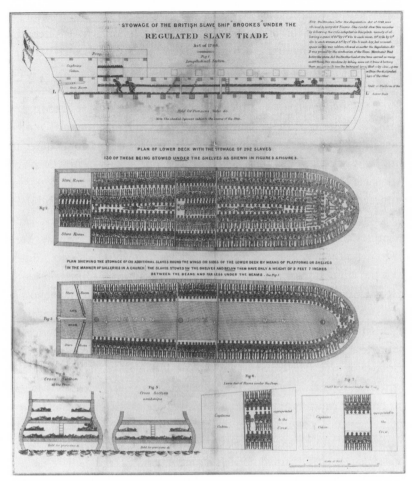

Ill. 2.1. "Stowage of the British Slave Ship 'Brookes' under the Regulated Slave Trade Act of 1788." The schematics of the appallingly close quarters of Atlantic slave ships suggest the horrific sensory world of the Middle Passage and reveal the contempt white traders had for African senses. (Courtesy of the Library of Congress, Prints and Photographs Division, Washington, D.C., LC-US262-44000)

their "eating with unwashed hands." Yet Equiano never offered anything resembling the ethnological arguments spouted by eighteenth-
century whites, preferring instead to locate how whites sensed and to
judge their use of the senses within a loosely conceived cultural context.[3]

Because southern slave society was a product of interaction between
black and white, slaves and masters sometimes shared the sensory delights of living in the Old South. They liked some of the same sounds,
shared an appreciation for some music, and heard pastoral quiet in
similar ways. They also liked many of the same smells. Millie Evans of
Arkansas (born in 1849) revealed that slaves, as much as slaveholders,
embraced cleanliness and its scent. Clothes were washed hard and then
perfumed: "The way we got our perfume we took rose leaves, cape
jasmines an sweet bazil an laid dem wid our clo'es an let 'em stay three
or fo' days then we had good smellin' clo'es that would las' too." Entry
into the white household on a permanent basis meant immersion into
the sensory world of whites. Sarah Debro of North Carolina was chosen
by her mistress from "de quarters" as "a house maid." This meant "a
clean apron every day" and introduced Debro to the taste and touch of
whiteness, the feel of "white sheets on de beds" and the taste of good
food, "even ham." "Us et jess whut our white folks had," recalled a
former slave from Georgia. "Dey didn't mak' no difference in us when
hit cum ter eatin'." And the memory of some of slavery's smells provided perverse comfort in the context of the sensory flintiness of the
Great Depression: "Dey ain't nothin' whut smells good lak' de cookin'
in dem days, I kain't smell no victuals lak' dat now."[4]

Slaveholders' doubts notwithstanding, slaves could and did appreciate sensory delights in other than animalistic ways. Former slave
Charles Ball, for example, waxed eloquent about the "Southern Magnolia": "No adequate conception can be formed of the appearance or the
fragrance of this most magnificent tree," and he marveled at "the air
when scented by the perfume of its flowers." Slaves also believed, with
their masters, that visitors to the South carried with them conditioned
senses. Just as William J. Grayson had lambasted the sensory bias of
Charles Mackay's work, so Samuel Ringgold Ward, a former slave, at-
tacked English travelers who failed to criticize slavery for having "sight-
less eyes" and deliberately looking for signs of slavery's supposedly
positive features.[5]

Even as owners called for sensory stoicism from their slaves, they tacitly acknowledged that slaves sensed like whites, at least when it came to sins of the flesh. "The slaveholders, masters and mistresses," recalled one slave, "had been educated to regard their Negroes as they regarded the furniture, or their cats and dogs, a species of domestic fixture, having eyes to see not, and ears to hear not, senses to feel and yet to feel not." "My God!" he continued, "When I look back upon those times, and knowing the warm, passionate, almost bestial propensities of my race, and the terrible temptations which the then prevailing, unconscious indiscretions of the southern mistresses, in the exposure of their charms, daily put before their slaves, I shudder even now at the danger and can only wonder that there were not more outrages, with the inevitable hanging or burning, or emasculation." Slaves were admonished to suppress their senses on some occasions and hone them on others even as their owners nursed beliefs about blacks' wayward passions. Masters were indeed confident in their authority.[6]

Slaveholder demands that slaves control their own senses, while plainly an effort to strengthen bondage, could produce the opposite effect. "The two senses of seeing and hearing in the slave are made doubly acute by the very prohibition of knowledge," recalled one bondman. Slaves also recognized that slaveholder talk of mutual trust was belied by the way masters used their eyes. Frederick Douglass maintained that the slaveholders' "safety depended on their vigilance. . . . They were constantly looking out for the first signs of the dread retribution. They watched, therefore, with skilled and practiced eyes, and learned to read, with great accuracy, the state of mind and heart of the slave through his sable face."[7]

Painfully aware of "the vigilant eyes of their masters" and of the various ways slaveholders used sound and listening to police their activities, slaves attempted to fool white senses in order to carve a degree of freedom from their bondage. As is well known, slaves used sound, especially music, to create spaces unavailable to whites, a way to preserve the soul and identity. They also smothered sound—prayed into upturned pots, learned how to walk silently, appreciated the importance of the whisper—to deny masters knowledge of slave religious and nocturnal gatherings. Slaves waited for "quiet, and the stillness of undisturbed tranquility," before venturing out. Quiet nights required careful treading and heightened senses, lest even small noises echo. Pricked hearing also sensitized touch. As Charles Ball recalled of a nocturnal skirmish with a man he was tracking: "Many of these bushes were full of dry leaves, which had been touched by the frost, but had not yet fallen. It was easy for me to follow him, for I pursued by the noise he made, amongst these bushes; but it was not so easy for me to avoid, on my part, the making of a rustling, and agitation of the bushes, which might expose me to detection."[8]

Some light-skinned slaves challenged white optics directly, using their visual ambiguity to "pass" from black slavery and, with a little luck, into white freedom. Toward the end of the antebellum period, just as slavery became whiter, slaves of mixed racial ancestry "ran away in greater numbers than their proportion in the slave population would suggest," "more than four times what would be expected," according to one study. Some of these slaves passed as free blacks but others almost certainly passed as whites. Newspaper advertisements listing such light-skinned runaways frequently warned that a particular slave would "pass for a white man." But there was not much that could be done to identify such slaves by sight alone. One had to listen, too. Slow speech, accent, dialect, stuttering—all functioned as aural markers of black slavery. Thus the most successful runaways, those who could fool whites most readily, were those with fluent "and smooth words," men and women "quick with speech." Coupled with light skin, the ability to sound "white" and free—or at least, not black and slave—posed significant problems for those hoping to catch runaways.[9]

Slaves' manipulation of the senses was also used to effect day-to-day resistance. Generally, slaves developed a "whispering habit . . . to guard against eavesdroppers by conveying information in whispers even when there was no one in sight to overhear the conversation." One sense sometimes bowed to another. For example, as former slave George Womble explained, when slaves wanted meat, they could sometimes steal a pig and satisfy a particular taste. But whites' sense of smell meant blacks had to taste clandestinely and in a limited number of ways: "As there was danger in being caught none of this stolen meat was ever fried because there was more danger of the odor of frying meat going farther away than that odor made by meat being boiled." Fried meat, then, was a taste better suited to freedom. Charles Ball suggested as much: "It was necessary to be exceedingly cautious in the use of our bacon; and to prevent the suspicions of the master and others who frequented our landing, I enjoined our people never to fry any of the meat, but to boil it." Ball understood that "no one can smell boiled bacon far; but fried flitch can be smelled a mile by a good nose."[10]

Although Ball could fool white noses at a distance, deception proved more difficult close up, especially when white eyes believed they could see what blacks had eaten. Ball's body betrayed his meat consumption to "the scrutinizing look" of his overseer. The overseer paraded Ball before a group of slaveholders whose "examination of my person," "a kind of leer or side glance," convinced them that Ball appeared to "live well" and had in all likelihood managed to eat outlawed meat. Ball protested his innocence, claiming that he consumed just the fish and rations allowed by his master. "Charles, you need not tell lies about it," said the overseer, eyes piercing Ball's skin, "you have been eating meat, I know you have, no negro could look as fat, and sleek, and black, and greasy as you, if he had nothing to eat but corn bread and river chubs." Ball's healthy look suggested wrongdoing to white eyes. Again, Ball protested his innocence. The overseer then invoked another of his senses to persuade the slaveholding elite that he could spot a stealing slave with his nose as well as his eyes: "None of your palaver," he snapped. "Why, I smell the meat in you this moment." To avoid punishment, Ball had to undermine the authority of the overseer's senses. Because his fellow slaves had also eaten the bacon and other meat, Ball invited the overseer and masters to accompany him to the fishery where he and the others worked, arguing that if the others looked like Ball, then it would prove that he had been eating just fish and plain rations. The slaveholders saw the other slaves and accepted the argument. Only the overseer remained unconvinced and was left ranting in the presence of gentlemen who believed the slave's story and doubted the overseer's ability to sense wrongdoing. In effect, Ball created a situation in which the "gentlemen now began to doubt the evidence of their own senses, which they had held infallible heretofore."[11]

If slaves could fool white senses, what were masters to do? Some found answers in relying on noses better than theirs. Hound dogs that tracked slave runaways were extensions of the master's nose, enabling him to continue surveillance out of his sight. Slaves thought dogs could smell "nigger blood" and so developed strategies to fool masters' sensory aids. Sensory evasion mostly involved fooling canine noses, using "remedies" so that "the hounds could not scent them, so they could not be trailed" even "within five feet." Runaways used "ointment made of

turpentine and onions, a preparation used to throw hounds off a trail,"
waded through swamps and other bodies of water, and "strewed . . .
snuff and ground cayenne pepper," which one slave said "caused them

to lose scent of me entirely"; he rubbed his feet "in some cow dung to
prevent the scent of the bloodhounds."[12]

Beyond the sensory feinting central to slave resistance was a powerful
critique of the slaveholders' use of the senses to mark race, one that
endured in African American circles well into the twentieth century.
Because they tended not to share the sensory racial stereotypes peddled
by southern and northern whites, southern slaves were the only constit-
uency able to expose and challenge the illogic of white views on black
senses. Heavy doses of common sense and a keen understanding of the
material basis behind sensory perceptions constituted the intellectual
architecture of the slaves' critique.

Slaves countered white charges of innate black stench, for example,
by explaining why black slaves might well reek and laying the blame
squarely at the slaveholders' door. Slaves worked appallingly long hours,
maintained John Andrew Jackson, a former slave in South Carolina,
sometimes shucking "corn till past midnight," then rising "with the sun
next morning." "They are not allowed a change of clothes," he explained, "but only one suit for summer, and the perspiration is so great
that they smell rank; thus they are robbed of comfort and cleanliness by
the cruelty and avarice of their masters." And so they were subjected to
the indignity of an infuriating self-fulfilling prophecy, whereby masters
argued that because blacks smelled their enslavement was appropriate.[13]

Slaves used the same hard logic and reasoning to expose other stereotypes, including the charge that blacks naturally had thick, tough
skin and so were well suited to manual drudgery. "As the slaves are not
allowed boots or shoes (except for a short time in the winter)," explained Jackson, "the combined action of the frost at night, and the heat
during the day, harden the feet; so that the outside skin at last cracks,
and is very painful to the Negroes." Yes, suggested Jackson, dead skin
dulled the sensitivity of black touch, but the condition was a product of
white cruelty, not black genes: "This outside skin is called 'dead skin,'
and the slaves cannot *feel* the rats eating it until their teeth touch the
more tender part of the feet." Black skin was, in fact, as sensitive as
white: "During the day, that part of the foot which has been skinned by
the rats is very tender and causes great pain."[14]

One challenge to the slaveholders' sensorium came from slaves, another from abolitionists. Abolitionists believed that slave traders and slave-holders were devoid of humanitarian sensibilities. In their efforts to refute "the opinion . . . that the Negro is essentially, and unalterably, an inferior being," abolitionists argued that "the Negro" was "bone of our bone, flesh of our flesh," that racial differences were "not organic" but a product of "climate and circumstances." In the course of their critique, abolitionists maintained that Africans shared in the human sensorium and that greed had numbed the senses of slaveholders and slave traders (abolitionists loved to conflate them). By remaining deaf to slaves' screams, slaveholders retarded civilization. To abolitionists' way of thinking, modernity was supposed to be more "refined" and sensitive to the senses. Slave traders were a grim, "cruel" bunch, emotionally calloused, indifferent to the sounds and sights of bondage. The aboli-tionists tried to refocus slave traders' senses by issuing necessarily over-wrought appeals to numbed emotions:

> Hark, to that shrill and agonizing cry!
> Gaze on that upturned supplicating eye!
> How the flesh quivers, and how shrinks the frame,
> As the initials of her owner's name,
> Burn on the back of that Mandingo girl . . .[15]

Radical abolitionists especially invoked the senses for political and moral effect, at once noting white southerners' professed disdain for black skin and their propensity for interracial sexual liaisons. They also stressed that they, as good abolitionists, showed no revulsion at the prospect of touching black skin. One of John Brown's last living acts— seeing "him stoop on his way to the scaffold and kiss that Negro child," as Wendell Phillips described it in 1859—was meant to demonstrate such progressive thinking, sensitivity, and compassion. The instruc-tion was obvious: one should contrast this kindly treatment with slave-holders' disregard for the tenderness of black skin.[16]

In truth, most antebellum northerners were not unlike most white southerners when it came to believing, inventing, and applying racial sensory stereotypes. Eighteenth-century statements on varieties within the "negro stock" and blacks' particularly thick skin and strong scent were regurgitated with little ceremony or revision in the antebellum

North. Johann Georg Heck's *Iconographic Encyclopedia of Science, Literature and Art*, translated from German and published in New York in 1860, acknowledged the variety of peoples within Africa but claimed a universal "Negro" type: "Most of the Guinea Negroes exhibit all the characteristics of the Negro race. Their skin is thick, like velvet to the touch, and secretes a perspiration of an unpleasant odor." Similar remarks offered by another European—Hermann Burmeister, professor of zoology at the University of Halle—were translated and then published in the New York *Evening Post* and as a book, *The Black Man: Comparative Anatomy and Psychology of the African Negro*, by a New York house in 1853. The African body, maintained Burmeister, has "a disagreeable property . . . which always produces disgust on the part of the European in his intercourse with colored people—I allude to the disagreeable smell emitted by their perspiration." Although "it can be diminished, but never completely destroyed, by cleanliness," the fact remains that "the more the negro perspires, the more apparent the odor becomes." Blacks sweat profusely, he argued, which is an olfactory and tactile shame. Not only would less sweat make them smell better but in areas of the black body that do not perspire, "the skin has a dull surface, and is very soft to the touch, quite as much so as the softest European skin. In fact, there is an agreeable, velvet-like feel in the negro skin, which is not found in the less stretched and stuffed skin of the European."[17]

Such beliefs were hardly embarrassing to northerners. Among the more famous efforts to hobble Abraham Lincoln's reelection bid in 1864 was the publication of a northern Democratic pamphlet titled *What Miscegenation Is!* The pamphlet is interesting not simply because it introduced the term "miscegenation" to the national lexicon but also because it fostered fear of interracial liaisons by playing on the power of the senses. The pamphlet's cover depicts a black man touching and kissing—tasting?—a white woman, their skins plainly in unison. Neither were Republicans immune to sensory stereotyping. In an article headlined "Stealing—and giving odors," the *Old Guard* magazine of New York reported: "The wife of a Republican Senator in Washington does not sympathize with her husband's admiration of negroes. She says, 'they steal everything they can lay their hands on, and leave such a foul stench on everything they don't steal, that she wishes they had taken that too.' The good woman seems not to be aware that this is the distinguishing, the poetic virtue of the Negroes." Benjamin Wade, an Ohio abolitionist, did not mince words on the same topic after taking his seat in the U.S. Senate in 1851. Food in the District of Columbia, he bellyached, "is all cooked by niggers until I can smell and taste the nigger." How Wade knew to distinguish the smell and taste of "niggers" is unexplained.[18]

THE "CRISIS" OF THE 1850S

Potentially the most serious challenge to the slaveholders' society came less from northerners and slaves and more from their own behavior. The time had come when "miscegenation" threatened to undermine the racial basis of slavery. By some accounts, in the early 1850s the incidence of race mixing by slaveholding white men reached a "crescendo," producing "clans of mulattoes." As sectional tensions became more acute, southern public opinion increasingly rejected these "legally white and socially black" people. Visually white slaves challenged the internal logic of southern slavery and threatened to give ammunition to ever more shrill and combative voices from the North. In effect, slavery in the 1850s "was becoming whiter, visibly so and with amazing rapidity." Numbers tell part of the story: between 1850 and 1860, while black slavery increased by about 20 percent, mulatto slavery increased by almost 70 percent, from 247,000 individuals to 412,000.[19]

So, why the turnabout, especially in places in the lower South that had formerly indulged race mixing or at least turned a blind eye to it? Why now the scrutiny? Why the increase in animosity during the 1850s against free blacks and especially free mulattoes? Broadly speaking, slaveholders thought they had a problem on their hands because the context tended to politicize (and exaggerate) the implications of race mixing. Thanks largely to the increase in sectional tensions, some slaveholders began to associate free blacks with sources of abolitionism and insurrection. Just as important, plantation mistresses and white women felt challenged by light-skinned women of color and began an earnest, intense criticism of the men—often husbands and relatives—responsible for the increase in free and enslaved mulattoes. As slaves became less visibly black in skin, features, and looks—the "white children of slavery," as Swedish traveler Fredrika Bremer denominated them—plantation mistresses were more acutely resentful of the elite men responsible for these ever-whiter, often attractive slave women. The apparent increase in such liaisons was simply too much for many planter women in the 1850s. As a result, they became a major factor in the push for "racial purity."[20]

In one respect, mulattoes and light-skinned blacks posed an intellectual problem that the slaveholders never fully resolved, even the brightest of them. For the most part, proslavery ideologues (James Henry Hammond comes to mind) tried to explain away the problem of enslaved people who looked white by denying it existed on anything but the smallest scale. More famously (and idiosyncratically), George Fitzhugh endorsed the notion that dependent, propertyless whites, too, could be enslaved, not least because organic southern slavery was a good deal kinder (and safer) than the form of wage slavery burgeoning to the north. But most defenders of chattel slavery barely mentioned mulattoes in their tracts, recurring instead to the assumption that slavery in the South was best suited to blacks, most of whom were readily identifiable by sight. If most proslavery ideologues were unwilling to hitch their wagon to Fitzhugh's thinking and if most quietly recognized that slavery was looking whiter by the year, they could either ignore the problem (which many did) or implicitly apply a one-drop rule to slavery—by which a tincture of African blood defined one as black (and, very likely, as slave)—and, finally, argue that mulattoes would eventually disappear because they were the unnatural product of a blending between white and black (an argument adopted by those enamored of polygenesis but rejected by theologians). By some accounts, the result was an anxious decade, one characterized by efforts to shore up slavery by invoking something like a one-drop rule and by loudly rejecting miscegenation. Slavery now had the power "to make all slaves black regardless of their seeming whiteness." It could be no other way, unless one wanted to join George Fitzhugh, and few wanted to do that by 1860.[21]

But slaveholders did not "solve" the problem by ignoring it; they readily acknowledged the matter and simply appealed to the authority of their other senses (in addition to sight) to ascertain racial identity. At root, of course, this was sheer fantasy—slaveholders thought they could determine race by listening, smelling, touching, and looking. In truth, they could do so only by contorting and exaggerating "black" cultural traits and reconstituting them as "natural." Quietly, of course, they knew this not least because they had immense trouble sensing racial identity in the case of "black" people light enough to pass. But, rhetorically, the strategy worked, and, at some level, whites did in fact believe what they claimed. Slaveholders had always professed to be able to tell a slave by sound and smell, especially; now these old authenticators were even more important because they had to detect a race that was becoming ever less visible. Slaveholders and southern whites generally did make mistakes, did treat some enslaved blacks as free on the basis of their appearance, and did undoubtedly have blacks passing under their very eyes, ears, and noses. But slaveholders could at least claim that blacks could always be spotted, if not in terms of behavior and gesture then in terms of smell, sound, taste, and touch, even if a few sensorily ambiguous cases occasionally eluded them. Unlike their forebears in the 1830s and 1840s—who wrote comparatively little on the sensory fingerprints of race—some proslavery ideologues of the 1850s pressed hard their claim that blackness could be detected by the other senses, thus at once perpetuating southern slaveholding paternalist ideology, making sensory dimensions of blackness and bondage indistinguishable, and stabilizing racial categories. While some of these thinkers ranked among the least sophisticated of the proslavery ideologues and while many of them were influenced by the kind of ethnological thinking most proslavery divines firmly rejected, what they said reflected broadly held assumptions in southern slaveholding society.[22]

We should be careful not to overstate the novelty of the proslavery sensory argument of the 1850s. Many writers simply restated what was common knowledge. Slaveholder appeals to non-ocular senses as a way to verify race were, in fact, perfectly consistent with standard daily—and historical—practice. Race had never just been a matter of seeing, and white southerners assumed that race could be heard, smelled, and felt. For example, Rosetta Clark of Spartanburg District, South Carolina, testified in 1859 that a black man entered her house around midnight and grabbed her around the throat. It was dark and she could not see him, but when she "pushed him away from her[,] in doing so she ran her hand through his hair and felt that it was a Negroe[.] She knew it was a Negroe from the feeling of the hair."[23]

But proslavery thinkers were important for clarifying and elaborating the sensory argument. George Fitzhugh tried to turn the tables on abolitionists and, in the process, explain slaveholders' sensory burdens. He argued in 1857 that "Negroes are so hideously ugly, that those not used to them, cannot help detesting an institution whose subjects are so disagreeable" and that "we have not the least doubt that the stupidity, ugliness, and bad odor of the Negro, are the true causes of hatred to the institution with which he [the slave] is connected, and always associated in idea." While bolstering notions of paternalist largesse, such an argument made little sense: why would abolitionists want to abolish slavery, and court the possibility of freedmen moving North, if they reviled blackness so much? Fitzhugh's response was that the abolitionist pretensions were just that: a sham. There was little point in trying to alter northern minds about the desirability of slavery. It was "as idle to attempt to change the Yankee's tastes and affections, as to blanch the negro's skin, or to sweeten his bodily odor." "Northern people loathe and despise free negroes," wrote the physician Alexander Woodward in his 1853 attack on abolitionists, explaining that the presence of blacks offended at least two of the northerners' five senses: "They cannot bear the sight or smell of them." Indeed, "the prejudices of the whites against the African race is stronger in the free states, than it is in the slave states."[24]

Second-rate thinkers added their voices. At a very basic level, some simply reiterated eighteenth-century tropes. New York's self-educated Josiah Priest, author of the 1852 *Bible Defence of Slavery*, invoked the senses to show that racial differences were divinely ordained. Priest gave the scriptural interpretation to support what Edward Long had implied with his comparison between the smell of goats and Africans in 1774. Quoting Matthew 25:33, Priest contended that the goat was "the symbol of all sinners," maintaining that "the goat is naturally quarrelsome, *lascivious*, and excessively ill-scented," a symbol of "profane, and impure men." Priest could not resist making explicit the comparison: "How very *similar* . . . were these two characters, the *goat* and the *negro*? They were alike in passions, in propensities, and in their *smell*, both disagreeable to excess."[25]

Priest also argued that black flesh, impregnated with black scent, was particularly inviting to animal palates, a point made a year earlier in slightly different form by the noted German–South Carolina scholar Francis Lieber. Priest advised: "We shall notice the very curious circumstance of the difference there is between the *nature* of the negro's *flesh*, and that of the white man's, the knowledge of which is afforded by the appetites of certain animals." If the heightened animal senses of sharks, lions, tigers, and leopards could tell the difference between the taste of black flesh and that of white flesh, suggested Priest, the distinction must be real. Such animals were attracted by "the strong odor of the negro's body, which, to the smell and taste, is more inviting than the white man's flesh." If black meat was different, then black taste and tongue must also be abnormal. One reason why blacks smelled different (though innate differences dictated that it could not be the only reason) was that "they can digest food of a much coarser and stronger character than white men can, such as the shark, the crocodile, the rhinoceros," and a host of other animals "of every description." Not only did white men taste different; they tasted differently: "All these [animals] are rejected by the white man, as abhorrent to his nature, tastes, and powers of digestion."[26]

Priest was not alone. Southern-born, northern-educated Josiah C. Nott—the antebellum American exemplar of ethnology—tried to temper his "scientific" finding that white and black were two distinct, innately different species with glossed-over appeals to Christianity. Ultimately, though, his findings show that polygenist accounts could not be squared with Christian doctrine or explained by reference to environmental factors. It hardly mattered much when it came to describing the distinctive features of blackness, for, like Priest, Nott, along with George R. Gliddon, maintained that black skin was "comparatively thick," the product of "an extra skin in the negro."[27] Thick, tough, strong: perfect skin for arduous labor.

New Orleans physician Samuel A. Cartwright created and reflected stereotyped images of black senses, his work adding scientific legitimacy to what many slaveholders already believed. In this respect, his ruminations serve as a useful, if uncomfortably stark, summary of the key beliefs of some of the defenders of racial slavery in the antebellum South. In his July 1851 *De Bow's Review* essay, "Diseases and Peculiarities of the Negro Race," Cartwright laid out in clear terms how and why black slaves were different and inferior to free white men. Among the main physiological differences between black and white, he averred, was the shape and extent of blacks' nerves. They had an "excess of nervous matter," especially those that "minister[ed] to the senses," which, in turn, partook "of sensuality, at the expense of intellectuality." This supposedly peculiar configuration of the black nervous system heightened the lower senses of smell, hearing, taste, and touch. Along with Thomas Jefferson, Cartwright argued that "music is a mere sensual pleasure with the negro," a pleasure divested of thought. "There is nothing in his music addressing the understanding; it has melody, but no harmony; his songs are mere sounds, without sense or meaning— pleasing the ear, without conveying a single idea to the mind; his ear is gratified by sound, as his stomach is by food." Cartwright shifted from hearing and tasting to touching, adding a twist to commonly accepted stereotypes from the eighteenth century. Whereas eighteenth-century thinkers argued that black skin was thick and, thus, largely dulled to touch, Cartwright contended that while "their skin is very thick, it is as sensitive, when they are in perfect health, as that of children, and like them, they fear the rod." Cartwright had to argue this tack not simply because of his larger logic concerning blacks' "excess" of nerves ministering to the lower senses but also because the imperatives of late-antebellum paternalism warned against excessive cruelty and required slaves to be, in the master's mind, childlike. The analogy was pushed further to include taste or, rather, lack of discriminating taste. "Like children, they are apt to over-eat themselves." It was not just that they ate too much; their palate reflected no discrimination in the quality or variety of food: "They often gorge themselves with fat meat." Neither could their senses be educated. For Cartwright, "the Negro is a slave by nature."[28]

Cartwright had more to say on the matter later in 1851. Still harping on the "larger size of the nerves in the negro than the white man" and the "harder" bones beneath his thicker skin, Cartwright maintained that "the negro's sense of smell and hearing is more acute." He then turned his attention to the eye, the most refined sensory organ: "The inner canthus of the negro's eye is anatomically constructed like that of the orang-outang, and not like that of the white man." Cartwright also challenged Benjamin Rush on blackness and leprosy, arguing that "the Mosaic history distinctly specifies an inferior slave race of people." Southern slavery arose "from causes imprinted by the hand of nature on the sons of Ham, so far back as the time when the catacombs were constructed." None of this was merely a matter of anatomy and science. After all, maintained the doctor, "the vulgar error that there is no difference in the negro's organization, physiology and psychology . . . is the cause of all those political agitations which are threatening to dissolve our Union."[29]

Like Nott, William H. Holcombe was southern born (Lynchburg, Virginia, in 1825), northern educated (graduating from the University of Pennsylvania in 1847), and trained as a physician (he moved back south to practice medicine in 1852). Holcombe also cast blacks as innately different and pointed to the different senses and sensory capacities of blacks to sustain his argument. In the popular *Southern Literary Messenger* in 1861, Holcombe first pointed to the exaggerated power of the lower senses among blacks. "The organs of sense are acute," he stated, "espe-

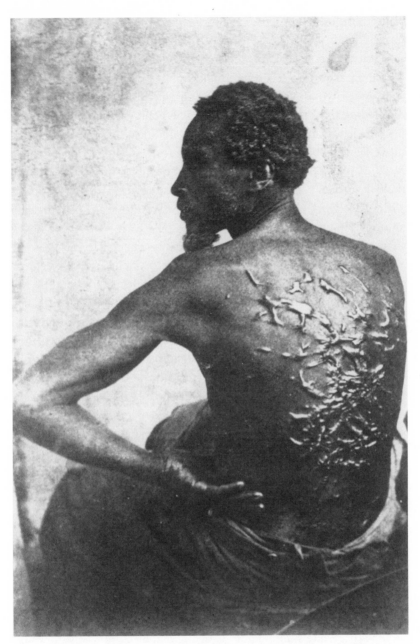

Ill. 2.2. "Gordon" the slave, circa 1863. The slave's sickeningly scarred back provides clear visual testimony to the belief that the skin of black slaves was especially thick and largely insensitive to pain. (Courtesy of the Abraham Lincoln Presidential Library, Springfield, Illinois)

cially those of hearing and smell—the conformation of the latter approaching the animal type." But not all the "lower" senses were refined in blacks, he maintained, preferring late-eighteenth-century thinking regarding black skin to Cartwright's contemporary analysis. "The nervous system is not so impressible as that of whites," Holcombe said, concluding that "they feel less pain." The point was critical in helping planters justify the need and desirability for stringent corporal punishment. Leathery black skin was also handy for wincingly hard labor. The black man's ability to endure "great heat qualifies him for labor amid the dense foliage of the cotton-plant and sugar-cane in a hot latitude, where such work would infallibly destroy the white man." Whites paid an olfactory price for using such labor: "The black skin of the negro exhales, especially when heated, a very offensive perspiration."[30]

"The animal propensities very largely predominate in the negro," continued the relentless Holcombe. The "aesthetic faculties are still in a child-like, or infantile condition," manifested in combustible passions, unfettered sensuality, and unthinking indulgence of the voluptuous. This amounted to tasteless tasting: "To eat, drink, sleep, enjoy the sexual relation, and wear fine clothes, undisturbed by any work, or dream of modern progression, would constitute the Paradise of the African." Although slavery had improved the behavior of southern blacks, they were, urged Holcombe, afflicted by these indelible African traits, sensory traits that remained intact even when black skins looked lighter and whiter. In this regard, the ways in which blacks smelled, sounded, felt, and tasted were much deeper, unalterable, and meaningful markers of race than the visual color of the skin. Lighter skin could only confuse—not erase—the fundamental aspect of racial identity.[31]

Even though their insights were hackneyed, having been bequeathed to them by an equally suspect group of late-eighteenth-century thinkers, in detailing the sensory dimensions of blackness Holcombe and the others achieved several things essential to the maintenance of their society. First, they made whiteness normative without actually discussing its sensory dimensions. By saying that black skin smelled, they implied that white skin did not; by saying that black skin was thick and tough, they implied that white skin was delicate, refined, gentle; and so on. Second, embedded in the sensory representations of blackness were clear and powerful justifications for the continuation of bondage. Lastly, and especially in Holcombe's case, by reciting the ways that blacks sensed and could be sensed, the apologists for slavery attempted to expand the definition of blackness beyond the eye. Blackness was not just seen—it could be smelled, heard, and felt. In fact, as Holcombe remarked, it was important not to trust the eye alone: "The black skin by no means constitutes a man a negro." Holcombe cited the example of albinos, "negroes [who] have been known to turn white," and doubtless at the back of his mind were light-skinned blacks, the products of interracial liaisons. Even though they may look white, "they remain genuine negroes." "The black skin," in fact, "is a very small part of that tout ensemble of physical and mental inferiority."[32]

There was wicked irony here. On one level, such reasoning helped stabilize racial categories in the 1850s, at least in slaveholders' minds. At another level, such thinking—half baked as much of it was—held decidedly nonintellectual implications. All this talk of the senses and race, both in the 1850s and for years to come, lessened whites' need to think about race: what it meant and whether or not it was, in fact, real. Instead, aspects of the Old South's proslavery defense—a largely intellectual project—ended up encouraging an emotional, visceral, and febrile understanding of racial identity. It was an understanding immune to logic, impervious to thought, and, as such, a perfect foundation for segregation.

3

Senses Reconstructed, Nonsense Redeemed

Precious sights, adored sounds, and fancied smells of antebellum life lingered for Frances Butler Leigh, "staunch Confederate" daughter of liberal British actress Fanny Kemble and, after the Civil War, mistress on two Georgia rice plantations. Following her father's death in 1867, Frances managed the plantations, alone at first and later with her British husband, James Wentworth Leigh. In the postwar years, she attempted to recapture and reimagine the world of antebellum slavery through the senses. "As I sit on the piazza," she wrote, nostrils open, ears listening, "the air comes to me laden with sweet smells and sweet sounds of all descriptions," scents so honeyed by nostalgia they masked the rice fields' "awfulness of smell." At other times, Leigh's eyes accompanied her nose in shaping her sense of southern serenity: "The orange trees are all in full bloom, now, and smell most deliciously sweet, and the little place looks its prettiest." Even aspects of freedom were tolerable, not least because freedpeople's behavior confirmed her assumptions about black inferiority. "They are the most effervescent people," she remarked, "and to see them in one of their excitements, gesticulating wildly, talking so violently that no one on earth can understand one word they say, you would suppose they never could be brought under control again." But as transgressive as black noise—that is what it was to her—could be, Leigh's own quiet authority, she liked to think, won the day. "At first I used to talk too, but now I just stand perfectly quiet until they have talked themselves out, and then I ask some simple question which shows them how foolish they have been, and they cool down in a moment."

Freedom changed everything. Black people breached rules of old, and their every action, sound, and silence combined to frustrate the woman. "Their whole manner was changed," Leigh moaned. "They took to calling their former owners by their last name without any title before it, . . . dropped the pleasant term of 'Mistress,' took to calling me Fanny . . . and tried speaking to me with their hats on, or not touching them to me when they passed me on the banks." Leigh was not having any of it, and threatened and scolded and cajoled. But her attempts to modify black behavior in the new context of freedom took their toll: "I felt sure that if I relaxed my discipline for one moment all was up." Leigh aimed to "improve" her plantation "by removing the Negro houses away from where they now are, close to this house, to where I can neither see, hear, nor smell them." If she could not control their sounds, sights, and smells, then she at least had the power not to have to witness and experience them as often as slaveholders had before 1865.[1]

Frances Butler Leigh voiced a process in which the old arguments about indulging sensory otherness took on deeper, more visceral meanings, feeding the gradual evolution of customary and, later, legal segregation in the South. No longer required, as they saw it, to support blacks, southern whites strove to separate the races, their paternalism evaporating with the end of the Civil War and their way of life. The perpetuation and reconfiguration of old stereotypes concerning black distinctiveness and inferiority were important to that process, and racial sensory constructions were reintroduced with a ferocity and frequency that slaveholding paternalism had muted in the antebellum period.

Understanding the role of the senses in the evolution of postbellum segregation helps us appreciate the ways in which southern whites reduced blacks to a position in which segregation seemed natural and essential. Once we begin to explore how whites reconfigured antebellum sensory stereotypes, we better understand both the continuity and discontinuity between the antebellum and postbellum periods (at least when it comes to attitudes toward race). Sensory history, in short, reveals the rabidly visceral nature of the white supremacist mind-set and exposes the fragile, contingent, and illogical nature of the system of racial segregation.

Slavery was an arrangement of convenience (and dominance) for whites, one that entailed close association with many of the people they enslaved. To search for patterns of Jim Crow segregation during the antebellum period one had to look north, not south. But the end of slavery meant the end of intimacy and closeness—physical and social—

and the senses were merely reconfigured for different ends after 1865. And yet, beyond its rhetoric, segregation, like slavery, was tied intimately to the senses, and some aspects of southern slaveholding society proved critical in guiding southern segregated society. Racialized sensory constructions allowed southern whites to monitor infringements on white physical and social space, to remind blacks of who authored and who suspended the rules, to animalize freedpeople, and, ultimately, to escape the legacy of the past. For by the 1890s, if not before, centuries of sexual liaisons between white and black as well as mulatto and black had created an unprecedented number of "black" people who did not look black, a group of people whose visual appearance jeopardized the very order segregationists were busily erecting. To avoid inventing a system of racial segregation based solely on an eye that no longer accurately told racial identity in every instance, southern segregationists resurrected sensory stereotypes and arguments that their fathers had used to stabilize race during the first, but less acute, visual "crisis," that of the 1850s.[2]

Segregation aimed to construct and then fix ideas of absolute racial difference by locating black and white bodies in different spaces, spaces with different social and political values and meanings, and the deployment of old sensory stereotypes was central to the process. But segregation was not just about the spatial and physical separation of the races. In sensory terms, whites used the very suspension of the rules of segregation—wholly necessary to the day-to-day functioning of the system—to further reinforce black inferiority. Southerners white and black understood that utter separation flew in the face of social and economic realities. Black and white did interact; they had to. Whites relied on black labor, and that dependence often allowed for a degree of intimacy and physical proximity that collapsed racialized space. Black sound, black scent, black touch, black taste—all penetrated the white world on a regular basis and with a frequency that sometimes shocked northern visitors. The point about segregation is not that it was a system of complete separation; the point is that whites derived their authority by defining when and where sensory intimacy was permitted. In short, whites were sensorily intimate with blacks even as they argued for segregation. Logic and consistency were not segregationists' strong suits, as black people never tired of showing. Then again, illogic was a luxury whites could afford.[3]

The transition to full-blown Jim Crow took time. Examples of sensory intimacy and the plasticity of race relations were apparent immediately after the war. It was possible to see "whites and blacks marching together, and in frequent instances, arm-in-arm." "The sight of white babies suckled at black breasts," of "the two races now eat[ing] together at the same table" immediately after the war, while hardly commonplace, nevertheless suggested that habituated segregation was still a little way off.[4]

That much said, the segregationist mentality was clearly present during Reconstruction, when separation was becoming a socially identifiable pattern. Although segregation sometimes actually improved black access to a variety of public services and accommodations (as slaves they had often been denied such access), and while blacks themselves set about establishing their own institutions—schools and churches especially—formal and informal segregation flourished in most places long before the end of Reconstruction.[5]

As freedpeople began claiming rights to education and geographic movement, as they began to behave independently, so white southerners reacted by passing a series of Black Codes in 1865 and 1866. The centrality of segregation to the Codes is clear. Statutes drawing color lines in public spaces partnered provisions for black apprenticeship and vagrancy laws. Blacks were excluded from first-class railroad cars in Mississippi, Texas, and Florida, for example. Congressional Reconstruction did much to undermine these early efforts to legalize segregation, and the Codes were dismantled in 1867; but Congress could not erase the cultural imperatives that gave rise to the Codes in the first place. Unspoken protocols of racial segregation prevailed during Reconstruction. It seemed to matter little who had political control in these years, for even with Republicans and black voters in control, schools were segregated and the races increasingly kept apart. Whether it was on horse-drawn streetcars or in bed, southern whites acted quite quickly to erect barriers. As early as 1867, southern states established provisions penalizing interracial sex or simply banned interracial marriage; some Republican Reconstruction legislatures struck down the provisions, but they reemerged in full force in the 1890s.[6]

Segregation and the mind-set that spawned it had a short gestation in war's echoes. Bitter, jaded, tired Confederates looked around and saw and heard and smelled a society in ruins, the most conspicuous example of that devastation less in the rubble of their beloved buildings than in the perceived impudence, independence, and freedom of their beloved slaves. Southern hatred for the freedmen and their Yankee aides (themselves hardly angels when it came to race relations) was probably as great as their professed paternal love had been for their slaves, and it was this intensity of emotion—this deep, abiding, and raw sense of betrayal—that caused southerners to express with such venom their antipathy to the new order and those who forged it.

The basis of informal and formal segregation was loathing, an almost unspeakable bitterness and stunned horror felt by Confederates who had lost a war at terrific cost. Evidence of loss was permanent, insistent, forcing its way into all the senses of an angry white South, acidic hate puddling in its guts. Sights, horrendous sights, things never before seen, affronted white southerners in 1865. Seeing the disruption of war's end, the physical movement of people whose previous activities had been regulated and surveyed, witnessing, literally, highways "crowded with wagons and teams, cattle and hogs, niggers and wogs" combined to produce an "afflicted gaze" for whites, whose loss of mastery was now mirrored in the visual disruption of the southern landscape.[7]

Remember Mary Pringle, the Charleston mistress who was greeted with "quiet silence" by slaves who lovingly "shook her hand" in 1859 at the news of her son's death? Remember Mary Pringle, the woman who, like countless others, received profound affirmation from such actions that all was right with her world, the woman who willingly touched back black skin, who must have reveled in the appropriateness—decorum and submission—of her slaves' voiceless expressions of loyalty and love? Six years later, her world had changed and with it her physical and sensory engagement with black people, particularly those men, newly freed, who refused to show her the respect she had long been used to. In October 1865, Mary Pringle approached the family coach house in war-ravaged Charleston. It was guarded by freedmen, black men, whose once quiet demeanor was now noisy, whose once tender touch she could no longer stand. There were "about a dozen seated before the door, howling, by note, a hymn—they did not even draw up their feet as I passed. I would have tread upon them but that I would not soil my own, by touching theirs." She still loved her maid, "our faithful Cretia," but

Mary thought most freedpeople ungrateful brutes. She did not mince her words. The sight alone of freed blacks induced "a loathing that I feel when looking at a venomous reptile." Free and backed by a federal government seemingly intent on crushing white southern authority, blacks quickly became "nasty, offensive." Old habits of intimacy died hard, of course, and new needs mandated old styles. Immediately after the war, the Pringles were so poor that Mary slept on "a mattress thrown on the floor," her delicate frame probably unused to the feel. Moreover, "we have eaten breakfast on plates borrowed from our Freedwomen," an act literally unthinkable thirty years on but, in the context of a world where paternal relations and memories lingered, still possible. But that world was dying, quickly. In May 1867, Charleston "announced that the street cars were open to the public." Mary wrote, "The 'Niggers,' of course, crowd into them, and the White people, not being citizens, keep out of them."[8]

"An inferior race cannot have the supremacy over a superior, more intelligent and cultured people," wrote Mary in 1868, "yet we must wait that this evil may correct itself." But the wait was long, punctuated by noisy elections, "painfully quiet and silent" rice mills, the only sensory comfort coming from the largesse of John Julius Pringle, who had profited handsomely from the war. He gave his father a "light, beautiful overcoat," one far more fitting his refined sense of touch than "the coarse, uncouth, striped one" he had gotten from a soldiers' store, and provided his mother and sisters with "delicate cologne" and "toilet soap, too."[9]

Foreign visitors confirmed what former slaveholders believed. Edward King's visit to Charleston, South Carolina, after the war introduced him to "numerous little shops frequented by negroes, in which one sees the most extravagant array of gaudy but inexpensive articles of apparel." Northern newspapers carried stories about what it was like to observe freedpeople, and the depictions were none too flattering. In Petersburg and Lynchburg in 1866, northern observers saw blacks adorned with "sham jewelry" and wearing "gaudy dresses and brilliant bonnets." "The Negro 'propensity to dress' is a rooted passion"; blacks betrayed their extravagant taste with their "showy" and "gaudy" clothes. What northern observers saw of freedpeople—or, rather, how they looked at them—was confirmed in how they heard them. Black religion was characterized in terms of "rants and rambles and howls," and "quietly talking" to preachers about appropriate aural decorum seemed like a waste of time since the noises were a mark not only of excitable zeal but also of "an aboriginal savagery of faith."[10]

Withdrawal was prompted by a desire for physical and social space, distances gauged by the senses. One Winnsboro, South Carolina, lawyer asked William Porcher Miles in 1867 how he could stand to live in the new world of racial equality. He found freedpeople "revolting" and measured and articulated that visceral loathing through his nose. Go to England, leave the South, he counseled Miles. There "you could succeed & at any rate wd not have as many Negro Clients & negro witnesses to offend yr nostrils as in these USA." Countless times, whites protested the sight of black men on juries and shivered at the thought of having "a negro sit next to you" in a theater. Immediately after the war, they made unusually heavy use of a word that became standard in the segregationist lexicon for the next century: crowded. At war's end, whites began to use "crowd," "crowded," and "crowding" as a shorthand for social equality, one they registered through bodily senses. Being "crowded" meant having not just to see blacks but also to feel, smell, and hear them (the inability to close nostrils or ears making "crowding" especially transgressive and invasive for whites). Instances of tenderness across the color line persisted, of course, some quite courageous, some touching to the extreme, some involving true love between white men and black women. But the mental and emotional chasm resulting from the war yawned massively. Smells, sounds, and touches, real and imagined, served to further isolate the white mind from the black body.[11]

REDEMPTION, SEGREGATION

For many white southerners, segregation was the permanent solution to the problem of black freedom. And as some blacks began to enjoy quiet, hard-won political and economic successes, so whites worried more deeply, envied with greater bile, and hated with edged loathing. White perceptions of closing social distance led some to ratchet up physical segregation by way of perverse compensation.[12]

This is not to say that there was no trace of interracial political cooperation even after Reconstruction. We know, for example, that black and white worked across race and class lines in North Carolina in the 1880s and in Virginia during the 1890s. Hoping to promote racial harmony, some white men established interracial organizations and clubs. But, on the whole, such efforts were nowhere near enough to stay what amounted to a wholesale disenfranchisement of the southern black electorate by 1910.[13]

Within two decades after the Civil War, white southerners bent on segregating received assistance from the U.S. Supreme Court. In 1883 the justices found most of the 1875 Civil Rights Act unconstitutional and argued that the Fourteenth Amendment could not be applied in instances of private discrimination. The Court was hardly in the vanguard of the segregation movement, though: several states prior to 1883 had already set about establishing separate but unequal accommodations for blacks and, in the process, eclipsed whatever modest moves toward equality that had been made under the Republican governments of Reconstruction. In 1877 black students were forced to leave the University of South Carolina and attend a separate college in Orangeburg, and in 1881 Tennessee began to segregate its public conveyances. Other states followed. By the early years of the twentieth century, every former Confederate state separated white and black in transportation.[14]

Of course, even in the 1890s blacks still voted, still held office, and still participated in the body politic, albeit on a much-reduced scale from the heady heights of Reconstruction. But such examples of black political influence only inspired white supremacists. Instances of black political authority fueled white hatred, legitimating violence, intimidation, and disenfranchisement of black voters. De jure segregation thrived in this environment.[15]

Black economic success and the patterns of consumption that accompanied it also challenged white sensory stereotypes. Blacks with carriages irked white North Carolinians: the sight alone contradicted cherished beliefs about black indolence and incompetence. Yet such images were often contorted so that they refined rather than undermined white sensory stereotypes: black carriages were gaudy and ostentatious, perfect examples of impossibly gauche black taste.[16]

Because segregation seemed to satisfy so many, often competing, demands in southern society, ways out proved elusive. For example, late-nineteenth-century structural changes created an excitingly fluid and progressive economic environment that ran headlong into white southerners' understandable concern for social order and stability. Segregation, though, controlled blacks, established order, and allowed whites to embrace modernity while having ostensibly solved what they referred to as the "Negro problem." The South would derive additional benefits from segregating the races, argued others. A new generation of blacks, one born since the Civil War, one not schooled in the racial etiquette of the old days, was becoming dangerously assertive, cheeky even, "uppity." Segregation would teach them their "proper place."[17]

Essentially, segregation took much of the thinking out of life. For many, it promised to make interaction between the races so automatic, so structured, that white and black would live tranquilly; all complications, abrasions, and contradictions were to be smoothed under the application of pervasive segregation. This was the real, psychological appeal of the system to whites. Segregation courted the southern gut and committed an outrageous infidelity on the southern mind. It was an attempt to regain a world lost, one destroyed by fire and war; an attempt to feed a deep hankering for the old days of racial etiquette, when, so memory said, social and racial order had reigned supreme. But whites could not have that world, so they tried to re-create one that maintained discipline and punished blacks for their perceived betrayal by keeping them (for the most part) distant and (invariably) unequal. Without slavery, though, the present was slippery, oily, and elusive. Such instability, combined with the horror of having lost the war and the ingratitude of blacks who left masters and mistresses, injected venom into this new system. Yes, a few paternalists and a few Populists protested the extremist stance that was emerging, but most embraced white supremacist arguments.

The senses were central to—inextricable from, really—this gut-driven society. Consider the evidence from southern literature—a supremely intellectual font of visceral racism. George Washington Cable's depictions of docile blacks gave way to a venomous, vicious, and enthusiastically racist genre pioneered by men born largely after the Civil War, men with few ties to the paternalist regime of antebellum America. In place of Cable's recognition of the range of black behavior—the existence of well-dressed and slovenly blacks, of blacks who smelled and blacks who did not—came statements touting absolute racial difference and invariable inferiority.[18]

Some of the era's most widely read authors affirmed and helped generate the accepted sensory dimensions of white racism. The first novel in Thomas Dixon Jr.'s Klan Trilogy—his 1902 *The Leopard's Spots: A Romance of the White Man's Burden, 1865–1900*—uses the senses to anchor white characters in the South and establish black inferiority. Dixon's former Confederates see, hear, and smell the southern homeland. "When I hear these birds in the trees an' see this old dog waggin' his tail at me, and smell the breath of them flowers," muses Tom Camp on his return from the war, "I'm at home." The same characters also use the senses to mark blackness. Camp—of poor white stock—loathes blacks in their entirety and thinks the planter class rather too indulgent of them. Uncertain if blacks are even human, Camp is certain that "I hate the sight of 'em," "their black ape faces grinnin'." He "always felt like they was crowdin' us to death on them big plantations" and resents that "I had to leave my wife and baby and fight four years, all on account of their stinkin' hides." He means "stinkin'," literally: "At night when they'd detail me to help the ambulance corps carry off the dead and the wounded, there was a strange smell on the field that came from the blood and night damp and burnt powder. It always smelled like nigger to me! It made me sick." Dixon also reflected the belief that freedom had let loose long-contained black emotions, now heard in "shouting and screaming," and seen in "streets . . . black with negroes."[19]

Dixon touched on what freedom really meant when detailing the lust and angst of his white characters. He has the lovelorn Charles Gaston, for example, ponder broad questions of social power. "Was a man full-grown until he had seen, felt, smelled, tasted, and heard all life?" "I will be free," Gaston rages, explaining, "I will sweep the whole gamut of human passion and human emotion. I will drink life to the deepest dregs of its red wine. I will taste, feel, see, touch, hear all!" The crescendo: "I will know for myself what it is to live." In the process, Dixon suggested that black people, too, would want to experience freedom in all its sensory glory, and therein lay a fear among white men. For surely to feel, taste, smell, and hear freedom, especially the forbidden, might well lead to miscegenation?[20]

Although Dixon tried to account for the high incidence of southern biracial children by emphasizing black rape of white women, he also blamed the South's earlier generation of white men for failing to tame their sexual desires (chances are Dixon had a biracial brother, courtesy of his father's assignations with his black cook in North Carolina). Not that even the noblest southern man stood much chance when confronted by powerfully sensuous black and mulatto women, women who knew how to play on the senses. In The Sins of the Father (1912), Dixon explained how white men were captured by black women's sexuality. Major Daniel Norton is lured by Cleo, an octoroon servant. Her white blood has done little, if anything, to dilute her sensory blackness. Dixon has "every movement of her body" serve as a "throb of savage music from a strange seductive orchestra hidden in the deep woods!" Norton's wife discovers that he has had sex with Cleo but is told by a physician not to blame her husband. The black woman's sensory lure was simply too much, too raw for Norton: "With that young animal playing at your feet in physical touch with your soul and body in the intimacies of your home, you never had a chance." There was a good deal of truth to the claim, often made by African Americans, that the real problem was not black men but, rather, white men unable to control themselves with black women.[21]

For men such as Dixon, the Civil War was not just about freeing slaves; it was also about the lowering of class standards and the rise of what antebellum southern slaveholders and American elites generally termed "the mob." "Prior to the Civil War," Dixon wrote in *The Clansman*, "the Capital was ruled . . . by an aristocracy founded on brains, culture and blood." With emancipation, the Fourteenth and Fifteenth Amendments, increasing immigration, and working-class activism, however, "a new mob of onion-laden breath, mixed with perspiring African odour, became the symbol of American Democracy." Time would not alter circumstance or character, just as "the odor of pomade on his black half kinked hair" was a mere olfactory veneer that did nothing to change the essence of the black man.[22] Blackness would always betray itself to white senses. It had to.

PUTTING SENSES TO THE TEST

By the turn of the century, segregation as a legal and cultural institution was well on the way to becoming an accepted, embedded, and unquestioned part of everyday life in the South. The sensory dimensions of segregation were everywhere apparent. Here, we consider just three areas where the sensory construction of race proved critical to the erection of full-blown southern segregation: gender and lynching, railroads, and late-nineteenth-century conversations about disease.

Lynching

Although white men had always harbored anxieties about sex between black men and white women, their fears became compounded in the context of a postbellum South, where sensitivities to slight and gesture were extraordinarily high and where the relationship between citizenship and manhood took on overwhelming political and emotional importance for all men. This is why touching a white woman, even an accidental brush on a sidewalk, as W. E. B. Du Bois and count-less others discovered, provoked furious reactions. Touch was critical to the white supremacist argument. Black men, argued whites, their lust freed from slavery's discipline, could not help but prod and ca-ress delicate white female flesh. Accidental brushes now would soon become eager groping and "crowding," and everyone knew where that would lead.[23]

Lynching was a response to such behavior. Yet, for lynching to work, segregation's sensory protocols had to be suspended. Rules against touching black skin were ignored as white hands branded black feet and cuddled severed black fingers and penises, the cozy, tactile reminders of ghoulish justice. New technologies captured the sound of such touch-ing. With the arrival of Edison's new talking machine at country fairs in the mid-1890s, you could hear an actual lynching, a black man's shrieks, crackling fire, and white anger. This was the soundscape of the New South, all for a nickel. Anyway, rules were relaxed when it came to men. Black men and white could box and fight because they were men. Cer-tainly, sensory indications of social equality were never countenanced, such as hand shaking, but masculine imperatives and practices allowed for a greater degree of interracial touching between men, nearly all of it violent. The firm injunction against touching was between black men and white women. And should even a rumor of such a touch gain currency in the white community, white men were perfectly happy to remind black men of a simple truth: touch whiteness, and whiteness will touch you.[24]

Old sensory stereotypes assumed new twists, in part to justify mod-ern behavior. Segregationists thought blacks especially prone to rape and particularly graphic, heinous displays not just because they lacked self-discipline and their sexuality was easily pricked (courtesy of height-ened senses), but also because, paradoxically, black senses were largely insensible. In the late summer of 1897, for example, George Brodie, a black man, was arrested for the rape of a white woman, Nannie Catlett, in North Carolina. At the trial, a white witness said that black on-lookers (and, presumably, hearers) "stood stolid, rather vengeful to my eye," during the rape. "These negroes cannot see the heinousness of the crime." In an ironic appropriation of the old abolitionist argument used against slaveholder insensitivities, segregationists maintained that blacks could see and hear terrible things and remain unmoved. Such stolid insensibility demanded the utter violence of lynching. To make blacks feel, literally, the enormity of their crimes, whites had to hit hard, harder than civility really allowed. That is why the witness at Brodie's trial recommended a lynching and nothing less since only extreme violence left a "sense of shock upon the race which even then seems to receive it all too dully." Brodie was hanged weeks later.[25]

Lynching stressed the inviolability of white space, skin, and bodies through violent, physical contact. It seemed that the only fitting punishment for a black man who touched a white woman was for white men to up the ante, to show, as if there was any doubt, who held ultimate authority in this society. The more than 2,500 lynchings recorded in the South from 1885 to 1903 showed that white men had the power to strip the black body, literally, of its senses, to possess it in parts. In April 1899, near Newman, Georgia, two thousand whites witnessed the lynching of Sam Hose for supposedly killing a white man. Their eyes saw the literal deconstruction of a black body: Hose's ears, fingers, and genitals were cut off; his face was skinned, and pieces of his skin and bone were sold as gruesome souvenirs. Legacies of other lynchings were olfactory, carried by whites long after the event. One woman in the Mississippi Delta noted detecting a "strong odor" from a white man and discovered the scent came from a black finger in his coat pocket. The daily injunction against smelling blackness notwithstanding, this man cradled the scent of black flesh and let it souse the fibers of his clothes, an odorous reminder of white power. But there were never enough body parts to go around, so visual reminders, specifically photographs, captured the moment. From these, postcards were made and sometimes mailed to critics of lynching in other states. The ferocity and sadism of lynching satisfied an emotional appetite among whites, but the event also revealed the contingent nature of segregation. Touch was, lynching thundered, a white man's prerogative.[26]

Railroads

During the 1880s especially, railroads became the contested terrain of segregation in the South. Embedded in that contest were conversations about the sensory dimensions of race. Not only did the trains introduce new sensory experiences to many southerners with their "strange and frightening sounds" and "the queer smell of things," not only did they help undermine whites' ability to read racial identity quickly, reliably, and effectively, but the "sexual charge that might be created among strangers temporarily placed in intimate surroundings," such as a railroad car, was also a worry for many whites. Efforts to segregate railroad cars before the 1880s were piecemeal, with local companies fashioning their own policies. Eventually, the trains fully came to heel; between 1887 and 1891 nine southern states enacted segregation laws for railroads.[27]

Preexisting divisions between first and second class lent themselves to a sensory demarcation of space. Prior to segregation, who sat in which class and car was tied very much to material comfort, the ability to appreciate that comfort, and the use of tobacco. Men and women who did not use tobacco sat in a sweeter-smelling first class, a place with quieting carpet and soft "velvet" seats, whose "heavenly feel" enchanted and caressed. Second class was a different sensory story: a noisy place with few tactile comforts, a place for bodies that could tolerate wood seats and probably would not appreciate softness and carpet anyway; a place where mainly men, especially tobacco smokers, chewers, and spitters, sat. This class was often behind the engine and filled with soot. Conditions were "the dirtiest, nastiest" some people ever experienced, and, increasingly, those who rode second class became associated with the conditions in which they rode. There was no real cause and effect— did the passengers create the conditions or vice versa?—but there was a definite association between second-class cars and sensory indifference, stench, coarseness (haptic and social), and dirt.[28]

Into this context stepped segregation, and, given the long association between blackness, smell, noise, dirt, and sensory numbness, it is hardly surprising that black men and women were pushed into the second-class coaches. White protest at black presence in first class was often articulated through a particular idiom of sense and space and proper place. Because first class was reserved for the clean, the quiet, the sweet smelling, whites reacted keenly to a black presence in what they cherished as "their" space. Not only would blacks jeopardize the sensory integrity of the space; they had no business consuming the softer sensory delights of first class.[29]

Whites were not shy about why they wanted to segregate blacks on railroads. During its 1891 session, the Arkansas legislature introduced a range of segregation measures, including "equal but separate and sufficient" passenger coaches, the Separate-Coach Law. A "visible and distinct admixture of African blood" meant being assigned to the black car. It was, as elsewhere, usually up to the conductor to detect race in such instances, using his eyes. But, as the editor of the Fort Smith *Times* wrote, the nose would do the job, too. "The people of Arkansas have borne with this negro nuisance on railroads a long time, hoping that the negroes would learn how to be decent." The "degree of offensiveness borne by respectable people at the hands of drunken, insolent blacks" was simply too much: "A Saturday night train out from Little Rock to Pine Bluff is hardly safe, to say nothing of the fact that not one in eighty uses Pear's soap or any other kind." Nothing in the editor's comments suggests that black smell was innate—soap would eradicate the scent, such as it was. But trying to change a smell to suit a nose that never wanted to be pleased was next to impossible. In other words, it was white stereotypes of blackness—not blacks' senses—that had become ossified.[30]

Gender complicated the picture and heightened the emotional stakes. In the close quarters of railroad carriages, argued a New Orleans newspaper in 1890, "one is thrown in much closer communication" with other people than in, say, a "theatre or restaurant." Without segregated cars, whites and blacks would be "crowded together, squeezed close to each other in the same seats, using the same conveniences, and to all intents and purposes in social intercourse." Here we encounter that word again: "crowded," even "squeezed." It betrayed a fear for southern womanhood. For a southern white man to even "see" his wife or daughter "occupying a crowded seat in a car next to a negro," to witness physical contact in what was perceived as almost private space, to eye the woman touching the black man was enough to inspire a "feeling of disgust" and get guts churning.[31]

At first, black women especially posed problems. Should a black woman be treated according to her race or her gender and, if the latter, allowed to sit with white women in the first-class ladies' car? Predictably, whites rejected black women's claims to ladyhood and tried to herd them into the black car. For their part, black women went to court, pushing for equality according to the standard provided for white women. Although they sometimes won, common carriers attempted to straddle a difficult middle position, satisfying state and federal court rulings while at the same time pandering to popular white prejudice, itself often expressed in modern terms of "emotional" damage suffered as a result of involuntary association with blacks. Carriers started to use neutral terms for their cars (front/back) instead of gendered terms (ladies'/smoking cars) and basically cobbled together a compromise by putting all blacks in the smoking car, except respectable black women, who were given the license to ride in the ladies' car. By the late 1880s and early 1890s, even this policy found its critics, and in defense of white womanhood and white supremacy, states began to segregate all cars by race alone.[32]

Integral to this process was a sensory de-gendering of black women. By arguing that they should sit with black men in the smoking car, a space filled with stench, replete with the visual evidence of tobacco chewing (bad taste in every respect), a space endured by only the dullest of senses (or, alternatively, where heightened senses would suffer), whites made black women sensorily something other than women. By subjecting black women to cars brimming with "filth," "cursing," and a choking "scent of smoke," whites used the senses to drive home the point about black inferiority, regardless of gender. White women, by virtue of their gender and race, out of fear for their physical safety, and out of a perception of their refined senses and sensibilities, were not directed to the smoking cars.[33]

That southerners were reliably illogical here was apparent to some northern eyes. Charles Dudley Warner observed in Louisiana in the late 1880s that while there was a good deal of mingling between the races, "there are prejudices remaining. There are cases of hardship on the railways, where for the same charge perfectly respectable and nearly white women are shut out of cars while there is no discrimination against dirty and disagreeable white women." The observation was too near the bone for many whites: in their invented world, only blacks were dirty, and those few dirty whites were either redeemable through soap or quietly consigned to the nether regions of the segregationist mind.[34]

Disease

Disease linked the senses and segregation. Part of white supremacists' association of blackness and disease was, of course, very old, but aspects of it were also very new and related to the advent of germ theory at the end of the nineteenth century. There was, in short, an emerging close relationship between racial segregation and medical segregation beginning in the 1890s.[35]

Tuberculosis was the key to the connection. The tubercle bacillus was discovered in 1882, and it was silent, invisible, deadly. Because it was understood to be the product of a germ, it was undetectable by the unaided eye. The disease, segregationists maintained, was spread by black maids and servants, the very people who came into daily, intimate contact with whites. In braiding blackness with TB, segregationists merely reframed and reformulated an old association between black-ness, dirt, and contagion. The disease, whites maintained, was spread through intimacy, which presented something of a problem: how to contain the disease while also successfully using black labor? Segrega-tionists never resolved the contradiction and instead accommodated their own tortured logic by arguing that while whites got tuberculosis too, they were victims of irresponsible blacks who were more prone to get the disease (and thus transmit it) because of their innate racial inferiority. To deal with black servants (and to somehow maintain their use by whites), whites employed a sleight of hand: black nurses did not "want to do harm," maintained Georgia governor William J. Northern, and they were often unwitting transmitters of disease to white children. White children could be loved to death by black nurses: "They kiss them over and over again and sow the abundant seeds of disease and death." So too with cooks. Well meaning though they were, "they expectorate when and where they please and we inhale the sputum; they prepare all that we eat, tasting as often as they like, and we taste what they leave." Washerwomen were also worrying, for they touched white clothes and often spat on irons to test the heat.[36]

Not segregating, in the estimation of the Virginia Sanatorium for Consumptives in 1905, therefore posed severe risks: "As long as our colored people continue irregular habits, and herd together in immo-rality and infection, their homes will be hotbeds of infection, fresh from which they will enter into intimate relations with our white people, drinking from public cups, spitting around kitchens and public places, as nurses fondling and kissing children, as cooks, waiters and barbers handling food, tableware and clothing, inevitably spreading infection broadcast among all classes."[37]

The association of black women with tuberculosis had its counter-part in the association of blacks generally with venereal disease. Both confirmed widely held white stereotypes but also posed challenges to the behavior of whites. Every instance of disease among blacks reaf-firmed prejudice; every instance of disease also worried white men and women that their sexual liaisons with blacks or their reliance on black labor had exposed them to disease. Black diseases (carried by unseen germs) and the products of interracial liaisons (in the form of ever-whiter and less-visible black people) challenged the effectiveness of white eyes to see their world reliably. But, as we shall see, this only encouraged whites to rely ever more heavily on what they considered—in fact, what they had to believe was—the authenticating power of their other senses. Black disease could surely be smelled as much as a black who attempted to pass as white. Equally vexing was the continued need to exploit black labor while also "protecting" whites from black disease. Plainly, accommodations had to be made. Segregationists therefore ranted about the association between tuberculosis and blackness while recognizing the hyperbole of their argument. Most of what they said was designed to reaffirm racial subordination more than instigate a revolution in public health. While they knew full well that segregation of public facilities provided only limited "protection" against the transmission of black disease, they were happy to further segregate public facilities as a putative precaution against the spread of disease and principally to bolster segregation itself. Several cities at century's turn passed ordinances meant to keep an eye on black laundresses especially (often assumed to be the most common transmitters of TB) by making them wear badges and, as was the case in Atlanta in 1910, urging that they undergo bimonthly physical examinations. If they passed the examination, they were free to work. In this way, white segregationists managed to leave black labor where they wanted it, retain the association of blackness with disease, keep in play the romance of the good black servant, and also ensure their health.[38]

All of this was by way of hideous preface to over a half century of segregation. Before charting the role of the senses in shaping segregation in the twentieth century, however, there is an important matter to which we must first attend, a matter that reveals with powerful clarity the tension inherent to the system of segregation. We must examine, with fresh eyes, ears, and noses, the history of the 1896 legal case that served as the basis of modern segregation, Plessy v. Ferguson. Only then will the developments that followed—how whites tried to "fix" race and how blacks tried to unfix it—make fullest sense.

Finding Homer Plessy, Fixing Race

Segregationists lived an illogical, emotionally powerful lie that relied on gut rather than brain to fix racial identity and order society. Their ability to make solid what was always slippery is annoyingly impressive. When it came to race, ordinarily thoughtful people contorted reason to fit a system of racial segregation riddled with so many exceptions and nuances that it should have imploded under its own nonsense. But that is not what happened. Sensory stereotypes—and the unthinking, visceral behavior they encouraged, even required—helped make the system seem entirely stable, reasonable, and appropriate to the people who sponsored it. This tension, along with the ability to reconcile the ostensibly contradictory, was present from the very beginning of formal segregation. As such, any discussion of segregation in the twentieth century must first address the legal foundation of the system.

LYING EYES, PASSING FEARS

Plessy v. Ferguson (1896) was a case in which the U.S. Supreme Court upheld the constitutionality of Louisiana's 1890 statute providing "separate but equal" accommodations for black and white passengers on its railroads. In a carefully planned event, Homer Plessy, a visually "white" "black" man, refused to sit in a colored car and was subsequently brought before the judge of the Criminal Court of New Orleans, John H. Ferguson. Plessy's attorney, Albion W. Tourgée, challenged the 1890 law on the grounds that it conflicted with the Fourteenth Amendment. In a 7–1 ruling, the U.S. Supreme Court upheld the Louisiana statute and maintained that the law did not violate the Fourteenth Amendment because it was merely a reasonable exercise of state authority and that separate but equal did not deprive Plessy of equal treatment. The lone dissenter was a former slaveholder, Justice John Marshall Harlan, who made the point that laws mandating segregation on the basis of race contravened the color-blind spirit of the U.S. Constitution.

So, here we have a black man who was not visibly black, who had to tell whites that he was black, who, in effect, told white eyes that vision alone was unreliable when trying to fix racial identity. From this, segregationists established a system that depended utterly on the separation of the races even if you could not always see who was "black" and who was "white." How on earth could white southerners have entrenched a system that seems so susceptible to failure? But segregationists would not have understood the question. Most never batted an eyelid in response to the visual ambiguity of race, their heavy reliance on the other senses bolstering their bravado, making emphatic their conceit. They had a long history of believing that they could sense race in other ways, ways that, when used with seeing, would allow them to establish racial identity with some certainty. Most of the time, they believed they could see blackness, and, in the cases where they could not, they believed they could use noses, ears, fingers, and tongues to verify what the eye thought it saw. The beauty of sensory verification was simple—it had the power of subjective authority. If a man was accused of smelling black, who was to disagree with the white nose doing the smelling?

To understand how segregation could be based on nonvisualist ways of understanding the world, we need to consider the *Plessy* case within the larger developments of the late Victorian era. Increasingly, doubts about the reliability of vision in the late nineteenth century brought into play the other senses, a return of sorts to a pre-Enlightenment experience in which vision tended to complement rather than dominate the other senses.[1]

If the eighteenth century connected sight with truth, seeing with balanced and reassuring perspective, vision with certainty, the end of the nineteenth century witnessed growing doubts about the eye's reliability. But there was no crisis of seeing because of the emotionally powerful appeal of the authenticating and stabilizing power of the other senses. Moreover, Enlightenment confidence in the truth of sight, in the certainty of perspective, in the very objectivity of seeing, did not evaporate entirely in the nineteenth century. In fact, several long-term developments even enhanced the prestige and power of the optic. The increasing availability of cheap print and, by century's end, affordable photographs, the ability to travel to places heretofore largely invisible, to see familiar sights from new perspectives (courtesy of the railroad and balloons)—all served to empower sight. But even in the midst of assurances that seeing was believing, some of these same technologies, especially those that rendered the formerly invisible visible (planets, stars, and germs, thanks to widely available telescopes and microscopes), challenged popular beliefs in the reliability of observations made by the unaided eye.[2] Indeed, doubts about the certainty of sight emerged at the same time that seeing was considered central to surveillance, codification, and classification. Even as the belief that types of character were physiologically identifiable gained popularity, the idea that people could dissimulate, cover, and alter the way they looked led many to pause before assigning judgments about inner worth just by looking.[3]

Late-nineteenth-century America was hardly immune to these trends. Despite an emphasis on essence, changeless and inscribed, worries about how to determine the true and the false, how to authenticate the authentic and detect the counterfeit were common and applied to a range of issues, from money to expressions of taste and culture.[4]

And to race. As African Americans began to exercise their newly found freedoms after the Civil War, as a few of them even began to prosper, many whites, North and South, found prevailing and emerging theories concerning intrinsic racial and sexual difference increasingly attractive. Arguments concerning racial intrinsicality were very handy, not least because they allowed those tiring of Reconstruction to claim, as did Maryland senator George Vickers in 1869, that efforts to "elevate or improve the physical, moral or intellectual condition of the negro" were beyond the power of government. These hearty claims about racial essence and the dangers of race mixing took place in the context of hard, physical evidence to the contrary: "miscegenation" had a firm place in U.S. history. Race, in short, was becoming a visually unstable category even as white Americans touted its permanence.[5]

Segregationists appealed to nonvisual ways to authenticate race at precisely the moment when their efforts to separate the races intensified.[6] And if color was becoming less important as notions of biological racial difference were gaining ground, whites had to be able to find compelling evidence of racial difference that was not always visible. Biological determinism, the racial imperatives of segregation, miscegenation, and an ever-whiter black population mandated that whites had to ascertain blackness independently of the eye, just as their ante-bellum forefathers had.[7]

Given this context, "black" people passing undetected into the white world, successfully becoming "white," posed an enormous problem for segregation. If race was innate and if white southerners could always identify it, how could blacks fool whites? Failure to locate passers meant that race was not genetic but environmental, and blacks who passed made a mockery of segregation.[8]

Of course, passing was not new—slaves had managed to fool white eyes for years. But the scale of the "problem," combined with the increased stakes of maintaining the color line under segregation, gave passing unparalleled urgency and emotional intensity. The "great age of passing" reputedly began "around 1880 and was over, practically, by 1925." Still, even in the 1940s between 2,500 and 2,750 people passed every year, "with some 110,000 living on the white side of the line at that time."[9] Passing focused segregationist minds in powerful ways, making them jittery even as they claimed utter confidence in their ability to sense race.

Modernization did not help the segregationists. Railroads, for example, created circumstances where people who could not know one another's genealogies came into contact on a scale and with a frequency not experienced before in the South. In this regard, Jim Crow called into question Enlightenment, modernist authority and replaced it with a growing reliance on "lower," even premodern, senses of hearing, smell, and touch. With strangers came doubts and qualms, and segregationists realized they sometimes had to know backgrounds to tell race, especially with light-skinned strangers. One effect of increasing geographic mobility among African Americans was to stir up ways in which whites saw race. Formerly, in less mobile times, whites just recognized an individual's race because they knew the individual's genealogy and history. But old histories evaporated in new faces.[10]

To know race was in part, then, to know genealogy, but in a South that was increasingly on the move and increasingly urbanized, that knowledge was not always certain. Trains and urban areas posed particular problems in this regard because both jostled people in space, tending, in the process, to muddy personal time and history. W. F. Penn—a black physician—told Ray Stannard Baker about an altercation on a streetcar in Atlanta around the turn of the century and suggested not only how white eyes were becoming unreliable but also how embarrassing—and infuriating—misjudging race could be for the segregationist. Penn got on a car and

found there Mrs. Crogman, wife of the coloured president of Clark University. Mrs. Crogman is a mulatto so light of complexion as to be practically undistinguishable from white people. Dr. Penn, who knew her well, sat down beside her and began talking. A white man who occupied a seat in front with his wife turned and said: "Here, you nigger, get out of that seat. What do you mean by sitting down with a white woman?" Dr. Penn replied somewhat angrily: "It's come to a pretty pass when a coloured man cannot sit with a woman of his own race in his own part of the car." The white man turned to his wife and said: "Here, take these bundles. I'm going to thrash that nigger."[11]

Other instances were even more embarrassing. Nashville, Tennessee, 1889: A "bright, good-looking colored girl (or rather an almost white colored girl)" boarded a train. A white gentleman, "flashily-dressed," started to flirt with her. To his eye, she was white. He bought her lunch, and they ate together for a couple of hours. The girl "was entirely innocent of any intention to entrap or deceive the fellow," and the gentleman discovered his visual mistake only after the girl reached her destination. "He was probably the maddest man in the State when he found it all out." The incident, while passed off with some humor in the local newspaper, revealed some sticky truths about the New South and the difficulty in actually authenticating race, segregationists' claims about their ability to sense race notwithstanding. The man's eyes were fooled, first, because the girl did not look black to him and, second, because she was a stranger, a person without a racial history he could read to verify or challenge what he saw. Critically, the failure of his other senses to correct his visual mistake exposed the lie that segregationists loved to use, namely: if we can't always see them, we sure as hell can sense them in other ways.[12]

Because of the profound threat passing posed to the segregated order, white reaction to visual uncertainty could be sickeningly harsh. Lynchings were most common in places with "strange niggers," blacks without history in a given community. Not every lynching was a product of fidgety whites worried that the black man or woman before them was fooling their eyes. Most blacks were visible to whites. The relationship between visual racial ambiguity and lynching was more complicated than that, but visual uncertainty helped create a twitchy atmosphere in which whites, leery of black strangers, became increasingly nervous about their own ability to authenticate race generally. Sometimes, as was the case of the man on the railroad noted above, they failed horribly, became embarrassed, and, in their quiet moments of reflection, must have wondered what on earth they were doing.[13]

One way to combat this uncertainty was to profile the visual, to shout the sights of race, to keep pummeling away at seen race, to capture and legitimate a caricatured view of race. This is where signs depicting white or colored came in, where visual posts directing whites and blacks to separate spaces—railroad cars, waiting rooms, so many public spaces—became very important. Signs took several forms though. Visual representations of race provided by northern business in the form of advertising, for example, reassured southern whites. Cartons and packages with gruesomely caricatured images of blacks sold goods, in turn making blackness even more visible. Beginning in the 1870s and 1880s especially, images of blacks dressed in gaudy clothes, with loud colors (sights were heard here), bolstered white authority. However, seeing alone was not enough, and the old argument about blacks' inherent odor found continued expression in scientific journals of the 1890s and in works of social inquiry at century's turn.[14]

Not all sensory arguments were long lived, however. While the contention that blacks smelled to white noses remained intact, the notion that blacks had a heightened sense of smell evaporated. Instead, late-nineteenth-century whites developed more sensitive noses. Segregation demanded as much, and those touting the system ended up using the putatively premodern sense of smell to bolster their modernizing society. As one nineteenth-century writer suggested, modern man's senses had been dulled and "contaminated with the smells of perfumery, distilleries, chemical works, and vile cooking," and it was only among "some savage tribes . . . whose senses are more cultivated . . . than those of civilized nations" that the sense of smell was more acute. Peruvian Indians, for example, "can distinguish the different races, whether European, American Indian, or Negro, by the sense of smell alone." The imperatives of segregation came perilously near to making white southerners who claimed they could smell blackness less than civilized. The belief that black noses were more sensitive had been helpful to slaveholders simply because such a claim placed blacks closer to animals. But segregationists very rarely argued that black noses were more acute simply because white noses were now doing so much sniffing in an effort to detect blackness. In the end, segregationists muted the contradiction by claiming that blacks were so fetid that any nose, refined or savage, could detect them.[15]

MAKING SENSE OF HOMER PLESSY

Given the visual slipperiness of racial categories, the increasing ambiguity in telling who was who and what was what, and the "problem" posed by blacks passing, we might reasonably wonder not only how legal, state-sanctioned segregation triumphed in the 1890s but also how it was to last for so long. A reexamination of *Plessy v. Ferguson*, from the standpoint of sensory history, offers some new insights into the legal establishment of segregation.

In the early 1890s a group of elite African American men in New Orleans decided to challenge emerging segregation in public life generally and on railroads in particular. (In 1890 the Louisiana legislature passed a law segregating railroads.) Albion W. Tourgée—a former Union soldier, judge in North Carolina during Reconstruction, noted author and social commentator, fine legal mind, and ardent supporter of equal rights—was brought on as chief counsel in the case, working closely with Judge James C. Walker and Louis A. Martinet, a prominent black attorney in New Orleans. Tourgée was blind in one eye but could see well enough with the other to know that Homer Plessy was so light skinned that he was an ideal candidate to test the segregation statute. The Tourgée-Walker-Martinet strategy was, as Martinet explained in December 1891, "for us to put a colored passenger on board and the conductor to direct him or her, for we may have a lady, to the Jim Crow car and any refusal to go into it to enforce the law by legal means, that is to make the proper affidavit against the passenger under their act." Homer Plessy was, according to the African American newspaper the *Crusader*, "as white as the average white Southerner," his racial identity too slick for the eye to fix.[16]

Tourgée seems to have advised Martinet on this point, asking for a light-skinned woman specifically. Martinet agreed but worried that it "would be quite difficult to have a lady *too* nearly white refused admission to a 'white car.' " He explained to Tourgée: "Walking up & down our principal thoroughfare—Canal Street—you would [be] surprised to have persons pointed out to you, some as white & others as colored, and if you were not informed you would be sure to pick out the white for colored & the colored for white." Visual standards of race were highly unstable in New Orleans. Plessy's attorneys knew it and planned to use that instability to contest the 1890 law. Although coordination proved difficult, Tourgée secured the cooperation of a local railroad company (the expense of segregated cars made railroad companies generally less than enthusiastic about the 1890 statute) and then orchestrated arrests, first of the light-skinned Daniel Desdunes, then of the virtually white, one-eighth "black" Homer Plessy.[17]

In court, James C. Walker explained to Judge John Howard Ferguson of the Criminal Court of the Parish of New Orleans the problem with the Separate Car Act of 1890. (A Massachusetts native, Ferguson had been appointed a federal judge during Reconstruction and was reputedly "friendly.") The law sought, Walker argued, to "confer upon a conductor the power to determine the question of race and to assort the passengers on the train." In Walker's opinion, this was an "invidious distinction and discrimination based on race, which is obnoxious to the fundamental principles of national citizenship" (his appeal here was to the Fourteenth Amendment). He also maintained that "race is a legal and scientific question of great difficulty and the state has no power to authorize any person," train conductors included, "to determine" it.[18]

Walker was quite right. The preamble to the 1890 act entrusted the conductor to "assign passengers" to appropriate cars, coaches, or compartments based on their race, ostensibly to "promote the comfort of passengers on railway trains." White comfort meant being out of sensory range of blacks and their filthy, smelly smoking cars. The conductor was key to deciding who was to experience that version of comfort.[19]

Louisiana's courts had no patience with such arguments. Not only were they dismissed by Judge Ferguson—there was, he said, no violation of Plessy's constitutional rights—but a subsequent appeal to a state court protesting the unconstitutionality of the 1890 statute was rejected in December 1892. In articulating the state court's position, Associate Justice Charles E. Fenner appealed to northern precedents allowing segregation in schools and on railroads and maintained that the law itself could hardly legislate away prejudice. He embraced the view that "following the order of Divine Providence, human authority ought not to compel these widely separated races to intermix." The court's largely dry legal decision is rife with peppery phrases regarding the dangers of the races being "thrown in such contact," the desirability of efforts to "avoid such contact," and the "unreasonable insistence upon thrusting the company of one race upon another." In his response to Walker, Assistant District Attorney Lionel Adams claimed that "interracial repugnancies, along with white inconvenience from the foul odors of blacks in close quarters," rendered the law reasonable. And if whites could legitimately demand separate railroad cars because of blacks' manifestly "foul odors," it was also possible to tell who was, in fact, genuinely black through inhalation.[20]

A petition for writ of error against the Louisiana court brought *Plessy v. Ferguson* before the U.S. Supreme Court in 1896. Walker and Tourgée's brief to the Supreme Court raised questions about the authority of the state to discriminate based on race and about the very workability of segregation and its daily enforcement. Tourgée particularly dwelled on the mechanics and reliability of discerning color. "Is the officer of a railroad competent to decide the question of race?" And what if the passenger in question differed with the officer's evaluation of his racial identity? Who had the authority to define race? "Is not the question of race, scientifically considered, very often impossible of determination?" Tourgée posed these questions in an attempt to configure race as property. Whiteness, he argued, was property, and the provisions of the 1890 act authorizing "an officer of a railroad company to assign a person to a car set apart for a particular race, enables such officer to deprive him, to a certain extent at least, of this property" without due process of law. Thus the conductor's power to define who was white and who was black held out the possibility of arbitrary discrimination. Tourgée kept on pummeling and kneading the doughy logic, pressing tenaciously the question of how to reliably ascertain racial identity: "By what rule then shall any tribunal be guided in determining racial character?" Of course, "it may be said that all those should be classed as colored in whom appears a visible admixture of colored blood." But, he asked, "by what law? With what justice? Why not count every one as white in whom is visible any trace of white blood?" "Justice," he maintained, "is pictured blind and her daughter, the Law, ought at least to be color-blind," not least because seeing race was increasingly problematic as a basis for racial segregation. Tourgée went on, building his case increasingly on the senses. While the Louisiana 1890 statute "requires the accommodations for the white and black races to be 'equal but separate,'" he maintained, "it by no means follows as a fact that they always are so." What of the black passenger who is forced to leave "a clean and comfortable car" for one "reeking with filth"? Surely, suggested Tourgée, there would be an inequality in the sensory comfort for the black passenger.[21]

The Supreme Court decision rejected Tourgée's argument. The 1896 majority decision offered by Justice Henry Billings Brown maintained that laws requiring the separation of the races did not "necessarily imply the inferiority of either race" and that, therefore, the provisions of the Fourteenth Amendment were irrelevant. Although Brown acknowledged the difficulty that conductors faced in identifying racial identity, he argued that "this question, though indicated in the brief of plaintiff in error, does not properly arise upon the record in this case, since the only issue made is as to the unconstitutionality of the act, so far as it requires the railway to provide separate accommodations, and the conductor to assign passengers according to their race." Here, the Court sidestepped the central question of how race was identified and, in so doing, allowed for the establishment of a modern system of segregation that necessarily conceded that sight alone was not always sufficient to establish racial identity.[22]

In no way did this concession startle segregationists. To maintain the color line, all southern states made mixed race marriages illegal and, in the process, described what made a black person "black." Virginia was an exemplar of sorts. The state toyed with various fractions: until 1910 one-quarter meant black; between 1910 and 1924 the fraction dropped to one-sixteenth; by the mid-1920s Virginia had gone to the one-drop rule. Even at one-quarter—certainly at one-sixteenth—it was "exceedingly difficult, if not impossible, to discern by eye" an individual's race. In fact, the evolution of the one-drop rule—hardly an exclusive southern development—suggests how very unreliable the eye had become to those trying to authenticate racial identity and, at the same time, how relatively unimportant seeing race was to segregationists. The one-drop rule relied on genealogy to ascertain racial identity—the history of fathers, mothers, great-grandfathers, a chronicle of color. The one-drop rule is, then, powerful evidence of the growing irrelevance of the eye in authenticating race.[23]

The sensory dimensions of race gained unprecedented currency at the end of the nineteenth century not least because, in the eyes of many whites, blacks had begun to approximate white behavior. In their economic and political standing, blacks seemed more white; in their consumption patterns, they behaved more white; and, in their very physical traits, some blacks were visually indistinguishable from whites. Segregationists' reaction to such developments was simple: in addition to claiming that blacks could only imitate whites, whites claimed that one did not always have to see race to know it. Innate racial characteristics spilled out, revealing themselves in behavior, dress, disposition—what was called "taste"—all apparently quite evident to the white ear, nose, and skin. Such beliefs were, of course, fiction, deeply cherished and entirely credible to those who held them. Whites could not always and invariably tell who was white and who was black because racial categories were socially constructed. Segregation, then, was built on nonsense, a lie, a deep illogic that Tourgée and passers came near to exposing. But such efforts were doomed to fail simply because the deep historical and cultural assumptions that created sensory stereotypes about black people precluded the kind of involved thought-process necessary to dissolve them. Twentieth-century segregation relied on sensory strategies that stabilized racial categories in ways that the largely intellectual act of seeing simply could no longer achieve.

FIXING BLACK IN THE TWENTIETH CENTURY

What twentieth-century segregationists meant by "black," how they constituted and defined it, was anchored by their senses. Segregationists fixed race sensorily, their projections editing and shaping what it meant to be black and, by default, nonblack.[24]

The Look-See

Casual, banal, everyday sights—often reflective of class but parading as racial aesthetics—were critical to marking and making race, rendering the process unthinking and natural. In his 1937 study of "Southerntown," Yale sociologist John Dollard saw racial seeing at work and recognized that access to the means of production reaffirmed the literal sight of blackness. "The contrast between the personal appearance of the Negroes and whites" was often shaped by economics: "The Negroes seem to inherit the castoff clothes, automobiles, food and social customs of the whites, and are marked off by a general sort of second-handedness." Although the "middle-class Negro homes are much better, . . . even there the limitations of income and taste are plain." On the black side of town, "a well-cropped lawn is a rarity. At night one sees kerosene lamps gleaming through the windows; in a few houses, electric bulbs. Only two paved streets traverse this area where fifteen hundred people live. In the evening groups of people sit on their front porches to keep cool, lacking the fans and electric refrigeration which are so useful in combating summer heat." Blacks inhabited the public space more fully and palpably through necessity. The overall impression of the black side of town was "dark and dingy." By contrast, the white side was visually appealing, aesthetically proper, thanks in part to whites' ability to consume modernity. White houses "[are] well painted, scrubbed, neat"; streets "are paved . . . and telephone lines run through the trees."[25]

In the countryside, too, whites had strict protocols when it came to what blacks should and should not be seen doing. A guiding light here was that "the only place in which they [whites] like to see them [blacks] is in the fields working." Off the farm, black bodies were supposed to obey other spatial rules. "The rule that a Negro should not enter the front door of a house is so taken for granted that many white people, when they go out for a short time, will lock the back door against thieves and leave the front door open," noted Hortense Powdermaker.[26]

Certain sights were forbidden, even to segregationists' eyes. In the 1940s the Mississippi writer David L. Cohn had lunch with a man in Memphis who "dilated angrily upon discriminations against Southern Negroes. Then, over coffee, he said, almost hysterically, 'But there is one thing I cannot stand. When I go to Chicago, I cannot bear the sight of Negro men dancing with white women.'" Going north generally was a visual affront for white southerners, for there teemed horrible sights, stabbing eyes at every turn. For one southern man, a trip north "made his blood boil . . . to see Negroes riding in streetcars side by side with whites, to see them eating in the same restaurants, to see Negro men and white women together." Even good, decent, self-avowed "liberal" men, men who would become actively involved in the Civil Rights Movement of the 1950s, were utterly shocked by what they beheld in the North. Prior to his involvement in the Montgomery Bus Boycott, Baptist preacher Robert E. Seymour Jr. attended Yale Divinity School in the 1940s, a place where white cooks and domestic servants served blacks. The "world seemed topsy-turvy as I watched the role reversal of white people waiting on black people!" Other sights just stung: "My shock upon first seeing a black woman kiss a white man reverberates within me still."[27] Of course, such things went on in the South but rarely in public or with the permission of the black woman.

Images of black competence and wartime bravery could provoke vicious reaction. Visual reminders of black courage, of black self-determination, rubbed whites the wrong way in Montgomery, Alabama, after World War II. Rosa Parks recalled, "I do know that white people didn't want black veterans to wear their uniforms," and some found that insignia, military badges, and chevrons could be ripped off on their return to the South. No occasion was overlooked for the reaffirmation of white difference and superiority. Just after World War II, the American Legion in Greenwood, South Carolina, proposed to erect a memorial to those who died, with the names of whites inscribed at the top, those of blacks underneath.[28]

In short, the preservation of southern race relations from the white perspective required constant calibration of things seen. It was a lesson outsiders learned quickly. A southern white "friend" of John Dollard said the sociologist had been "criticized for sitting on a porch with 'niggers,' to which Dollard responded, "I told him that I did not remember sitting on any porch with Negroes." No wonder Dollard felt he "was under constant surveillance by the white group." Possible visual transgressions were everywhere and applied to black and white behavior alike. Dollard was instructed not to "tip your hat to a Negro, man or woman."[29]

What segregationists wanted to see, then, were visual displays put on by the likes of Sam Eades, a "good Negro," a black man who reaffirmed what whites wanted their world to look like. Sam

> behaves strictly in accordance with the race-caste code when dealing with white people. . . . By inclining his head, Sam shows the white man that he acknowledges him as superior. He tips his hat to white men and women. He does not look a white woman straight in the eye. . . . Sam treats all whites, from the "sorriest" poor white to the wealthiest "high type" white from the plantation, with the same deference. . . . He says "sir" or "ma'am" at all times. . . . Sam would not sit and eat with white people even if he were asked to. . . . Sam is even careful not to call other Negroes "Mr." or "Mrs." before white people. . . .[30]

What Was That?

If seeing Sam Eades reassured segregationists, then hearing his deference functioned similarly. White southerners liked to hear harmony, black and white sharing and shaping southern serenity: "On Sunday mornings the air of the little towns vibrates with the ringing of church bells as the faithful of many sects and both races gather for worship." The soundscape sculpted southern race relations. Here, "whites and Negroes dwell in peace and amity," or so David L. Cohn claimed even as modernity rasped ever louder: "The brawling world is over the horizon's rim. Its alarms and revolutions do not reach us." Mississippi summers came "alive with the chatter and laughter of Negroes wielding hoes," and black music and mournful harmonica notes "scarcely seem[ed] to disturb the stillness of the night." "That music must always have been there." Thus did Mississippi Delta towns appear in their "peace and quietude always to have lived happily and serenely." And if black and white sometimes sounded a little alike, there was no real shame to it, for a southern lilt echoed a braided history. "Children learn extreme forms of the southern dialect early," wrote Morton Rubin, explaining that "the influence of Negro nurses and association with Negroes affect white speech at all ages. White adults resort to Negro dialect and expressions in dealing with Negroes." The "plantation area dialect is a source of regional pride, and foreign accents (northern United States or European) are quickly noticed and meet with disfavor."[31]

But outside of such aurally constructed serenity and its attendant metaphor of racial harmony, whites frequently heard blackness as emotional and bruisingly loud. Towns were described in the 1930s as having a quiet white side and a "noisy" black side, and the following 1910 evaluation of the sound of blackness by southern sociologist Howard W. Odum spoke for the listening ears of many a white southerner: "And just as jealousy leads to intensity of the animal passion peculiarly in the case of the negroes, so with this emotion go laughter, shrieking, singing and various expressions of wanton recklessness and morbid pleasure in the pouring-out of the animal passion."[32]

There might have been some truth to the argument that black culture was louder than its white counterpart, not least because material factors were relevant not only in shaping the production of sound but also in influencing how sounds were consumed. Whites' ability to afford fans and the electricity that ran them enabled a retreat from the heat, even at night, so that white culture became increasingly interior. The effect on the ear was marked: "Another feature of life on the two sides of the tracks is immediately striking," wrote John Dollard: "In general the white side is quieter, especially at night; there are fewer people moving on the streets, although the number of whites and Negroes in town is about the same. A sense of discipline and order is more apparent. People are more likely to move about in cars. There is less walking, loitering, and laughing than on the negro side."[33] Material conditions were one thing; whites' characterization of black laughter and merriment as noise—and their relative silence on the noise of their own cars—was part and parcel of the daily ritual of stereotyping black sound and behavior in particular ways and for particular purposes.

Fragrance

If eyes and ears could spot which side of town was black and which was white, so could noses. Hortense Powdermaker suggested an olfactory dimension to "Cottonville," Mississippi, in the 1930s. The visual "trimness" of the white side of town contrasted with the smell of the black side, where some residents gave "off a strong odor of stale perspiration and whisky." Similarly, Cecil Cook, a white Mississippian, associated pronounced odor with a black area of Columbus in the 1920s: "The smell of overfried catfish and the hickory smoke smell of the barbecued pork chops usually permeated the air in the area."[34]

Too easily, such cultural associations—that blackness could be smelled through food preferences—slid into preexisting categories touting an intrinsic, identifiable "black" smell. When a social worker visited the house of Ruby Bates—one of the two girls at the center of the infamous 1931 Scottsboro case—she entered the "clean unpainted shack . . . in a Negro section of town," paused, and said: "Niggers lived here before you, I smell them. You can't get rid of that nigger smell."[35]

The argument that blacks smelled was tied closely to assumptions that they were irretrievably dirty. The association was a powerful one. As the Group for the Advancement of Psychiatry pointed out in its 1957 study, *Psychiatric Aspects of School Desegregation*, in American culture "yellow, brown or black [skin] tends to be associated with ideas of dirtiness or destructiveness or unpleasant smell, while light colors, especially white and pink, tend to be associated with ideas of cleanliness, purity, innocence, and chastity." In the 1930s John Dollard found that "the fact that the Negro seems 'unclean' to white people is frequently stated in reference to personal hygiene, body odor, and the like." And Morton Rubin concluded in 1951: "To the question 'What is a Negro?' the white man will answer, 'He is not a real human being like you and me. He smells bad; he is sexually promiscuous; he is filthy and ignorant.' "[36]

Whites thought blacks should endure their own stench. In the late

1920s Robert Moton observed that on segregated streetcars "accommodations for Negroes are combined with the baggage compartment or the smoker for whites, which in effect makes the negro section a smoker too, as it is impossible to confine tobacco smoke and odour to the white section." According to Moton, olfaction helped explain the use of large partitions on streetcars separating the races: "Where coloured people ride in the rear it is said that it [the partition] is to keep unpleasant odours from the nostrils of white people; that is also the section of the car which gathers the most dust on unpaved streets."[37]

Plainly, the notion that black people harbored an innate smell was a vicious fiction. The very few scientific studies done between the 1930s and 1950s proved as much. An early unpublished experiment in the 1930s comparing the sweat of blacks and whites found not only that noses could not distinguish the race of the sweat but also that sweat from a black person was often ranked by whites as more pleasant than the smell of white sweat. In 1950 George K. Morlan reported in the *Journal of Genetic Psychology* the results of a more detailed experiment in which white students (mostly, but not exclusively, northern) smelled black students. Morlan found that "neither the mass nor individual data support the theory that Negroes have a distinctive body odor that whites can identify." He went on: "If a peculiar odor is a racial characteristic that can be noted, it exists in every individual of any given group and can be accordingly identified. If it does not exist in a single member of that group or cannot be identified with complete accuracy, it cannot be considered racial."[38]

However manipulated the olfactory fiction, it was very likely that poor people, because of their living conditions, did have a distinct, often unpleasant odor. And since African Americans were often appallingly poor and subject to atrocious living conditions, there is a good chance that many of them did, in fact, reek. Interviews of former slaves collected as part of the Federal Writers' Project, for example, tell us a good deal not only about memories of slavery but also about white attitudes concerning black living conditions during the Great Depression. "Such a hovel, such squalor," wrote FWP interviewer Margaret Johnson of Mary Smith's Augusta, Georgia, home in the late 1930s. "Mary was a squat figure, her head tied up in a dirty towel, her dress ragged and dirty," continued the description, the house ripe with "the odor from chickens." Laura Bell's interviewer was even more candid: "I cut the interview short thereby missing more facts, as the odor was anything but pleasant." But what else could one reasonably expect from a "little two-room shack with its fallen roof and shaky steps," the yard "an inch deep in garbage and water" following a heavy storm? Even in homes of the black middle class, bathrooms "seem to be very unusual, as is indoor plumbing. The worst cabins are miserably plain and poor; they are very hot in summer and hard to keep warm in winter."[39] Being poor was, of course, no guarantee of being ripe, but material deprivation combined with sweaty manual labor did make it difficult to maintain standards of hygiene.

The consolidation of segregation in the South's legal structure coincided with sociological, anthropological, and psychological work stressing the racialized nature of the senses, a trend summarized and explored in Otto Klineberg's 1935 study, *Race Differences*. At the time, Klineberg's study represented a scholarly reformulation and summary of what had been written by ethnologists and pseudoscientists for a couple of hundred years, the findings of which had already percolated deep into the mind-set of southern white supremacists. But Klineberg's work is revealing not just because it pointed to the continuity of scholarly work on the sensory dimension of racial differences but also because it expressed some deeply held and unquestioned beliefs about blackness in twentieth-century America. Klineberg noted that "members of any one group often find the odor of a strange group disagreeable," observing, quite correctly, that "this has frequently been regarded as an insurmountable barrier to free racial intermingling, for example, between Negroes and Whites." Klineberg dismissed, quite wrongly, the impact of this tendency. "Since miscegenation between all racial groups has been going on since the beginning of history, it is not necessary to attach much significance to this notion," he argued, adding that people gradually adapt to smell "so that the odor is no longer observed." Klineberg misread the segregationist mind badly because he failed to appreciate the fact that whether or not the racialized smell was real, segregationists made it real by virtue of a priori association and constant invocation of the stereotype. As George Morlan remarked in his 1950 study, "If Negroes had any peculiar body odor that whites noticed, it was probably due to whites looking for that odor."[40]

Two years after Klineberg's book appeared, John Dollard made similar points but with greater specificity: "Among beliefs which profess to show that Negro and white people cannot intimately participate in the same civilization is the perennial one that Negroes have a smell extremely disagreeable to white people." "This belief," he continued,

> is very widely held both in the South and in the North. A local white informant said that Negroes smell, even the cleanest of them. It might not be worse than other human smells, but it was certainly different. It was asserted to be as true of middle-class Negroes as of others, at least upon occasion. Another informant swore that Negroes have such a strong odor that sometimes white people can hardly stand it. He described it as a 'rusty' smell. This odor was said to be present even though they bathe, but to be somewhat worse in summer. Another white informant described the smell as 'acrid.'

Dollard then made the critical point: "White people generally regard this argument as a crushing final proof of the impossibility of close association between the races."[41]

Touching Tales

"Since the skin and its extensions—the hair and nails—cloak the entire body, it becomes part of a person most quickly accessible to superficial perception and evaluation," ventured psychologists studying school desegregation in the 1950s. As a result, "the association of particular meanings to certain colors and textures of skin," coupled with the notion that dark skin holds an "unpleasant smell," frequently "determines the manner in which one person relates to another."[42]

Fourteen-year-old Hubert Eaton understood what this meant. In the summer of 1931, Hubert committed a tactile sin, one he would not forget. Hubert was black and worked Saturdays in a Winston-Salem Woolworth's. A young white woman, a waitress with whom he worked in the soda shop, "leaned over the counter. . . . and I noticed the watch on her arm. Wanting to know the hour, I placed the tip of my little finger on her arm just above her watch so that she would turn to me." Her reaction: "She jumped back and screamed, 'Nigger! Don't touch me, you nigger!' " Hubert remembered the dire detail: "Her face contorted with rage. . . . As the redness of her face increased, I felt vibrations of hate." Then it dawned on him what had happened, the significance of his unwitting touch, his moment of forgetfulness or, in his estimation, his ignorance: "I knew I had violated a taboo of the South: Thou shalt not touch a white woman. In the ignorance of youth, I had desecrated the pale flesh of this undereducated, underpaid woman by impressing upon her, however innocently, my darkness." Hubert Eaton left, quickly.[43]

White southerners who grew up in the 1950s still remember the importance of touching and not touching. In an interview that I conducted, a white South Carolinian recalled the first time black skin touched her. As a child, she had an accident, her head was cut, and her father handed her to his black handyman, George. "And I screamed and screamed" because "he was black and I was afraid it would come off on me." "You would rarely touch anybody black," remembered Kip Carter, another white southerner with whom I spoke. In the 1950s, said Kip, whites "might" have patted black men on the shoulder, but they were "very conscious" of shaking black hands and touching black bodies.[44]

Outsiders sometimes had difficulty appreciating the depth of the prohibition against touching. Dollard had been in Southerntown five months before segregation managed to contort his reflexes: "When meeting Negroes I would feel the twitch of the shoulder muscles tending to put my hand forward and instantaneously the countervailing caste pressure against giving the Negro such a sign of social equality." Had Dollard been a southerner, there would have been no such twitching. No wonder he "heard many criticisms of the way northern politicians have fraternized with Negroes, and repeated mention of the visit of a Republican president who got off his train in a town and shook hands with various Negroes."[45]

Social and racial equality lingered in a handshake, but other haptic brushes touched a rawer nerve, one with a sexual undercurrent. When white mothers saw their sons touching the black maid, they reacted strongly, as Anne Moody recalled of an experience during her adolescence. When cheek touched cheek, when, within sight of the white matriarch, a black woman could feel a white boy's "warm breath on my face," the reaction was predictable: apoplexy.[46]

Black skin was not to be touched directly because it was suited only for hard and dirty labor. A common refrain in the 1940s was that the black man "is good only for work with his hands." Mississippi middle-class whites in the 1930s similarly held to "the conviction that manual labor is for the Negro, and that the Negro is designed for manual labor." White women made clear their contempt for black senses in the kind of work they assigned their maids. As one South Carolina black maid recalled of the 1930s, before the widespread use and availability of washing machines: "One woman named Miss Essie used to wash clothes, including the filthy, soiled clothes used by white women during their menstrual cycle. She would wash those dirty, bloody clothes by boiling them and getting them as white as snow. She couldn't refuse them since she needed [white women] as customers." Economic need required black women to touch and scrub the clothes, and doing laundry was "especially unpleasant in the South's already hot climate." That white women required black maids to perform such duties speaks volumes about how they perceived blacks and their suitableness for dirty work.[47]

Money, markets, and the power to consume barely grazed the tactile embargo. While blacks were free to enter white space in stores and buy hats, gloves, dresses, shoes, and other apparel, they were frequently prohibited from trying them on. Even the most generous policy made blacks try on clothes over other clothes, and most stores never let goods touch black skin without making the black customer buy the item. According to a 1941 sociological study: "The idea of uncleanliness is also extended to any clothing worn by Negroes, as was dramatically shown when a Negro customer returned a coat which she had bought from a white clothing merchant. The clerk was unwilling to accept the coat and when the assistant manager accepted it, the clerk said to another clerk: 'This is perfectly terrible; I think it is awful. We can't put that coat back in stock.' The latter said: 'I know it. Who wants a nigger coat?' " The clerk explained the power of indirect touch: " 'Some little white girl will probably come in and buy it and not know it is a nigger coat.' She hung it up very gingerly and didn't touch it any more than necessary."[48]

When a black woman went to try on shoes and "the clerk would hand them to her without offering to help her try them on," one could glimpse the sensory dimensions of segregation, a place and instance where sight and touch met to shape the clerk's reaction. How, after all, could a serious segregationist really entertain the sight of a white person kneeling at—and touching the feet of—a black woman? Little wonder black-owned shoe stores—businesses involving the tactile generally—blossomed. Black undertakers "are especially favored by discrimination. If it is in any way avoidable white undertakers generally will not handle the bodies of Negroes. . . . It was the ambulance corps from a white undertaking establishment that in one city left a Negro railroad worker to bleed to death rather than carry him in the ambulance used for the accommodation of white patrons."[49]

There were, of course, exceptions. "The depression has wrought a definite change in the policy of most white shops toward the other race," argued Hortense Powdermaker. Financial need made white shopkeepers more accommodating. During the Great Depression blacks were "permitted to try on garments rather than, as before, being required to buy shoes, gloves, hats, without first finding out whether they were the right size or shape." Also, "white gas-station attendants . . . began the practice of tipping their caps to upper-class colored patrons." Powdermaker's conclusion, however, is not borne out by later evidence: "Once such concessions have been granted, they cannot easily be withdrawn."[50] They were.

Segregation's haptic protocols were specific and involved. Here are some rules of "caste etiquette" that a "white friend" explained to Dollard: "Don't shake hands with a Negro (except in the case of an old Negro friend who has been gone for a long time, and this would be rare)." Mammy-like figures, echoes of a surer past, were allowed—probably encouraged—to hug ("clasping and kissing") little ones without social censure. The limits, however, were clear: "A colored mammy may kiss her charges, perhaps even on rare occasions after they have grown up. But colored people and white people do not as a rule shake hands in public."[51]

Some touches, though, were mandatory and important for preserving the segregated order. Black bodies were required to touch their hats when "greeting respectfully any white, even a stranger." Conversely, the "white person may return the greeting with a nod but will never touch his hat." In some instances, white failure to touch black skin was condemned. During the 1930s it was "considered entirely correct for the white person to resort directly to physical attack upon the Negro. Thus, if a Negro curses a white, the white may knock the Negro down; and failure to do so may even be considered as a failure in his duty as a white." In a similar vein, Cleveland Sellers recalled a case from his South Carolina childhood regarding the trial of some Klansmen: "Two informers testified that the black man was castrated because one of their members, Bart Floyd, was willing 'to get nigger blood on his hands' in order to prove that he was worthy of a promotion."[52]

If the prohibition against cordial touching marked a departure from the practice under slavery, some other sensory stereotypes regarding black skin died hard. The notion that blacks had to sustain a beating—and that their skin was suited to it—if they were to learn lessons properly proved remarkably enduring. While physical punishment of children among white working-class families seems to have been de rigueur, the harshest beatings were reserved for blacks, also considered childlike. "It is a common belief of many whites," observers noted in the 1930s, "that Negroes will respond only to violent methods. In accordance with their theory of the 'animal-like' nature of the Negro, they believe that the formal punishments of fines and imprisonment fail to act as deterrents to crime." Hence the benefit of a "whipping" or a "paddling." Blacks needed to feel punishment. It was an old notion, one bequeathed to each southern generation and still discernible among white high school juniors and seniors in 1953 in Charlottesville, Virginia. Several of these students considered "ability to stand pain" and "able to stand hard work" chiefly black characteristics (they did not think the traits desirable). That such old stereotypes still had purchase, especially among the young, suggested that white southerners would be slow to change their racial attitudes voluntarily.[53]

But such beliefs were necessary to that world, and, perversely enough, they are helpful to us too as we seek to understand the past. How else are we to make sense of the Texas lynching of "Big Nose" George? Whites skinned his corpse, making his "leather" into razor strops, bags, and shoes.[54] A sensory history of segregation, the way the senses numbed minds and agitated guts, helps explain that and other enormities. Not much else does.

Trippingly off the Tongue

Social anthropologists studying southern race relations in the 1930s concluded: "The belief in organic inferiority of the Negro reaches its strongest expression in the common assertion that Negroes are 'unclean.'" The association was most obvious in "a strong feeling against eating or drinking from dishes used by Negroes," with many whites providing "separate dishes for the use of their servants." "The taboo against eating with a Negro" was widespread. "Eating with a person," maintained Hortense Powdermaker, "usually signifies social acceptance." Although white children may "on special occasions eat with Negroes . . . for colored and white adults to eat together under ordinary conditions is practically unheard of." Even "mammie" and trusted servants were not allowed to eat with the "adult whites or in the dining-room." "Kissing and embracing" mammie was fine; eating with her was not.[55]

Taste could be closely linked with touch and sight. John Dollard described "the one drugstore in Southerntown where both colored and white may drink at the same soda fountain, an unusual state of affairs since most drugstores exclude Negroes from the soda fountain." Yet separate sets of glasses were kept for each race, "thick glasses for colored, thinner ones for white people." Black people's skin generally, tongues included, was considered too rough and unrefined for thin glasses. Even seeing one another eat was deemed visually offensive, the sight of blacks consuming presumably too sexually suggestive and menacing: "Negroes are not in general allowed in restaurants where whites go; in the case of some of the poorer restaurants, there is a separate entrance for them and a curtain is drawn so that whites and Negroes cannot see one another eating."[56]

Again, old sensory stereotypes died hard, some too savory to abandon. Like antebellum slaveholders, twentieth-century white storekeepers and landlords revealed a set of beliefs about the black palate when they reserved, for example, "the lowest grade of flour" for black families. Because whites believed black tongues appreciative of only very strong tastes and foods, many thought it did not matter what blacks ate: "It is a general practice among white employers to buy a poorer quality of food for their servants than for themselves. Ground meat, pig tails and feet, and cowpeas are usually given to servants." But, just as with white charges of innate black smell, claims about black taste were wrongheaded. After all, upper-class whites doubtless had a better diet than poor whites, and middling blacks probably had a more varied diet than poor ones. Indeed, the diets of rural black and white Mississippians in the 1920s had much in common. A 1928 survey by the Mississippi Agricultural Experiment Station found that out of thirty-two foods just nine "were used in more generous quantities by negroes": flour, rice, cornmeal, cane syrup, lard, salt pork, fresh fish, dried peas, and cabbage. Also, blacks consumed more fish, rabbit, and opossum than whites. Cooking styles did not differ appreciably between the races; frying and boiling were common to both. There were some differences, though. Whites preferred beef while blacks opted more often for fish or pork, and the "use of pepper, spices, catsup, [and] pickles" was more popular among whites. In fact, whites tended to eat tarter, more pungent food principally because "the white man has had more opportunity to develop tastes for these abnormal flavors"; the survey did not reveal "any distinct difference in sense of taste between these two people."[57]

Such evidence had little purchase with the segregationist. Blacks had no social taste because they had no taste at all. Like their rough skins that could not handle the relative delicacy of a thin glass, their tongues could not fathom the more toothsome things in life. Witness Dollard's remarks in this regard: "A white informant bought a quantity of ice cream for a picnic, much of which was not used but was returned to him. He hailed me one day in the street and said he wanted to show me something interesting; behind his house a group of his [black] tenants were eating ice cream which had soured by now. The assumption seemed to be that they could not tell sweet from sour ice cream and that they would feel that they were getting a whole-hearted treat."[58]

THE LOGIC OF HYPOCRISY

While the prejudices concerning sensory aspects of blackness were crucial for anchoring race, it was difficult to maintain the segregationist line absolutely, given the extent of actual social interaction between the races in the South and the fact that poor whites often shared sensory characteristics usually attributed solely to blacks. But the segregationists managed to square the circle to their own satisfaction so that blackness, whiteness, and the rules governing interaction remained intact. As Hortense Powdermaker said of the set of southern white beliefs about blacks: "Like all creeds, this one does not depend on facts and logic for its support, nor is it directly vulnerable to them. An article of faith is seldom disturbed by arguments and experience."[59]

Superficially at least, it does seem stunning that segregationists managed to mouth one thing while doing another, and the lived contradictions seem impossible and unfathomable. Some contemporaries, especially those from outside the South, saw the tension and did not quite know what to make of it. "In spite of their widespread use as nurses and servants," argued a group of sociologists in the 1930s, "there remains a strong feeling that the color of the Negroes is abhorrent and that contact with them may be contaminating." Black maids touched white food all the time, cutting bread and preparing meals, and they caressed white clothes when doing the ironing; yet they were not allowed to touch a white person directly or eat with whites. Northern psychologist George Morlan threw up exasperated hands at what he considered resolute hypocrisy in 1950: "If color makes them undesirable neighbors, it makes Negroes even less desirable servants, but those who insist on residential segregation rarely object to having as servants those who are not good enough to be neighbors." Similarly, white men protested loudly against interracial sex but happily indulged their own desires with black women; and the contradictions went on, and on, creasing the fabric of southern daily life at every turn.[60]

Whites recognized that many of the most vehement voices against race mixing belonged to those that did most of the mixing. "Our own people, our white men with their black concubines," offered District Attorney J. H. Currie in Meridian, Mississippi, in January 1907, "are . . . raising up a menace to the white race, lowering the standard of both races and preparing the way for riot, mob, criminal assaults, and, finally, a death struggle for racial supremacy. The trouble is at our own door." Hence the formation of Anti-Miscegenation Leagues in Mississippi at around the same time. But the temptations were many and great and complicated by envy. The authors of the 1941 sociological study *Deep South* argued that "white people often think of the negro as completely free from all irksome social controls and obligations," especially with regard to "enjoying to the fullest all physical satisfactions. The Negro can eat hugely with no thought of manners; he can laugh loudly; he can express his joy or his anger in direct verbal and physical action; and he can seek and enjoy his sexual experiences completely free from external restraints or personal inhibitions." Blacks, then, were animalized in terms of their sensory sophistication even while whites quietly coveted the very traits they publicly abhorred. In such a tortured logic, there was ample room for unwitting, unexamined contradiction.[61]

Paternalist, close, and intimate relations between white and black people helped ease the contradictions and gave smoother edges to rough logic. In his examination of the September 1906 Atlanta race riots, Ray Stannard Baker offered insight into the black and white mindsets that governed relations between the races. "It is highly significant of Southern conditions—which the North does not understand—that the first instinct of thousands of Negroes in Atlanta, when the riot first broke out, was not to run away from the white people but to run to them. The white man who takes the most radical position in opposition to the Negro race will often be found loaning money to individual Negroes, feeding them and their families from his kitchen, or defending 'his Negroes' in court or elsewhere." Of course, Baker referred principally to affluent whites, those who could afford, financially and socially, demonstrations of largesse. But Baker thought it misleading to describe such acts as relations between the races: those acts were premised on white perceptions not of black people as a group (which they disliked) but on individual blacks (whom they could like very much). As Baker put it: "Southern [white] people possess a real liking, wholly unknown in the North, for individual Negroes whom they know."[62]

But for every paternalist gesture, there was at least one mindless, visceral one. Reactions to blackness were knee-jerk, inducing actual physical contortion of white bodies. Listen to Robert Moton describe a scene in a southern city in the late 1920s: "At the street car the conductor is busily assisting passengers aboard, especially women. A coloured woman appears in the line, perhaps 'an old black mammy,' and suddenly he stiffens, his whole manner changes—no coloured woman must be assisted under any circumstances." Moton believed this to be "embarrassing alike to the colored passenger and to the white conductor." So why go against "the natural impulses of kindness and courtesy," why not give the black woman a hand? Answer: because "his whole white world shouts in his ears, 'Don't do it! Don't do it!' And the kindly impulse is checked: his soul is dwarfed; he humiliates himself in denying the service."[63]

Did all of this entail a contradiction of the most staggering proportion? Undoubtedly. Some at the time could not reconcile white men's practices with their ostensible principles: "A Negro woman reported with indignation that a number of white men in Southerntown have Negro mistresses. She had been surprised to learn of the fact because some of these very men are the ones who insist on segregation, and preach that the Negroes should have their own life separate from that of the whites." Segregation was anchored in shifting terms whose standards were applied and reapplied by those who defined them. True, whites who transgressed too much, too often, with rather too much fervor and enjoyment, could be reprimanded. But the quick, quiet kiss, the crafty caress, the clandestine indulgence of heady scent—they were permitted. The fingering of black female skin was even appropriate to white men of power, as was the ability to bruise and scar a black man's skin. Segregation was often suspended by those who had the authority to transgress it; the suspension itself reaffirmed white power.[64]

The suspension of rules was, in fact, paradoxically helpful for refining segregation. What was prohibited in public was often permitted in private, especially in white homes and especially when it came to black maids. Whites had several strategies to explain away the apparent contradiction. Some simply claimed that a maid's help was exceptional.

Echoing their antebellum forebears, segregationists said that, yes, their maids might smell, but they did not smell as much as the great black mass; or that they tolerated a maid's odor because they loved her so. Black maids and nurses—such as the woman who, in Lillian Smith's recollection, "fed me . . . let me fall asleep on her deep warm breast"— enjoyed such a sensory intimacy with whites that larger claims about black inferiority and the need to segregate look absurd. Yet even as the presence of black maids in white homes was the "crucial exception" to segregation, the "white home," according to one thoughtful interpretation, "became a central site for the production and reproduction of racial identity precisely because it remained a place of integration within an increasingly segregated world." Whites "had paradoxically created the color line as permeable, as transgressable by their own desires."[65]

RACE RULES

One way to maintain segregation was to insist on the primacy of race as regulator of life and to mute whatever class distinctions existed within black and white southern communities. Often, though, class consciousness fractured the lie. Instances of cooperation between elite whites siding with blacks against lower-class whites were hardly unknown, and tensions within the white community usually simmered just beneath the serene surface.[66]

Middle-class whites often expressed their contempt for lower-class whites using sensory stereotypes usually applied just to blacks. To middle-class eyes and ears, poor whites dressed incorrectly, were slovenly, and were prone to passionate, voluble outbursts. The tone, tenor, and volume of white working-class religious expression especially sounded (to middle-class ears) remarkably like African American services. Among white Baptists and Methodists, the "lower-class ministers preach with apostolic passion, attempting to stir their audiences to genuine personal remorse and to give them a thrilling emotional experience." Liston Pope's 1943 study of a North Carolina mill village depicted white working-class religious expression as appealing "to the hands and feet more than to the head," contrasted it to the "more restrained worship of the 'respectable people' uptown," and considered mill-hand religious music as especially "rhythmic," with a set of oral and aural registers not unlike that of "Negroes in the South," whose "emotional needs are comparable in many respects to those of the mill workers." This " 'special music' " appealed "to the simpler emotions of the hearers."[67]

Class differences and tensions within the white community were especially apparent in mill villages. Here, the middle class depicted poor whites as noisy, emotional, "filthy," and disease ridden. In his 1958 sociological and anthropological study of "Kent," a Piedmont mill town of about four thousand, John Kenneth Morland remarked: "In the late forties the [white] mill workers were in many respects actually more segregated than the Negro elements of Kent society. . . . If one were a member of a mill village, he had no more chance of being invited to dinner by 'respectable' white families than had a Negro, nor could he entertain much greater expectations of marrying into a 'respectable' white family." That white supremacy "did not mean white equality" had long been apparent in southern society.[68]

Townspeople not only saw and heard but also smelled mill hands. Morland found a Kent doctor who dismissed several patients from his office "and with great disgust told the next person who entered (a townsperson), 'God damn it, I hate these mill people. They're the dirtiest, nastiest people in the world.' Thereupon, he raised the window for a few minutes 'to let the air clear' before talking to his next patient." Moreover, some townspeople would not "use the [city] pool because of the large number of mill people who swim there." They believed that mill workers went to the pool to bathe. Kent mill workers were caught in a habitual quandary. While elites described them "as innately low," they also expected them "not to 'live like a Negro.'" And they knew very well what elite whites thought of them because the middle class sometimes let slip offensive remarks. Yet lower-class whites were hardly passive, and they fought back when they could. John Dollard overheard this conversation during a political campaign:

"I won't vote for the lady."
"Why?"
"She said the other day, 'I'll be glad when this election is over and I won't have to shake hands with sweaty rednecks.'"[69]

If mill workers in particular sometimes shouted too loudly or came home sweaty and rank, it was the result of the nature of their work. The mills lacked air-conditioning and were "hot, moist, lint laden, and noisy." Morland said of the aural dimension: "The hum of the spinning room and the clatter of the looms can be heard some distance from the mill, and inside the mill itself the noise is deafening." Many mill hands loathed their work and considered their senses assaulted by it. Some quit and chose to pick cotton, itself back breaking, but preferable to the deadening influence of the mill on ear and skin: "At least the air's fresh and I can feel the sunshine." Others gave up the work because "the noise was so frightening." Most had no choice but to endure the sensory assaults, however, and thus could not help but confirm the opinion of elites that poor whites were suited to such labor.[70]

Class differences were, then, important to southern society. Yet no matter what separated, say, poor whites from wistful southern aristocrats in economic and cultural terms, no matter what divide distanced poor from elite blacks, no matter what temporary accommodations some southerners made to dull the impact of segregation at the edges, a stubborn, numbing fact remained: race ruled the South, and significant, long-term deviation from the color line could not and would not be tolerated. The point of Jim Crow was, after all, to make a previously contingent, complex world simple to the point of unthinking when it came to race. Whereas the old paternalists liked to invoke their exceptions—the beloved "auntie," the cherished "uncle"—Jim Crow lumped all blacks together and all whites together, regardless of class.[71]

Race had to trump class if segregation were to remain viable. Even if they were "members of the upper economic group," blacks could not "eat in white restaurants or live in houses in white neighborhoods of the same economic level as their own." They could not "receive accommodations equal to those of even the poorer whites in theaters or trains." Blacks, no matter how affluent or refined, were kept from eating with whites to such an extent that "well-to-do colored persons of the professional group [could not] even wait inside white restaurants . . . for sandwiches to be eaten outside." Even material similarities between poor whites and the majority of blacks were not enough to suspend race. Yet despite the fact that poor whites undoubtedly smelled—descriptions of their living conditions are rife with stench—elite whites hardly ever attached the stigma of odor to that group, at least publicly or loudly.[72]

The idea that black skin was suited to certain tasks held enormous influence among poor whites and helped to confirm whiteness—and all of its sensory associations—as the currency of the segregationist realm. "The mill worker, with nobody else to 'look down on,' regards himself as eminently superior to the Negro. The colored man represents his last outpost against social oblivion," argued Liston Pope in 1942. As a result, white mill hands distinguished between what their working hands should do and what the hands of working blacks should do. Ideally, jobs suitable for black skin involved touching, seeing, and smelling filth. As a group of mill hands tried to explain to management, "We think un-stopping Toilets is out of a White Man's Class of Work, it ought to be done by Negroes."[73]

Even the Great Depression could not effect radical change in sensory stereotypes and class consciousness. In the 1930s white hands were in danger of becoming black: "With regard to unskilled or 'common' labor, there was a decided change in the operation of the caste system. . . . Until the 'depression,' unskilled labor was the province of colored men." But during the Depression, especially from 1930 to 1935, "a large number of whites" entered "into the field of 'common' labor," so that white hands now cleaned streets, touched garbage, dug holes, and pushed laden wheelbarrows. The result was not lost on blacks, many of whom for the first time saw white bodies working like black ones. "Let um know how it feels tuh swing that pick!" smiled one black man. But the result was to further refine the caste system so that labor-saving devices, such as tractors, were given to white laborers, not to black ones, thus rescuing white skin from becoming black.[74]

When all was said and done, white southerners lived in a binary world where, to their way of feeling, black and white were absolute and where absolute differences were mediated and reaffirmed through all the senses. Whites convinced themselves that they had learned to sense race and minimize class by going beyond the eye, shoring up and, in the process, naturalizing the sensory order of southern racial life and reducing it to an unthinking, automated choreography. As Gayle Graham Yates recalled of her Mississippi childhood in the 1940s and 1950s: "Around Shubuta when we were children ironclad ancestry was racial and racial identity definitive. People were either black or white. Even if some tanned white people might be darker than some blacks and if some blacks were whiter than whites, we all knew instantly who was which—a gesture of lowered eyes, a specific fragrance, a footstep of a certain kind, an inflection of speech or word choice, a choice of hair style, dress or vehicle . . ." In short, "physiognomy told only a little of the story, but a person was clearly one or the other, no doubt about it." That lack of doubt and the sensory basis supporting it, fiction though it was, proved absolutely essential to the segregated order.[75]

5 The Black Mind of the South

Black challenges to segregation and the sensory stereotypes underpinning it owed much to a steadfast logic honed during slavery. Unlike the system of segregation, this critique was a product of the mind, not the gut. When blacks "passed," for example, they revealed that whites' senses could be fooled, that innate sensory racial characteristics were invented. Equally commonsensical and embarrassing to segregationist sensory conceits, African Americans also employed what we might call a materialist critique of segregation, a remnant from slavery. Yes, said blacks, we smell; if you worked as hard as we do in the conditions we do, you would smell, too. Some also argued that ostensibly racial differences in, for example, sound and smell were really a product of culture and history. The effect of this hard-headed critique is difficult to gauge. The arguments had no purchase among segregationists, unsurprisingly. When black people pointed to the visual ambiguity of race, segregationists simply nodded and argued that one did not necessarily have to see race in order to authenticate it. But the intellectual consistency and logic of the black critique did seem to make moderates listen. For the most part, though, black reason was not intended to persuade anyone. Theirs was an argument that allowed blacks to get the intellectual upper hand on a daily basis and shielded them from the mind-numbing effects of the relentless mantra of white superiority. In other words, the black form of critique—materialist, logical, historical—preserved the life of the mind in a society where thinking on race of any real caliber and consistency had long gone out of style.

Hard thinking did not, of course, preclude other behaviors, and sometimes southern blacks found it easier and vastly safer to bend, in pragmatic fashion, to white expectations. There were some frighteningly good reasons why blacks sometimes accommodated sensory demands made by whites. As children, blacks learned not to "look a[t] white folks in de eye," to avoid the presumptuousness of direct eye contact, to avert a gaze whenever possible. "Negro men walking along the street seem careful not to look at the white women sitting on the porches they pass," thought John Dollard. Not looking was one way "to avoid the too-ready suspicion of the white men." Just as masters had watched slaves closely, so blacks in the early twentieth century learned to watch whites with precision, what Richard Wright referred to as observing "their every move, every fleeting expression," learning "how to interpret what was said and what left unsaid." When it came to white men looking at black women, however, white eyes happily scrutinized black bodies and dress.[1]

Neither were black people always united in the ways they dealt with segregationists. If understandable fear was a factor in making blacks look and train their eyes in particular ways, so was class. While the racial imperatives of segregation tended to hide class differences within the black community, "in situations of emotional stress individuals from any of the classes were apt to express antagonisms toward other classes." For example: "Upper-class colored persons, when angered by the behavior of lower-class individuals, accused them of being black," by which they meant "boisterous, murderous, stupid, or sexually promiscuous." Middle-class blacks were especially critical and cast lower-class blacks as smelly, dirty, noisy, and lazy. How one looked echoed how one sounded. African American "women of higher social status deliberately avoid bright colors and are offended if clerks in the stores assume that they want something 'loud.' " Thus "the upper-class Negro who dresses with quiet good taste is not only demonstrating that he possesses this attribute of breeding" but also divorcing himself from "the inferior type of Negro."[2]

None of this was new. Class consciousness had always played an important role within the black community, both before and after the Civil War, and it was a consciousness often articulated in terms of sensibility. When a white doctor insulted a black woman for brushing past him on a Charlotte, North Carolina, street in 1882, a group of young black men, apparently from respectable backgrounds, beat him up.

These same black men and no few women saw themselves as distinct from black lower classes. The black middle class insisted that whites "must not look upon us *all* as boys and wenches." Such men and women led by example, depicting lower-class blacks in visual terms not far removed from white stereotypes. Poor blacks, especially young ones, lacked decorum or taste, "strut[ted] like a peacock," were showy, gaudy, and vacuous.[3]

Although all southern blacks were subject to the strictures of segregation, the middle class, like all bourgeois, thought their aesthetic sensibility superior. Classical music figured prominently in their church services, illustrating that their class was "not deficient in appreciation of 'the best' in music." Hence, upper- and middle-class blacks adopted some of the perceived sensorial refinements they deemed fitting to their class by sounding like middling whites and, simultaneously, quarantining their senses from the black lower class. In short, they aimed to show themselves as having better, more refined ears and to be more in tune with good southern white society.[4]

Like whites who characterized black religious expression as loud and full of swollen, bursting noise, many middle-class blacks considered poor blacks too fond of rhapsodic emotion. For John Dollard, the middle-class black churches "in town are much more reserved and have much more the frozen, restrained characteristics of the white churches. There seems to be also the perception among middle-class negroes that the emotionalized patterns of lower-class religion have a sexual element in them and that there is something orgiastic about the high-tension performances of the preachers and congregation."[5]

The other senses bolstered class feeling. Again, there was nothing new here. Recall the Fort Smith, Arkansas, newspaper editor who in 1891 justified segregation of railroad cars on the basis that blacks stank. The response of the state's black leadership to such criticisms generally, and to the 1891 segregated-car law specifically, revealed operational sensory stereotypes within black society. At one of several meetings to protest emerging segregation, Arkansas black leaders confronted claims about black scent head on. Professor Joseph A. Booker, president of Arkansas Baptist College, denied that blacks wanted social equality and argued that whites needed to note the differences between educated, propertied blacks and those less fortunate. If the separate-coach bill were defeated, blacks "proposed to buy soap even if they couldn't get bread." Booker especially objected to segregation's tendency to treat all blacks alike and, in the process, conceded that some black people, especially the poor, probably did smell. Another black leader, dentist Dr. J. H. Smith, put the argument this way: "To force the better negroes into contact with the more degraded would be to force the race backward." Booker T. Washington likewise argued that many blacks were, in fact, dirty and that toothbrushes and cleaning would lead to black improvement and, ultimately, acceptance by whites.[6]

The sensory stereotypes that middle- and upper-class blacks applied to "rough and common nigguhs" could be as nasty as those applied by whites. One maintained that association with lower-class blacks made her "feel sick"; another, an "upper middle-class colored woman, a dental inspector, was averse to handling the colored school children and constantly washed her hands during inspections." Sociologists pondered such a reaction at length. In their 1941 study, *Deep South*, based on participant observation research conducted in the early 1930s, Allison Davis, Burleigh B. Gardner, and Mary R. Gardner were surprised to find a reaction of that kind, principally because they believed that the middle-class blacks who voiced such sentiments "may be no different in color, odor, hair-form, or other physical characteristics from" the black working classes. The sociologists explained the difference between white and elite black reactions by arguing that white people "testify to a feeling of sickness or nausea in regard to colored people only when social or sexual intimacy between white and colored persons is observed or imagined" but that outside that context "the most intimate physical contact is acceptable, as in the cases of white adults who embrace and kiss their colored 'mammies,' or white patients who are bathed and attended by colored nurses. . . . Between upper-class and lower-class members within the colored society, however, the most intimate of even these physical contacts are rigidly avoided, such as sexual intercourse or marriage with a black or lower-class woman." For that reason, "colored people of the upper class and upper-middle class constantly express surprise at the ability of . . . white men not only to have sexual intercourse with 'black and common' women but to love them."[7]

Lies told again and again, so outrageously, relentlessly, and easily, made believers of even thoughtful people. "It is an often unrecognized fact," ventured a 1957 report on the impact of integration, "that the Negro may come to believe in the prejudicial myths about him and frequently be as unaware as the white person that he is reacting defensively to inner impulses in an irrational, self-destructive manner." As a result, "many Negroes feel driven to spend on cosmetics, deodorants, clothes, and automobiles in efforts" to counter white stereotypes and approximate "the supposed white middle-class standards." "Paradoxically, even this is used as propaganda against them. The complaint is voiced that they have become 'uppity,' that they do not know their place." The common belief that "the Negro aspires to whiteness" was, many thought, reflected in efforts to mirror and acquire ostensibly white senses and sensibilities.[8]

Seeing and looking by African Americans took on white forms—at least as whites expressed ownership of those forms. Blacks, thought one observer of southern race relations in 1908, wanted to look white—have straighter hair, to marry "whiter." "The ideal is whiteness" because "whiteness stands for opportunity, power, progress." Such thinking, of course, was white, mere proxy for black opinion and hardly reliable. But black people themselves offered comments that tacitly endorsed some of the fiercest sensory stereotypes. Efforts at lightening were indeed apparent. "Photographs sometimes reveal the tastes of their subject more accurately than they indicate his appearance," so Hortense Powdermaker found in her 1939 study of a black Mississippi community: "They are invariably lighter than the original, and sometimes the features and hair are made to appear less Negroid. . . . One of the blackest and most African-looking women in the community has hanging on the wall a large photograph of herself which it would be almost impossible to recognize as the same person. The hair is straight and soft, the features thinner, and the complexion many degrees lighter." And those who did not wish to "whiten," who were proud of the way they looked, were often the target of criticism from other blacks who heard a visual flatulence in the wearing of loud clothes, something that confirmed white stereotypes about the inability of blacks to contain passions. But black people could not win for trying. According to one black woman in the 1930s, whites "seem to resent seeing a colored person dressed up and looking nice." White criticism did not always have to be spoken to be effective: "She often feels criticized by white eyes when she goes out in a tastefully designed dress." Black people walked a thin line, and missteps were not unknown.[9]

So-called accommodated Negroes not only tried to "smell" white—the application of "Pumpkin spice" fragrance apparently achieved that for women—but they also reiterated the olfactory mantra regarding blackness. A Mississippi prostitute in the late 1930s, a woman "who . . .

had many white men, [said] that colored men 'stink' to her." Another prostitute made identical claims publicly. Approached for sex by a black man, the woman "told him she 'wouldn't have no nigger,' that 'all niggers stink,' and that she'd have only white men."[10]

Texture was another way that southern blacks showed a desire to imitate whiteness. John Dollard found some Southerntown blacks bemoaning excessive darkness of skin, quietly celebrating lightness, cringing at "bad" hair (excessively kinky), and applauding "good" hair (thin and straight, "of the white type"). In 1951 an advertisement in Ebony magazine for Queen Supreme suggested that, without its "LIGHT, CREAMY, WHITE" lubrication, black hair would remain "brittle and excessively dry" thanks to "hot combs" used for straightening hair. Queen Supreme, instead, would make hair "feel silky soft and lovely," thus undermining a commonly held white stereotype about the natural coarseness of black hair.[11]

PASSING BY, PASSING THROUGH

Superficially, passing endorsed every white sensory stereotype concerning blackness. Plainly, though, passing did not mean that black people accepted the legitimacy of these stereotypes. In some ways, passing exposed them as patent nonsense and also demonstrated that at every turn, with every gesture, blacks who passed as white thought—not felt—about the form, legitimacy, content, nature, and meaning of the very stereotypes they used. Senses, passers showed, could be manipulated. Thus passing was less an affirmation of white sensory conceits and more a challenge to the wobbly logic underpinning them.

Anecdotes suggest that almost every black person seemed to know someone who could, or actually did, pass, that nearly everyone knew a "Mr. Jim," "one of those almost-white colored men whose skin would burn from the intense southern sun." Passing in the rural South was more difficult than it was in northern cities. To pass in a southern community, you had to be new, unknown, without a local past. Because the one-drop rule meant that blackness was no longer visible, whites had to rely on history, contacts, and genealogies to help them ascertain blackness, which is why southern legal minds argued that if "it is known that an individual" has black blood, then he stands as black. Where genealogies are known, "it is almost impossible for persons to 'pass for white.'" As Morton Rubin explained, "Almost everybody's kinship is known by everybody else, white and Negro." There were aural difficulties, too, at least in rural areas in the 1940s: "There is such a cultural difference between Negroes and whites that the lightest skinned 'Negro' is soon detected when he opens his mouth to speak." Whites fancied themselves masters of such detection and, in the absence of knowing an individual's history, brought to bear all the senses in searching for race-truth. "It is not surprising that 'passing' is much more frequent in the northern cities, where the individual can most easily lose all contact with his past and where the penalties for discovery are not so great." That much said, passing was hardly unknown in the South, and the evidence that it occurred throughout the region in the first half of the twentieth century is clear and compelling. Some whites were, of course, fooled on occasion, but deception by a "white nigger," if detected, was usually punished.[12]

Passing took several forms and involved various motivations. Most obviously, light-skinned blacks could pass into white society deliberately. Those who were darker could also pass "by moving to a proper locale and taking Spanish, Portuguese, or other Latin names that explained their color and features well enough." There was also inadvertent passing with whites taking exceptionally light blacks for white and treating them as such. Mamie Garvin Fields remembered that blacks in the early part of the twentieth century "used to pass for white right in Charleston, when they were around strangers. If they got on the streetcar and decided they would pass on the streetcar, they'd just sit anywhere." The conductor "would stop the car and say, 'You don't belong back there with the colored, come up here.' They let the conductor do the passing for them." "Certain families were well known for doing that," said Fields, but local histories and known genealogies meant that "the Negroes on the car generally knew and took whoever did it for a laughing stock." Among those who passed deliberately, some passed sporadically, especially to take advantage of decent accommodations while traveling or to get a better job. This was particularly the case in large northern cities, where some light-skinned blacks passed for white during the day and became black at night. And "sometimes they passed for simple revenge—to trick the whites."[13]

Passing was an optical illusion, and, as such, it could be complicated. White eyes could be fooled, provided that black skin was very light and, as Reba Lee who passed for white in Chicago and New York in the 1940s recalled, one had "real curls, soft and silky," not "kinky hair" and "fuzz." Sartorial elegance was also key. Reba's high-minded, light-skinned grandmother "had taught me that it was good fashion to dress simply and not wear loud colors and earrings and fake jewelry. I was at the age when girls love flashy stuff, but Gran called that 'niggery.'" Reba knew "niggery" when she saw it and so altered her own presentation of self. At a mixed school in Chicago, she encountered "as 'niggery' a colored girl as I had ever seen, with a purple silk blouse, big gold hoop earrings, and thick lips and nose." Dresses and colors, Reba knew, had to be chosen with care: "I was afraid of pale blue. I don't know why, but it made me just a little yellowy. Beige was better."[14]

In her 1929 novella, *Passing*, Harlem Renaissance writer Nella Larsen suggested the importance of the other senses to the passer. Unknown to Hugh Wentworth (a white man), Irene has passed into white society. When Wentworth says he sometimes feels that he cannot tell if a person is black or white, Irene replies:

> "Well, don't let that worry you. Nobody can. Not by looking."
> "Not by looking, eh? Meaning?"
> "I'm afraid I can't explain. Not clearly. There are ways. But they're not definite or tangible."

Irene means that race is not simply visual. Light-skinned blacks passing for white could not rely on fooling white vision alone—they also had to sound white. The "noise" and loudness of "field-hand stock," Reba Lee's grandmother told her, gave them away. At her Chicago school, Reba heard blackness and knew not to echo it: "Some colored girls went past me, screaming with laughter." Reba was from the South and used her southern accent to "explain my way of talking." Policing one's voice—thinking about the production of sound and the ears that would consume it—was essential to the passer and entailed constant monitoring. As a black friend told her: "You know, that drugstore clerk said he thought you were a white girl at first. Till you got to talking." The comment made Reba deliberate on her own sound: "I knew I was talking carelessly, now, less quiet and refined." "Singing was another thing to be careful about," remembered Reba at a party. "My stories had prompted Sallie to bring out records of Southern spirituals, and then one of the men sat down at the piano and asked me to sing some, and I did those spirituals too well, I was afraid, with too real a voice."[15] Passers always had to think carefully about what they were doing and understand the content and meaning of white stereotypes without necessarily accepting their legitimacy.

Because passing exposed the loopiness of beliefs in absolute racial difference, it constituted a powerful critique of the segregationist order. Passing, after all, was something that white senses supposedly precluded—blackness would invariably betray itself sensorily went the logic. Whites liked to claim, as did South Carolina newspaper editor William Watts Ball in 1932, that passing by a black person was impossible. But Ball and his ilk were often unable to detect blackness. When light-skinned blacks who had left for the North returned to southern communities, racial confusion reigned. Clifton Taulbert recalled the return of a red-haired, "well-dressed lady" to a funeral in Glen Allan, Mississippi, in the 1950s. "As she walked up near the front, the ushers were confused. They didn't know if she was white or colored." This woman had not been to the town for forty years, and no one could sense her race without her history. "My grandfather was very light complected, with straight hair, and sometimes people took him for white," recalled Rosa Parks, explaining: "He took every bit of advantage of being white-looking. He was always doing or saying something that would embarrass or agitate the white people. With those who didn't know him, when he was talking with them he would extend his hand and shake hands with them. He'd be introduced to some white man he didn't know, and he'd say, 'Edwards is my name,' and shake hands. Then people who knew him would get embarrassed and have to whisper to the others that he was not white. At that time no white man would shake hands with a black man."[16]

Some African Americans could have passed but chose not to. That they could choose their racial identity exposed the intellectual poverty of segregation. In a wicked twist of the *Plessy* case, Charles Johnson recounted an example in Georgia of a light-skinned black man undermining a train conductor's ability to tell his race. The conductor thought the man white and could not understand why he was riding in the colored car. The man asserted his "color" as black. Doubting him and his own eyes, the conductor "examined the man's hair and hands, but without helpful clues in his association of speech and dress," and therefore "had to take the word of the passenger." Such examples worked to embarrass the segregationist logic, so much so that whites became edgy about labeling people who confused the eye. Whites, according to one man in the 1930s, "are pretty careful before they call a person a Negro," just in case they were wrong. Look at the photograph of Cecil J. Williams and Leroy "Bunt" Sulton (illustration 5.1), and you'll see why. Even

Ill. 5.1. Cecil J. Williams (left) and Leroy "Bunt" Sulton—
two young "black" men in South Carolina in 1957—illustrate
the visual ambiguity of "race." (Photograph reproduced with
permission of Cecil J. Williams)

though Leroy's known history and genealogy classified him as "colored"—as "colored" as Cecil—"he looked 'white.' "[17]

Passing allowed some African Americans to improve their economic lot. The desire for improvement, argued an essay in Ebony in 1952, led many who could pass to do so, but only temporarily. These were people "passing as white during the day to hold decent jobs and returning to their Negro families and neighborhoods at night." The essay reaffirmed the unreliability of sight in identifying "race."[18]

There were other ways to interpret passing in the black community. In the 1950s the Chicago-based magazine Tan Confessions (published by the Johnson Publishing Company, which also put out Ebony) included a number of stories critical of passing. In essays titled "I Hated My Race!" and "I Wanted My Daughter to Pass," Tan Confessions argued that although passing was possible, the psychological and social damage was immense. Fear of being caught always took a huge emotional toll in these stories, and whites, once they discovered the true "race" of their passing husbands and wives, always rejected the passer. The message was clear: passing was not worth it; it demeaned the black race; and, anyway, as Sarah Vaughan declared, "Dark girls can make it too!"[19]

COMMONSENSE RESISTANCE

"Whatever the strains arising from differences within the group," argued Hortense Powdermaker in 1939, "the social distance they interpose among its members is dwarfed by the greater gulf intervening between Negro and White." Fissures caused by personal taste, self-hate, human jealousy, and the grinding pressure of segregated society were certainly present in southern black society, and to pretend otherwise would be to flatten a people and a region. But historians must balance evidence and offer some sort of "in general" evaluation, lest they slip into the easy habit of overqualification with the ever-finer slicing of the past that is of interest to no one but the antiquarian. And so, "in general," it may be said that southern African Americans, across classes and genders and over time, developed forms of resistance to the daily deployment of sensory stereotypes that might authentically approach a "black" experience in its consistency and regularity. This resistance was a powerful and wholly commonsensical critique of segregation.[20]

Black southerners challenged the warped logic underpinning segregation in many ways. Often, they were simply practical. Blacks used segregation to suit their own ends, carving social, cultural, and economic space from a system designed to stymie them. After all, segregation offered opportunities for black professionals—doctors, nurses, businessmen, and teachers especially. Immediately after the Civil War, when memories of exclusion from education, theaters, and a variety of social services under slavery were fresh, African Americans pressed hard for an end to exclusionary measures. Sometimes they made headway, and when they did not, many accepted segregation as an improvement over exclusion. Under customary and legal segregation at least, they could participate in areas that slavery had denied them, and they used separate black institutions to nurture independence. Where adequate facilities were not forthcoming, freedpeople sometimes used the courts to lobby for improved, albeit separate, conditions. Black southerners continued to use such tactics long after the legal consolidation of Jim Crow. Irony peppers southern history, perhaps even guides it; that segregation, a system designed to undermine black independence, was used by blacks to establish a degree of autonomy is deliciously glaring.[21]

The black sociologist Charles S. Johnson called this world "ultraviolet" because it was largely invisible to whites. The black middle class was in the business of "body-oriented services," including barbershops and funeral homes. As state and local ordinances began to prohibit the most intimate sensory contact—white nurses were barred from touching black patients, white undertakers from handling black bodies—so African Americans began to take over such jobs, sometimes profitably. And, with that profit, they bought increasingly standardized goods— clothes, cars—that made them ever more like whites, the "shock of racial sameness" unnerving segregationist eyes.[22]

African Americans relied on all the senses to counter segregation. In response to white arguments about black sensory numbness, their general sensory constipation, blacks responded by profiling their humanity, employing the sort of tactic slaves had used to limit physical punishment. Whites, they argued in the 1890s, should know that "the Negro race" had "bodies and feelings like other races." Southern blacks did not see fundamental differences between the races. "Aren't we all alike, aren't we all made by the same God?" asked one Mississippi mulatto woman in the 1930s, explaining: "If my skin was scraped off wouldn't my body be like the body of any white woman my size?"[23]

African American magazines played an important role in challenging white sensory stereotypes by showing that blacks could embrace cleanliness on their own terms and not smell better just to impress whites.

Scientific evidence was relevant here. *Tan Confessions*, a magazine devoted to exploring the "emotional, intimate" aspects of black life, and, like other black periodicals, often available in the South, offered readers a primer on olfaction. The January 1951 issue included a piece on "Body Odor" by Dr. Julian Lewis, "Author of 'The Biology of the Negro.'" Lewis devoted most of the article to explaining the cause of body odor, regardless of race. You might not be able to smell your own scent, counseled Lewis, "because the nose is relatively insensitive to one's own odor." Bathe, shower, take particular care to wash hair and remove dead skin, he said, and do not rely too heavily on "oftentimes harmful de-odorants to attain desirable body hygiene. The free (and even lavish) use of soap and water is all that is necessary to prevent objectionable body odors." Under no circumstances, Lewis said, worry about the putative racial dimensions of smell. The notion that smell was racial was bunk, he maintained: "This discussion naturally brings up the question of racial characteristics of body odors. Some white people declare that Negroes have distinctive odors, and Negroes equally insist that white people have specific smells." In terms of biologically dictated odors, Lewis reassured his audience, "carefully conducted scientific tests have exploded such distinctions."[24]

In moments when black people felt they could not beat the sensory stereotypes of whites, they simply indulged in their own. Some countered olfactory stereotypes with a visceral tit-for-tat. Richard Wright recalled a boyhood conversation in Jackson, Mississippi:

> "Man, you ever get right close to a white man, close enough to smell 'im?"
> "They say we stink. But my ma says white folks smell like dead folks."
> "Niggers smell from sweat. But white folk smell *all* the time."

The argument that "Negroes find the odor of White women to resemble that of cadavers" was not uncommon.[25]

Such countering covered all the senses. For example, as a black student at the University of Michigan in the 1930s, southerner Hubert Eaton "found myself surrounded by white faces; I was the only nonwhite student in my courses at graduate school. I found to my dismay that, after spending all my life in a colored community, I could not dis-tinguish white students from one another." It took him months to learn how to see white faces, and he "began to understand the dilemma of white people who claim that all blacks look alike."[26]

But applying sensory stereotypes to whites went only so far. The argument—one expressed by Wright—that whites smelled, day in and day out, was relatively unusual, not least because such a critique played too readily into the logic that race had an indelible scent. This kind of implied endorsement of race as innate, not environmental or social, was comparatively rare among blacks. Anyway, few accepted such stereotypes uncritically. According to Henry Louis Gates Jr.: "One thing we always did was smell good, partly because we liked scents, but partly because white people said we smelled bad *naturally*, like we had some sort of odor gene. 'Here come you niggers, funking up the place'—even we'd crack that kind of joke a lot. So one thing colored people had to do around white people was smell good." Quite. "But it was white people who smelled bad, Mama always said. When they got wet. When they get wet, she said, they smell like dogs." Gates checked for himself: "I do hate the smell of a wet dog, I have to confirm. But I don't think white people smell like that when their hair is wet, I have done a lot of sniffing of wet-headed white people in my time." Gates sidled up to "my favorite classmate, Linda Hoffman, one day at the swimming pool—which had integrated in that same year, 1955—nostrils flared, trying to breathe in as deeply as I could, prepared for the worst." But nothing. No whiff of whiteness. Gates's "mother would not have believed the result of my researches, even had I shared them with her. That these doggy-smelling white people should cast olfactory aspersions upon *us* was bitter gall for her."[27]

Arguably, the most powerful critique of the segregationist sensorium came from blacks who pointed to the material basis of sense perception and thereby exposed the idiocy of the segregationists' essentialist argument. Yes, our hands are rough, blacks argued, as yours would be if you hoed cotton; yes, we might smell, but so would you if you labored hard and sweatily, without decent plumbing; yes, we might not have refined taste, but we can hardly demonstrate otherwise on the pittance we earn.[28] In other words, many blacks argued that they did, in fact, often reek because they did, in fact, live in squalor—and squalor stank. In one of the poorest parts of Knoxville, Tennessee, black housing was especially bad. According to James Robinson, who was born there, the houses were "hardly more than rickety shacks clustered on stilts like

Daddy Long Legs along the slimy bank of putrid and evil-smelling 'Cripple Creek.'" The stench from nearby slaughter pens made the area mephitic, a sensory precinct, "a world set apart and excluded" from the white world. Live here, Robinson seemed to say, and you would reek too. Mamie Garvin Fields explained the basis for segregated streetcars in Charleston, South Carolina, in the 1920s by referring to the local fertilizer mill and its "terrible smell." "Naturally," she commented, "the smell got on the people who worked there, and that made a special type of segregation." "The majority of the workers in the mill were Negroes," recalled Fields, elaborating: "Since the company made no provision for them to take showers or change clothes, they had to come to Charleston on the streetcar just as they were." Black laborers carried the smell of the plant with them, and so authorities "decided to put on a special car, segregating the Negroes from the mill from their own people." Fields then made a telling point, one that deracialized the olfactory and exposed the tortured logic of segregation: "I wonder what they did with the whites (and including the whites who were supervisors, too), because not just the blacks working there took on the stench of the rotten fish cooking up with the chemicals."[29]

The same materialist thinking exposed the haptic stereotype. Blacks explained that hard labor, not genes, left hands thick as leather. Anne Moody recalled of Mississippi Delta poor blacks: "The only thing most of them knew was how to handle a hoe. For years they had demonstrated how well they could do that. Some of them had calluses on their hands so thick they would hide them if they noticed you looking at them." Clifton Taulbert recalled "Poppa's calloused hands" pulling "me up just in time so we could step aside and let the white people pass" during their trips to Greenville, Mississippi, in the 1950s. Heavy skin helped prevent accidental touch, which in turn avoided the possibility of a violent pummel. Drawn by the "smell [of] hot French bread" those same calloused hands then went into a bakery. " 'Anything else, preacher?' the baker asked, handing us the wrapped package. Reaching out to accept our money, the baker made sure his white hands did not touch Poppa's strong colored ones." Neither were women exempt, their hands toughened by domestic service and sewing, especially. Taulbert called his mother's hands "calloused."[30]

African Americans confounded segregation as soon as it began. Black leaders in Arkansas during the 1890s criticized a separate-coach bill using raw common sense and relentless logic. John Gray Lucas, the chief black spokesman in the Arkansas House of Representatives, made his case in the House on February 17, 1891. His rhetorical strategy was simple. First, take the segregationist logic to its extreme—what next, he asked, separate residential areas, "all white people to live in one particular portion of our cities and the colored people in the other portion"? Second, he dealt with the cleanliness question. "Is it true, as charged," asked Lucas, "that we use less of soap and God's pure water than other people, that it is sought to isolate us from other fellow citizens?" Is it right for the Democratic Party to say that "the negro is not so clean and pleasant to the eye as he should be" and to institute separate carriages on that basis? Lucas doubted it and thought, quite rightly, that he detected a ruse. It was not smelly black people whom segregationists found offensive, he maintained; rather "it is the constant growth of a more refined, intelligent, and I might say a more perfumed class, that grow more and more obnoxious as they more nearly approximate to our white friends['] habits and plane of life." If this was not the case, if it was not the sensory whitening of blackness that was the issue, continued Lucas, if it was really black stench, how to explain the incredibly close contact between the races? Lucas's logic is worth following in detail. "Who," he began, "are employed as your servants throughout the South in preference and to the exclusion of every other class?" He continued, paying particular attention to the sensory intimacy of race relations: "Who is he that attends to the very delicate duties that bring persons in closer relations than any other; that sits by the side of yon delicate and refined white lady, laughing, chatting, covered by the same lapcloth?" Then came touch: "Who is the scraper of your chin with his face and breath close as the 'lover sighing like ballad'?" Lucas wasn't finished. Taste came next: "How about those cooks who handle all that goes over your delicate palates and the baker who is said to knead the dough with feet as with hands?" His white hearers were, in all likelihood, horrified, the imagination filling noses and tongues with the smell and taste of sweaty black feet. He went on: "How about those nurses that must sleep with the children, go traveling with you, occupy the room with you and the bed with your loved ones?" Then the devastating, rhetorical answers: "Do you stand all this (and I have not half portrayed it), and yet you can't bear to ride upon the same car, though in a separate seat from your colored fellow citizens?" How, then, to explain white behavior? His answer was bold and must have shocked: "It is the dissatisfaction of some of our neighbors [whites] with their own, it would seem, that for their own restraint (which does not restrain) they must have laws to prevent this race antipathy of which they love to prate."[31]

Other black leaders used similar strategies. On June 4, 1890, in speeches concerning the Louisiana legislature's effort to segregate railroad cars—the so-called Separate Car Bill—black representatives C. F. Brown and Victor Rochon exposed the illogic of segregation. Rochon put it this way: "Why, Mr. Speaker, the idea that you and your family would not be offended in traveling hundreds of miles with a dozen or perhaps more negro servants, but would be insulted to travel any distance with me and my family on account of our color. The logic of this proposition is beyond my understanding."[32]

This style and form of critique continued into the twentieth century. Born the son of a slave in Virginia in 1865, Wendell Phillips Dabney wrote in 1918: "All people have a natural odor." Dabney was especially confused by the common claims made by whites that putative black stench justified segregation. After all, he pointed out, "since Negroes were first brought to this country they have been extensively used for cooks, waiters, sick nurses and wet nurses etc. etc."[33]

Those most trusted by whites—mammies, cherished and loved—were also very sensitive to the hypocrisy of the segregationist conceit and among the most devastating when it came to lampooning white logic. Old black servants in the 1930s "contrast[ed] the intimate nature of their services to white families (i.e., in cooking their food, nursing, and often suckling their children, and caring for adults, male and female, in the sickbed) with the taboo of social uncleanliness which their employers recognize[d] in their public relations with them." "One old colored servant ridiculed the fact that her employer was active in supporting measures in the state legislature 'to keep Negroes in their place,' because she had always had complete charge of his children and often slept in the bed with them."[34]

Black maids were especially attuned to white hypocrisy because of the sensorily intimate nature of their labor. An exasperated Aletha Vaughn noted that even though her employers had her prepare food, they insisted she use a separate bathroom; that while she was allowed to clean the white indoor bathroom, she had to use the outside one; and that "they had certain dishes you could eat out of. You ate out of certain dishes, and your particular plate and fork and spoon went in a certain place." Even taste was regulated: "I've had them tell me, 'Now anything that's here you can have except the things I've marked.' She'd mark an X on things she didn't want you to have. That would be the best food." Most maids responded with the mask of deference—anxious not to lose their income—or quiet acts of resistance, including disrupting schedules.[35]

Black magazines also applied hard logic to combat sensory stereotypes. Don't be ashamed of black culinary taste, argued an Ebony editorial in November 1953. "Few are the Negroes who have become objective enough to do what they wish, act as they feel and say what they want without fear of perpetuating some so-called Negro stereotypes," read the editorial. Sensory stereotypes lacked real grounding, Ebony argued, not least because many whites had begun to "eat foods we like," "wear the colors we admire," even "give vent to emotions we feel." "If figures were available," continued the editorial, "they would show that proportionately more white people eat watermelon, fried chicken and pork chops than do Negroes." "Cornbread . . . Spareribs . . . Chitterlings" also graced the white palate. In short, white appropriation of black styles made a mockery of putative racially determined sensory characteristics: "Whites have out-eaten the Negro right down to Saturday's neckbones and Sunday's red beans and rice. They have aped his style of music so well that it is sometimes impossible to tell when the blues are black or white. . . . Red cloth is now so attractive that its appeal is no longer attributed solely to dark races of African origins. The master race has even got sinners singing about being happy in a chapel."[36]

Black intellectuals living outside the South used the same style of reasoning to deride segregation's logic. This is precisely what James Weldon Johnson did in the 1920s during a series of public talks. After one lecture, "a man rose and said, 'I want to ask you a frank question. Isn't the chief objection to the Negro due to the fact that he has a bad odor?'" Johnson agreed that "there were lots of bad-smelling Negroes; but, in turn, I asked my questioner if he thought the expensive magazine advertisements about 'B.O.' were designed to attract an exclusive Negro patronage. I remarked that I did not think so, since they were generally illustrated with pictures of rather nice-looking white girls."[37]

Black people pushed the segregationists' argument to corners from which it could not escape, to conclusions that just made no sense. The main point about blacks' challenges to white sensory stereotypes is that a good deal of their critique was intellectually devastating precisely because it was based on hard and fast common sense of the kind that had helped slaves survive bondage. Their arguments were exactly of the sort one heard from liberal southern whites in the years surrounding the 1954 *Brown v. Board of Education* decision.

The *Brown* Concertina

On April 4, 1956, a Norman, Oklahoma, schoolgirl wrote to Alabama governor "Big Jim" Folsom asking his counsel. In careful, adolescent penmanship, she explained: "We are having a debate at school on segregation. I have the affirmative side; that is, that segregation is good." But she was stumped and needed his help: "Although I firmly believe in segregation, I find it hard to say why I am prejudice[d]." In this respect, the schoolgirl was wholly and sadly typical: people supported segregation without really thinking why. They simply "felt" it was right. Feeling, not thinking, was segregation's best friend.[1]

Cherished sensory understandings of race shaped white attitudes in visceral ways. "I would like to furnish you with an instance of the Negroid depravity and loose morals of these people," Randolph McPherson counseled Virginia governor Thomas B. Stanley in 1956. Look and listen: "To see them in action, one would think they are fresh from a jungle, with the beat of the Tom Tom's sounding in the background." Such depravity was innate, since "one hundred years of civilation [*sic*] in the United States" had done nothing. If you doubt me, ventured McPherson, listen to my experience at the newly integrated Center Theater in Norfolk: "At a recent performance of 'HOLIDAY ON ICE,' Negroes were observed in the toilets of this theater acting in a lewd manner . . . so foul white people were unable to look on." Black sound confirmed the spectacle (because, of course, white eyes could not bear to look): "These niggers were using the bowls in the toilets, and then shaking their appendages at each other and in a loud mo[u]th manner" boasting of sexual prowess.[2]

The 1954 *Brown v. Board of Education of Topeka* decision and the federal mandate to integrate public schools was understood by southern segregationists as a forced sensory folding or collapsing—a sensory concertina—in which whites believed they now had to see, hear, smell, touch, and, God forbid, taste blackness in contexts defined by African Americans. This revulsion at sensory crowding is clear from reading sociological and psychological literature concerning integration published during the 1930s, 1940s, and 1950s and, more especially, little-used letters from a broad spectrum of people—not just the much-studied formal organizations behind massive resistance—written to southern governors in Texas, South Carolina, Virginia, North Carolina, Georgia, and Alabama between 1953 and 1957. These letters, hundreds of them, written by whites and blacks, integrationists and segregationists, southerners and nonsoutherners, children and adults, clergy and newspaper editors, farm hands and housewives, the educated and the barely literate, help explain how and why white resistance could be so powerfully emotional. Although whites who protested integration ranged enormously in their socioeconomic background, they—and no few white southern "liberals"—shared a common sensory idiom concerning racial identity. This sensory dimension to race-thinking gave a gut-wrenching quality to white reaction over Brown, a quality that far outweighed the intellectual component of massive resistance. Theirs was a self-contained logic—more of an instinct—premised on fear of sensory assault that they associated with school integration. The sheer venom of the segregationists' reaction to Brown and the ferocity of their hatred in letters to southern governors suggest why southern politicians tended to wed themselves to an anti-integrationist stance. The political price for doing otherwise must have looked astronomical.[3]

Brown brought all sensory stereotypes into play with searing focus. Even old stereotypes that had lost currency in the early twentieth century, ones suggesting that blacks had a heightened sense of smell, rushed to the surface of everyday discourse in this moment of unbridled venom. Taking the sensory dimension of segregation seriously reveals the utter radicalism of the Civil Rights Movement and the power of the Brown decision. But the meaning of "radical" to the segregationist was by no means the same as it was to the integrationist. For whatever the white supremacists were wrong about—and there was so very much—they were right about one thing: federally mandated integration could not change with any reasonable speed deep-seated attitudes about race, especially when those attitudes had for so long been shaped by the senses.[4]

Had a small but committed group of southerners had their way, integration—fully meaningful and operational—would have come quickly. The South was, after all, home to some white southerners who styled themselves "liberal" on the race issue. Academics, writers, labor leaders, members of the National Association for the Advancement of Colored People (NAACP), Communists, and New Deal radicals actively critiqued their region and its past, embraced interracial unions and civic committees, pushed hard for black voter registration, and lobbied for black uplift. Although the best chance for such a broad and varied group to effect change was probably in the five or so years immediately after World War II, they had, in various guises, been actively campaigning years before the war, particularly during the New Deal. By the 1920s some white moderates had formed groups, such as the Commission on Inter-racial Cooperation (the CIC was out of Atlanta), in an effort to soften segregation. Never really challenging the basis of segregation, the CIC was hardly radical, but it did help open up a dialogue whereby questions could at least be posed about the desirability of the existing southern segregated order.[5]

According to Morton Rubin in his 1951 study, *Plantation County*, "These liberals are evolutionists; they are 'liberal southerners,' rather than 'southern liberals' in the accustomed usage. They operate through existing race-caste behavior patterns rather than attacking them directly." While "none of them believes in the innate inferiority of the Negro," and while they "are willing to grant the vote to the educated Negro group at once, . . . they feel the masses should be educated before the vote is completely extended." Membership was diverse and included labor leaders, teachers, lawyers, clergy, newspaper editors, and just ordinary working men and women. They also often felt obliged to defend their sanity and southern pedigree. Mrs. Martin Waldron, who told Alabama governor Gordon Persons in 1954 that he "might be surprised at the number of intelligent people in Alabama who feel that segregation is costly, outdated, immoral, and downright silly," concluded her letter: "I pray you do not think this a letter from a crank. I am a sober, non-radical, ordinary housewife."[6]

The liberal persuasion often stressed the safeness of interaction between the races and the idiocy of sensory racial stereotypes. Witness interracial experience in the U.S. military. Beginning with U.S. Navy policy in 1946 and then with President Harry S. Truman's executive order in 1948, the armed forces began to introduce "equality of treatment and opportunity." Blacks gave orders to whites, whites to blacks; on base after base, black and white were permitted to school together, eat together, and swim together. There was, according to one soldier, "no apparent antipathy," and men left the armed forces and reentered civilian life with thousands of memories of interracial association. Even as the war itself gave rise to absurd rumors about black aggressiveness and activism on the southern home front, some white men returned to the South with the conviction that segregation was nonsense. After all, they had now "saluted Negro officers," "slept in the same barracks, [eaten] at the same table, bathed in the same showers," and the world had not ended.[7]

Religion was important to the liberal position. For many, integration was the only Christian thing to do. "The 'problem' which you feel faces Alabama is indeed a large one," wrote Mrs. Francis Walter of Spring Hill, Alabama, to Governor Gordon Persons in December 1953, "but the 'problem children' are white instead of black. You would do well to start a campaign in the press urging the white population of this state to go to their Bibles for the answer to this 'problem.'" She concluded: "We thank God that our children will welcome their dark brothers- and sisters-in-Christ to their superior school facilities." "Let us keep Alabama free from bitterness and hatred during this period of advancing Christianity," offered W. P. Ingram of Birmingham in 1954.[8]

Like African Americans, white liberals often applied hard logic to lampoon segregation. David F. Conrad of the National Lutheran Council in Montgomery, Alabama, argued that "our greatest action as citizens in the South is to admit the truth that segregation has been a farce." Conrad peeled away the public fiction of segregation and revealed how it was highly contingent, applied and suspended as whites saw fit, not the ironclad custom that white supremacists now insisted it always had been. "Show ourselves and others that there has been no segregation except where we have 'insisted' that the law demand it," maintained Conrad, arguing: "In public places like banks, post offices and on city streets, segregation has never been practiced, at least in my life time. In our southern homes most of us learned to eat while sitting on the knee of a beloved Negro housekeeper." "Let us be honest with our Negro friends," he concluded: "They are clamoring for something we all would clamor for if we were in the same situation."[9]

Using the kind of materialist critique favored by blacks, other liberals pointed to the conditions creating the appearance of black inferiority. Geoffrey Birt of the Advertiser Company, which published both the Montgomery *Advertiser* and the Alabama *Journal*, told Gordon Persons: "From a fiscal standpoint, the decision of the Supreme Court will—or should—make little or no difference except, perhaps, that a continuation of separate but equal facilities will prove somewhat more costly. . . . As a guarantee of good faith in this doctrine, certain counties in particular should start putting lavatories and water, etc., in the Negro schools, and, in general, start getting these poor little Negro kids out of the leaky, unsanitary, dirty, dingy, rotten fire traps cynically called schools." It took guts to make such points, even when they dripped with paternalism. "I am afraid to sign my name," "Just a Friend" scribbled from Stonewall, Mississippi, to Governor Folsom in 1956. His or her angst was understandable: "I am a white Southerner Born and raised . . . negroes . . . are not strangers to us. Some of our finest people have them in their homes servants cooks, side by side with them. We are living in 1956 not 1909. We have made Progress since that time so have the Negroes. They are better Educated they have learned to keep clean."[10]

White liberals—some of whom were more properly described as "radicals"—were also important for their continued efforts to expose the stupidity of segregationist thought. Virginia Durr was particularly good at revealing its warped quality. In the context of the Montgomery Bus Boycott, she wrote to Nathan David, a Washington, D.C., attorney and friend: "To show you how silly this whole thing really is, Maxwell Field [Air Force Base] is now completely integrated, and thousands of white people from here work out there and accept negroes in the Library, Cafeteria, work by them, and even in some cases, go swimming with them, BUT let them get back to Montgomery and they go nuts." Her explanation for this "schizophrenia"? "It is not a fear of the negroes but a fear of each other, what people will think about them."[11]

Alabama blacks agreed with all of this—in fact, had pioneered the form and substance of the critique—and used the talk surrounding *Brown* to articulate with increasing force and clarity what they had always been saying. Willie James Russell, a junior at Alabama State College, asked Gordon Persons, "Didn't God say that we all were his children and we were brothers and sisters in one world?"[12] Others framed their arguments within the larger context of African American economic advancement, specifically with regard to black consumption patterns and the senses. In 1955, for example, Jesse J. Lewis, head of an African

American advertising firm in Alabama, sent Governor Folsom a copy of his company's newsletter, with particular focus on "Greater Birmingham and It's [sic] Enormous Negro Market." Although Lewis's precise reasoning for sending Folsom the material was unclear, in the context of the intense debate over *Brown* and school integration, what was essentially a marketing report took on special significance, pointing to the rapid assimilation of blacks in southern society not by dint of politics but, rather, by virtue of "Birmingham's Negro buying power." The document showed that since 1948 black consumption of household items had undergone considerable change, and Lewis pointed to, for example, the increase in Birmingham's African American population owning washing machines (15.1 percent in 1948; 61.7 in 1954). He also explained that Birmingham's blacks bought products that whites traditionally did not associate with black consumers. Lewis reported that 100 percent of the city's black families used "Bath Soap," that 95 percent used toothpaste, and that 94 percent of black women and 83 percent of men used deodorant. Lewis tried to demonstrate the purchasing power of Alabama's blacks and suggest that their buying patterns—and their aesthetic sense—were hardly any different from those of whites. Lewis argued, in effect, that blacks would soon be smelling nicely, if they were not already: "The perfume manufacturers of America and the world have long closed their eyes, ears to a market right under their noses that within itself has an income twice as large as Canada. . . . The first of '56 will see several of the bigger fragrance houses entertaining proposals."[13]

Blacks from outside the South joined in and helped expose segregation's faulty logic concerning interracial contact. In 1955 Governor Folsom received a copy of an article published in the Joliet, Illinois, *Negro Voice* pointing out that southern blacks "have served as domestics around your home, have fondled your children and taught them the meaning of 'The Lord's Prayer.' " In a thoughtful, intellectually powerful essay on the logical fallacies of segregation, Malcolm Henry Christian of Chicago asked: "If Negroes, as a whole, are so diseased, immoral, criminally inclined and generally unacceptable for close contacts then, to truly segregate them, it would be necessary to completely set them apart from *all close contacts*," but, he continued, southern blacks in fact "have close contacts with whites in numerous circumstances other than in schools." Christian then suggested that segregationists' real fear was the effect of integration on fostering a "mutual understanding" and the explosion of cherished myths: "White supremacists realize that mutual understandings, gained in school interactions, would reveal the half truths, exaggerations, distortions" of their claims. Anyway, he concluded, it simply made no sense to assign characteristics to either race when, as was well known, "there are greater differences between individuals of the same race than exist between different races."[14]

Rampant and equally long-lived instances of northern racism did not prevent the critique of southern segregation from taking on a national quality in the years surrounding *Brown*. Is a "colored man without prejudice," a New Yorker asked Jim Folsom in March 1956, "what the white race is afraid off [sic][?]" It was a rhetorical question designed to expose the hypocrisy of segregationist claims: "Is it because they fear that the colored man is going to take away his woman. Lets look at the record." He pointed to the incidence of "mullatoes" and explained: "In nine out of ten cases the father is white. It is plain to see that it is the white man that does the mongrelizing." The writer was dogged: "I am still asking what is the Whitman [sic] afraid off [sic]. You allow the colored woman to cook your food, care for your children, and nurse you when you are sick, yet at the same time you are afraid to sit beside this same person in a street car." "If Negroes are good enough to raise your children, and feed you your food, and be trusted servants in your homes," offered Kitty from Buffalo, New York, "they are good enough to be treated as any other human beings. We have Negroes in practically all our schools and industries up here and none of us has been polluted by them and the black doesn't rub off!!!"[15]

While nonsouthern support for desegregation was important, many hopes rested on forces within southern society to effect meaningful change. But whatever their undeniable courage, southern white liberals were too few in number (hence their courage). Many were also plagued by quiet doubts about the reliability of their own critique. A powerful liberal foe was the liberal psyche itself, burdened with the enormous weight of history that accompanied being a white southerner. White liberals were gutsy, thoughtful, but, quite sensibly, careful, and they often had difficulty escaping the history of their own senses.[16]

Seeing segregation unravel was hard, even for white liberals sympathetic to integration. Change threatened to rend tried and tested race relations with which many liberals were quietly comfortable. For Rev. Thomas R. Thrasher, a member of the biracial Alabama Council on Human Relations, the Montgomery Bus Boycott ruptured the intimacy of race relations almost beyond repair. "Time after time during these past weeks," he told the New York *Reporter* in 1956, "I have felt as if I were living in a nightmare, one of those where you speak and nobody hears. . . . This nightmare extends to the whole community. White and black stand on opposite sides of an invisible line, and there seems no possible way of communicating across the barrier, a barrier which is there and isn't there, which in a sense both of us have made and of which we are both victims. The Negroes are people who have helped us, taught us, nurtured us, made us laugh, made us weep, and have given us depth of understanding. But the patterns of our past communication are breaking, and new patterns are not yet formed. . . . The nightmare persists even as we hear words and see gestures. They speak. We do not understand."[17] At times, the future seemed impossible to imagine.

Liberals had a difficult time evading their region's history. Its inherited and unquestioned credo concerning racial difference lodged like emotional shrapnel in the gut. Breaches of sensory racial etiquette made even reasonable people gag. As a teenager, Melton McLaurin of Wade, North Carolina, harbored what might reasonably be characterized as "liberal" sentiments. He recognized that segregation was cruel, and by his own estimation "a developing intellectual curiosity set me apart from many of the white residents of the community." A year or so before the *Brown* decision, McLaurin was playing basketball with black and white friends, among them James Robert Fuller Jr., known as Bobo, a black. The basketball was unreliable and kept deflating, and the boys kept taking the ball to a nearby air compressor, inserting a needle into it, and pumping it up. In one instance, Bobo "stuck the needle in his mouth, applied the usual lavish amount of saliva" and handed the needle to another boy who proceeded to botch the needle's entry. McLaurin became agitated by their incompetence, "pulled the needle from the valve, and placed it in my mouth," an act that was "one of the most shattering emotional experiences of my life." In short, the white boy had tasted and ingested blackness, the "Negro spit" threatening "to defile my entire being." Silly fears ran through him, fears with a long history. Bobo's spittle "threatened me with germs which, everyone said, were common among blacks," and would give him "diseases from the tropics, Congo illnesses." Even as the fear gripped him, McLaurin knew that a good deal of his reaction was irrational. After all, "I often had drunk from the same cup as black children, dined on food prepared by blacks," and he had just been playing basketball with Bobo, a game involving touch, none of which he had perceived as violating "my racial purity." But tasting black spit, ingesting it, tipped an emotional scale inside McLaurin for reasons that were unclear to him then and can be explained only in terms of visceral impulse. Bobo's spit "placed in jeopardy my racial purity, my existence as a superior being, the true soul of all southern whites," producing nothing short of "emotional turmoil" in the boy. "The urge to gag, to lean over and vomit out any trace of the black saliva that might remain to spread its contamination throughout my body, was almost unbearable."[18]

But McLaurin could not vomit or even gag. To have done so would have betrayed a white southern past and jeopardized a white southern present. He explained: "More than the poison of Bobo's saliva I feared the slightest indication of loss of self-control, the merest hint that this black child I knew so well had the power to cut me to the emotional quick, to reach the innermost regions of my being and challenge the sureties of my white world." McLaurin's own particular background—stressing the supremacy of whites within a paternalist idiom mandating that "superior people never treated their inferiors in an unseemly manner"—made him hide the impact of tasting and swallowing black spit. Less disciplined people, whites less concerned with class status and behavior, would have revealed their loathing. McLaurin's reaction to Bobo's spit revealed the tension facing liberal southerners, people who wanted to use their intellect to explore the inconsistencies of the system of segregation but whose own history, upbringing, and racial privilege rendered them hostage to raw feeling and the compass of the gut. White liberals struggled between emotionally conditioned reactions and their desire to appeal to the head. Segregationists experienced no such turmoil.[19]

MAKING SENSE OF BLACK AND BROWN

The Brown decision was so important to segregationists precisely because they believed it would end in mandated racial intimacy. Not only would whites now have to see blacks; they would also have to hear, smell, taste, and touch them, no longer on their terms but on terms set by federal authority and enacted daily by black people. This sensory concertina was important for shaping segregationists' anticipation of, and reaction to, the Brown decision. That the senses of smell and especially of taste and touch figured so prominently in white reaction to Brown is easily explained. As one Virginian believed, "Social intercourse between the races always implies sexual intercourse." Cast an eye over the hundreds of letters written to southern governors between 1953 and 1957, and it is clear what boiled just below that serene southern surface: anger, raw and bitter.[20]

Religion played a role in shaping that anger. While integrationists appealed to both a reasoned and an emotionally charged theology to help justify why segregation should end, white supremacists invoked a visceral, primitive form of religious agitation, one largely devoid of careful theological reasoning, to justify why integration should not take place. Sensory arguments held center stage in this argument. "I have Gods proof we are different," wrote one supporter of segregation in 1955: "My eyes and ears tell me we are different." Faith, after all, came through hearing as well as seeing. And smelling, too, apparently. The Lord Himself had impregnated stink into black skin, argued Ben Howard of Athens, Alabama, in 1957. "No one wants there [sic] Child to go to School with Stinking [Negroes] they stink they all do God Put that Sent [sic] on them." The future smelled bleak, too: "Why if the Negroes force Integration our next President will be a Stinking Negro."[21]

Appeals to God did not preclude appeals to pseudoscience. Blackness was genetic, and you could hear it. "In the white man the alveolar arch and palatine area of the mouth became shortened and widened and the tongue became shortened and more horizontally flattened which allows for greater refinement in pronunciation," read a particularly nasty piece of segregationist propaganda out of Florida. By contrast, "the Negro palate and tongue remained ape like (macrodont) and he is unable to pronounce sibilant sounds. Sibilant sounds are unknown in the Negro dialect." The danger of mixing was enormous, not least because "the black genes of the Negro are more powerful than white genes."[22]

Black assertiveness inspired vicious responses from segregationists, some of which played up sensory stereotypes, attributing black characteristics to the influence of an African past. Segregationists referred to the Montgomery Bus Boycotters as "black slimy, juicy, unbearably stinking niggers," whose increased presence on the street reaffirmed established stereotypes. "I tell you," went the rant, "they are a group of two legged agitators who persist in walking up and down our streets protruding their black lips." These "African flesh eaters," distinguished by their demonic sense of taste, "have an ancestral background of Pigmies, head hunters and snot suckers."[23]

Anyway, some maintained, segregation was good for blacks, not least because they were not—and could not be—like whites. Blacks would loathe integrated schools, their sight and sound making them feel uncomfortable. Martha Holman of Evergreen, Alabama, told Gordon Persons in 1953: "The colored children, some of them doesn't bathe often as they should. Their dress would be looked down upon in a white school by some white children." Moreover, "the whites are quiet. The Negro could not possibly be happy in a white school." No, she concluded, black "feelings would be hurt in many, many hundreds of ways."[24]

Segregationists fingered a number of culprits behind the growing move for integration. They believed, not unreasonably, that national forms of communication, television in particular, affected the way people thought about race, and they did not like the visual images and sounds of televised interracial intimacy. The Ed Sullivan show came in for harsh criticism especially. " 'Sullivanism' is rapidly becoming a trademark by which disgusting spectacle of mongreli[z]ation propaganda is measured on television," Big Jim Folsom was told. The sensory messages were repulsive: "The program is used as a stage to sell integration to the nation, as Negro after Negro is paraded across, hugged, kissed and praised for their 'rock and roll' type of animal 'entertainment.' " Corporate America was equally culpable, using visual images of interracial touch to sell goods and shape black consumption patterns. "Johnnie, the Phillip [sic] Morris trademark, seems very happy to have his arms around two Negroes."[25]

The U.S. military was also to blame. Integration at American military bases, argued the Southerner: News of the Citizens' Council in February 1956, had started slowly, even quietly, a "silent, fist-of-iron movement," and then accelerated, leading to mixing in all areas, including the cafeterias, where "white girls" were "forced to serve" black soldiers. "The degrading movement of integration was taking effect." Witness the process at Fort McClellan, Alabama. The paper had the pictures to prove it, and the editors offered commentary, sound-tracking the visual horror of interracial touching: "And as the evening wears on, one can hear the music rising in tempo, the beat growing into a jungle throb, the courtesies grow more lax, until the woman is accorded no visible respect. And there in the course of a few hours is capsuled before the viewers' eyes the road America is taking, away from civilization; downward into the mire of mongrelization from which no race can return."[26]

But good southern whites always resisted such pressures, even when in the army. "A Rebel Friend, John," wrote to Gordon Persons from

France in January 1954, arguing for continued segregation. He spoke, he said, from firsthand knowledge, and the matter of eating with blacks figured prominently in his reasoning: "You see, I know because I have to eat with them and stay in the same barracks they do, but there's nothing I can do, I know of many white men here that don't want nothing to do with the colored race. Lots of them here are from the North and if you want to eat around them and work with them, I will guarrenty [sic] you one thing, you'll never want nothing to do with them, and that I suppose is how they are taught in Northern schools." Thomas M. Taylor of the air force echoed those sentiments in a letter from Korea in July 1954 to Texas governor Allan Shivers. Taylor thought "less of the negro now than I did before I enlisted."[27]

Very occasionally, southerners blamed themselves for their predicament. "A Citizen" from Houston wrote to Folsom: "The whites in the U.S.A. have become too familiar with the Negroes in every way. Everybody know[s] that white men sweetheart with Negro women. They will hire them in stores to get a chance, or as a housekeeper. . . . We whites," he (or she) concluded, "need to reflect and reform. . . . No under the cover doings."[28]

Because of its old associations with sex, disease, nearness, and invasiveness, smell preoccupied segregationists during the years surrounding Brown. "My association with the colored people," Mrs. John F. Watlington of Reidsville, North Carolina, wrote to Governor William B. Umstead in June 1954, "has been very pleasant. . . . The reason for this," she explained, "is it has always been in airy places—plenty of fresh air." Extravagant smells could, then, be diluted. But integration meant black invasion of white space, which would affect not just the visual world of whites but also their olfactory one. According to Mrs. B. B. Tart, "In working with Negroes here on the farm in open air is all right but get in a tight place like gradding [sic] tobacco . . . you have to get out in the air for their oder is like Cloriform, now think of closing up a warm school room, & you will see, & hear of more & more disease." This was olfactory "crowding." Mrs. Lella M. Galvani of Nashville wrote a letter to Alabama's Gordon Persons and Virginia's Thomas B. Stanley in 1954, listing sixteen objections to desegregation. Point two reads: "If race segregation laws were broken down, it would mean white people would be pushed out, imposed upon or be made to bear the very offensive odor of negro people under crowded conditions at work, study, rest, recreation or play. Our country is large enough that we do not have to be crowded up with thousands of negroes." Making blacks wash would not alleviate the problem because, as Mississippi segregationists believed, the "characteristic odor of the Negro's skin . . . is inherent and not caused by uncleanliness."[29]

If southern governors ever had cause to doubt the extent and intensity of the olfaction argument, they received confirmation from people far removed from the South. Carlos H. Allen of Santa Ana, California, sympathized with white Alabamians. "In keeping with you," he wrote Folsom, "we are not Negro haters." Nevertheless, "we are thinking of two major factors that should operate to keep the two races apart." First was the visual: "We object to their color." Second, the olfactory: "We can't tolerate his body odor." Ergo: "So we think the Blacks should be excluded from all buildings where the whites congregate." Southerners who had moved but who occasionally came home confirmed the argument and suggested what an integrated future would smell like. Mrs. Eulalia Mangels of San Jose, California (a native Texan), told Governor Folsom of her experiences riding integrated trains from California to Texas. On "the train, I won't even ride the Pullman for fear I'd be somewhere close to a Negro." But regardless of where she sat, aspects of blackness penetrated her body, seeping into defenseless nostrils. Even though she would "take a walk" out of the main car, she had to "come in the car again and all I smell is Negroes, oh that oder!! How can Congress or Supreme Court force that on us?" She dreaded each journey: "I am making a trip to Texas in June . . . am afraid I'd have a berth below or above me containing a Negro. And if the Negro oder makes me ill as it did last time (and it was that) I'd be tempted to sue Congress and Supreme Court." But the association of sickness, blackness, and odor was nothing new to the woman: "Their oder sure made me sick when I was growing up and my family hired them as servants."[30]

Segregationists forced to travel on integrated interstate buses complained loudest of all, arguing that close spatial proximity to black people, not so much the time of enduring the proximity, was the issue. "How would you like to take a trip of several hundred miles, or even just for one mile," asked a "poor bus driver" of Georgia governor Marvin Griffin in March 1955, "with a smelly Negro sitting beside you, blowing his or her breath in your face, or trying to get up a conversation with you?"[31]

If olfaction measured space, black stench also confirmed animalism and sex. The *White Sentinel* of Fort Lauderdale, Florida, made the following acidic observation: "The Negro carries stench glands as does the dog and in his natural state these may serve as a means of identification in place of a name. . . . This stench (from extra sweat glands) is partly under control and is put out when the Negro is excited." Readers who still failed to get the point could examine taxingly explicit cartoons rife with haptic and olfactory stereotypes. One (illustration 6.1) depicted the "Animal Smell" of both "The Negro" and "The Ape," with arrows pointing to a bottle of poison, in turn labeled "A Warning."[32]

Old stereotypes concerning race, smell, and hygiene were trotted out with extravagant delight and loud desperation in the years surrounding the Brown decision. Mrs. John E. Schmidt Jr. of Valdosta, Georgia, believed that "most of our 'darkies' take too infrequent baths and consequently have a decided unpleasant odor about them." She and others of her ilk tried to help, of course, but their hands were tied by their respect for black personal freedom. White noses simply had to suffer: "Aside from insisting upon cleanliness while in our homes and trying to teach them the value of cleanliness we can do nothing—it is not for us to make laws saying how often one is to take a bath." Bath or no bath, black people just smelled, and they would do so as long as segregationists believed what they felt. The statement of one white man from Alabama in 1955 captures the clumsy power of the stereotype: "I was learned & reared in Ala. Have been around Negroes all my life and am sure I have Never smelled a Negro I wanted to Call Bro."[33]

School integration focused the olfactory discussion. Disease and smell informed some complaints, leading one Alabama man to claim, "When the negros [sic] stay in their own school the white children do not have to set [sic] beside them and smell them all day and catch their disease." Governor Folsom was advised in 1955, "You could ask the blacks which school they wish to go to. They will pick the white school. Then the whites could go to the abandoned black school, after freshening it up, of course." "I am a white school girl and I strongly oppose outlawing segregation," Kathie Rose Swoop told Virginia's governor in 1954. Her reasoning was based on family tales: "My brother told us of a colored school in Fla. where he helped put on a roof. The school was new, he went past it in a year and it had a terrible odor, the shades and windows torn and dirty." Scent lingered in segregationists' nostrils, ripe with meaning.[34]

School integration, argued one Virginia woman, would lead to the laceration of refined white skin at the flinty hands of rough blacks, who

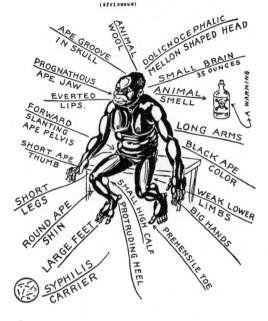

Ill. 6.1.
"The Negro, The Ape."
This explicit white
supremacist cartoon
from the 1950s
animalized black people,
particularly with regard
to smell. (National
Citizens Protective
Association, St. Louis,
Mo., J. D. Rowlett
Collection, 1954–1972
and n.d., ac 1971-0299M,
Folder 3: *White Sentinel*,
Georgia Archives)

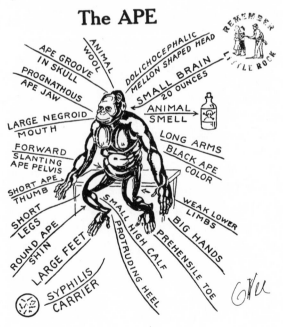

showed no love of human hide, even their own: "I'm afraid . . . the Negroes will bring knives to school and stab our children as more Negroes get in cutting scrapes than do the whites." Segregationists had long connected blacks' desire to touch white skin with violence. Central to such thinking was the apparent contempt that blacks had for their own skin, which they naturally extended to white skin if given the chance. In the context of the *Brown* decision, such arguments were offered eagerly and dutifully.[35]

Alabama governor Gordon Persons received a pamphlet outlining the tactile dangers of integration in 1953, extra copies of which could be ordered from the Christian Nationalist Crusade out of Tulsa, Oklahoma. The unidentified author explained: "Jim Crow must remain. It is a realistic program of transportation. It is bad enough for our daughters and wives to be crowded and pushed around and squeezed on busses and trains by the occasional white moron without them being subjected to this offensive physical contact by black men."[36] Crowded, pushed, squeezed: Reconstruction was but yesterday.

White women confirmed it all, speaking of unbridled black touching, especially after the *Brown* decision. In November 1955 Jane Revill of Sumter, South Carolina, reported what she considered an epidemic of touching. Some of it bordered on violent—black elbows "used to punch a stiff blow while passing"—while other forms were plainly sexual. Here is how she described the minuet: "One white lady standing just back of a negro man in a cue-line, up steps another negro behind her and pushes forward to the point where the white lady drops out in self-protection to prevent what a colored schoolteacher called 'putting the pinch on.'" "*Some* white women," of course, "do not mind"; but this one did. She had been subject to "wedging" by black male bodies in line, bodies that "wanted to take the space" around queuing white women. "I do not hate them," she concluded, "I just don't like to come in contact with them." And, in their own way, black women were just as bad. In March 1956 a Georgia nurse sighed that integration had already gone too far in Savannah. Black women "go up town & try on the same clothes & hats that we white women have to try on."[37]

Want to know where integration ends? asked Representative James C. Davis in his November 1956 address to the States' Rights Council of Georgia in Atlanta. Look no further than already integrated schools in Washington, D.C., which revealed the "well-known differences between whites and blacks which no amount of glossing over and covering up by

subversive so-called 'anthropologists' and pseudo-scientists can hide."
Davis lamented "that colored boys touched white girls in a suggestive
manner when passing them in the halls." By 1958 Davis's predictions
were borne out: the Augusta *Courier* ran a front page story proclaiming,
"Negroes Put Hands over Girls; Hugged Them, Young Lady of East Point
Says," in reference to a parade at Russell High School.[38]

Integration, then, meant forced encounters not just with black smell
but with blackness in toto, culminating in sex. An "Unreconstructed
Southerner," who fancied himself "a student of physical anthropology,"
explained that integration meant bleeding black into white, a wholly unnatural state of affairs since the African American was "a being apart."
Witness: "wide and straight nasal passages so he drips inside; wool instead of hair," and "a *body-odor* that bathing will not suppress." These
characteristics, plus "a skull about 40% thicker than normal," and
other features reminiscent of "primitive man," were intimately linked to
blacks' "sexual maturity at a very early age, and sexual organs of exaggerated size with a corresponding intense sex-urge difficult to control."
A black man's touch meant sex and rape, and his thick skin, uncontrol-
lable passion, and animal lust were good cause for visceral shudder.[39]

Integration moved along the senses—seeing, hearing, smelling, and
touching—and ended in tasting blackness. In 1956 a young Georgia
woman wrote to the U.S. Supreme Court protesting integration, her
words disconcertingly fretful. "If they sit side by side in classrooms—
why not at school parties? We certainly cannot draw the line at that
point. They will dance with and date each other and eventually go into
marriage." She concluded with a metaphor that reveals the close association between sex and the tongue and the segregationists' revulsion at
the prospect: "A child does not come to like a disliked food anymore
when parents force him to eat it—he gags on it and consequently hates it
more and more." But what if she was wrong and taste buds were stimu-
lated, aroused, and teased to further consumption?[40]

The activities of some white women made the worry real. Kissing
held such power because it was the culmination of the closing of distance between the races. Liberals who willfully flouted segregation came
in for some vicious criticism. In 1950, for example, Arthur Stoney accused Elizabeth Avery Waring, wife of South Carolina's prointegration
judge Waties Waring, of "kissing . . . one of them" during the course of
her much-publicized championing of civil rights. Elite as she was, her
kissing of blackness, combined with her northern origins (she was a

native of Detroit) now consigned her to the status of "White Trash," a "buckra woman," as Stoney called her.[41]

To drive the point home about the meaning of kissing, segregationists produced crude but very precise cartoons. The *White Sentinel* out of Fort Lauderdale, Florida, included a drawing representing the ultimate sensory sequence of integration (illustration 6.2). The artist's pen was at once rough and scruffy yet delicate and precise, especially when it came to drawing the lines of black and white lips. The white woman's lips are pursed, her head angled to suggest both latent longing and mild hesitation; the black man's lips, full, open, hungry, are near enough to hers to suggest both touching and impending taste. Lest anyone remain in doubt over the picture's meaning, the artist titled it "The Kiss of Death."[42]

Similarly, a flyer issued after *Brown* by the National Citizens Protective Association of St. Louis, Missouri, asked: "How would you like it if your exquisitely formed White child was no longer White?" How would you like it if the child's body was "no longer beautiful but black and evil smelling?" The dangers were everywhere, especially with "Youth Movements," including the Scouts, which preached the desirability of integration to the young and impressionable. Such "adults who are unduly attracted to White children and wish to mix them with Negroes are suffering from a Freudian Complex that gives them a sex thrill at the very thought of mating your lovely child with the evil ape like body of the negro." The unholy trinity of pedophilia, Communism, and integration lured white girls into black hands. The flyer was capped with a cartoon (illustration 6.3) whose ambiguity was intended to reflect both the sexual lure of interracialism and what the National Citizens Protective Association hoped would be the natural instinct of white repulsion at the prospect. Examine the woman's face closely. It contrasts with the black man's protruded lips, drawn to emphasize his desire, craving, and lasciviousness. But her reaction—or, perhaps, action—is complicated. Is she smiling or repulsing, responding or initiating? Her leg is raised, higher than his. The cartoon was a warning—tempted though you might be, white women of America, resist the feel and taste of black lips and avoid association with the leaders of youth movements who would lead you to abandon that resolve. And the message to white men was even louder: white women and black men might enjoy such encounters. Stop them now before it is too late.[43]

Metaphors revealed the relationship between taste, proximity, and

Ill. 6.2. "The Kiss of Death" was a 1950s segregationist cartoon depicting the social "dangers" of interracial touching and tasting. (*White Sentinel*, Ft. Lauderdale, Fla., n.d., J. D. Rowlett Collection, 1954–1972 and n.d., ac 1971-0299M, Folder 2: Annotated Handouts, Georgia Archives)

Ill. 6.3. "Youth Movements." Interracial contact among impressionable youth worried segregationists. Here, a 1950s cartoon details the dangers of touch and hints that white parents should be concerned, lest their daughters be led astray. (National Citizens Protective Association, St. Louis, Mo., Integration: The Right Wing Response, 1956–1964, ac 1968-0187M, Folder: Broadsides, Georgia Archives)

federal force. Integration as throat-stuffing became an increasingly common metaphor as the Civil Rights Movement gained steam, revealing a deeply held association between integration and the most intimate, sexual, raw sense of taste and forced feeding, a crowding of the mouth. "If it is a mixed race of the people that you are in favor of then," wrote a jeweler from Mobile to Gordon Persons in 1954, "then you should be in favor of 'Stuffing the Darkie down the Throats of the Southern People.'" In throats resided taste and, possibly, desire. "Do not be lulled to sleep with soft words," wrote G. W. Hanna, acting secretary of the National Citizens Council in Birmingham, Alabama, "or they will ram mongrelization down your throat and make you like it." "Now lady, I'll tell you the whole thing in a nutshell," offered a Montgomery, Alabama, bus driver in his late thirties during the bus boycott: "They are just trying to cram this down the people's throats and do it in a hurry." Or as "A Christian Grandmother" from Texas implored her governor in July 1955: "You can raise a protest against these negroes being cramed down the white peoples throats."[44]

The visceral nature of segregationist reaction to the *Brown* decision led to all sorts of contradictions. On the one hand, school integration and all that it stood for must not take place because of the innate—and therefore irreconcilable—differences between the races. This much was clear from segregationists who held firmly to the argument that racial identity was not solely visual. As a Tulia, Texas, resident argued a year or so after the *Brown* decision, "You're a fanatic! . . . that's the charge against us for holding on to the Southern tradition that pumpkins and melons should be grown in separate fields; for tasting, smelling, or seeing besides color, basic differences between the two and saying so." Yet, in almost the same breathless rant, segregationists argued that some aspects of race were, in fact, not inherited but decidedly learned and, moreover, transferable. Whites who supported integration, for example, assumed black sensory characteristics, and while the comparisons were metaphorical, they nevertheless showed race to be fungible. Those sponsoring integration were almost as rank as those they championed, and indulgent whites who had been lax in maintaining the color line were in real danger of becoming black. Beyond the old fear of passing was an additional concern with whites' adopting black sensory qualities. To protest integration, segregationists had to make race transferable—so that enemies could be accused, reliably and authentically, of behaving like blacks, down to their sensory core. Such an argument represented an expansion of the segregationist position. Race was now both biologically fixed and, ironically enough, plastic. Here segregationists happily borrowed from the loathed disciplines of sociology, anthropology, and psychology to defend their embattled world.[45]

For example, the ironically named Emitt Daniel of Phoenix, Arizona—who "used to live in Alabama"—wrote several southern governors in 1956 querying the origins of the integrationist impulse. "It certainly didn't start in the South," he offered, "but it does have a strong garlic like smell and accent of the Northern 5th Columnist." All enemies, then, smelled, and, in the case of blacks at least, the aroma was indelible: "God made the Negro black, and gave him the peculiar odor for good measure, and regardless of any High Court order, the fact remains he is a Negro and smells like one just the same."[46]

Becoming black did not apply just to outsiders. It was happening within, courtesy of patricians. In a particularly vicious letter to Jim Folsom, an Alabama woman argued that paternalist laxity was part of the South's problem: "You said after a Negro had raised us how come we couldn't be good to them. You may have sucked Old black Negro tit but I want to let you know we sure haven't. That is the trouble we have been good to the nasty things." Her conclusion was shrill and steely: "You would look nice kissing your sunning laws & daughter law and little black grand children Old black lips. When they cross it is just like a cure dog between a hound and a Shepard." Naturally, then, "all them that takes up for them looks worse than a Negro."[47]

Ultimately, though, the blacks were to blame for the whole bloody mess. Black efforts to eat with or touch whites were perceived as attempts at blackening. B. T. Matthews said as much in recounting his experience in Brookgreen Gardens, near Myrtle Beach, South Carolina, in April 1957. Matthews went to the gardens to have a picnic with his friends and family. Hovering around the tables was a "great throng of Negroes." Their intention, believed Matthews, was to take picnic seats and force whites to eat with them. Whites would have offered them a seat but, he argued, "they knew if they just got up and left that the negroes would get it and that we would be forced to eat with them or do without." Even walking around the gardens was dangerous: "Only about ten percent were white, which made it very embarrassing to walk around, a Negro in front, one in back, and if you weren't careful they would walk right side of you, your wife or friends." Such proximity, black brushing white, meant "they acted as if you were black too."[48]

Psychologists understood that fundamental changes in segregationists' attitudes toward race were hardly likely to happen overnight. Evidence of prior interracial contact mattered not to the "emotional" temper of the segregationist. "The fact that the great majority of American 'Negroes' and a large minority of Southern 'whites' are of mixed ancestry," offered sociologist Arnold M. Rose in 1955, "plays little role in the thinking of the whites." The segregationists' problem and the basis of their commitment were fundamentally historical in nature. Based on his examination of 383 Louisiana adults in 1952, E. Terry Prothro concluded that "the problem of 'the American dilemma' cannot be solved by approaching it from the level of personality dynamics alone. Situational, historical, and cultural factors appear to be of considerable, perhaps major, import."[49] History mattered—a lot.

Belief systems, argued Harvard psychologist Gordon Allport in 1954, "have the slippery propensity of accommodating themselves somehow to the negative attitude" that prevails despite evidence to the contrary. Beliefs have "a way of slithering around to justify the more permanent attitude," not least because original beliefs, especially when historically grounded, were largely "ideational and emotional." In the case of segregationists, "contrary evidence is not admitted and allowed to modify the generalization; rather it is perfunctorily acknowledged but excluded." This kind of mind-set lent a profoundly emotional quality to the segregationists' position, enabling them to sustain an understanding of the world by denying the need to think of the validity of possible alternatives. Mr. F. C. Owen, a retired Durham, North Carolina, attorney, was in a distinct minority in this respect. Although he remained a firm supporter of southern segregation, he refused to let emotion dictate his reasoning. Yes, he argued in June 1954, "through the years we have lived with a system of segregation and have managed to prosper amazingly well," but that alone "is not adequate cause for its continuance." "Neither," he continued, "is the fact that we may not like the looks, or the smell, or the behavior or even the mentality of the Negro" sufficient reason to continue segregation. Precedent and custom were not enough to justify the system. Instead, "there is but one valid and enduring reason to continue segregation"—the preservation of "the purity of the races."[50]

Mr. Owen was rare in that he thought. Most segregationists allowed instinct and unquestioned history to guide action. Imagining the visual consequences of integration inspired a visceral reaction in Mrs. Ruth

Barnett. She told Gordon Persons in January 1953: "Deep down inside of me there is, 'No, oh no, it must not happen.'" This was her gut reacting: "The thing goes further than mere separation of races. When something is physically, and morally, distasteful to a human being, no amount of legislation will ever change that person. . . . The mental picture of seeing young white girls forced to wedge themselves in among a school-bus full of negro youths is simply revolting."[51]

Segregationists recommended emotion as a sure compass and blue-print of action. Viscera and passion ruled the day because they had to. Five months before the first ruling in the *Brown* decision, a Mississippi man told Persons: "You say this is not a time for hot heads and flag waving but for clear, cold thinking. We need these hot heads, just as we always have when our liberty is threatened. Let's let the hot heads be the forge and retemper the bright shield of segregation which is our heritage. I, for one, would gladly lay down my life to prevent mongreli-zation. There is no greater cause." Now was the time to revel in the ferocity of southern whiteness, proclaimed Birmingham, Alabama's the *Southerner: News of the Citizens' Council* newsletter in February 1956. Exult in your "cracker" and "red neck" sound, the paper advised, revel "in the high whine of the fiddle's bow that calls up the sound of the fierce Scot blood that sounded the bagpipe of battle and lamented in the ballads of yore."[52]

Passion was essential if segregationists were to understand the true source of their fears. So, at least, argued Richard W. Edmonds in his 1957 *Foundation for Segregation*. To become exercised, emotional, and passionate about segregation was natural and desired. "Feeling on such a subject is not necessarily wrong. Those who advocate integration are actuated by feeling also, and their feeling runs as high and is just as irrational as the feeling of the most ardent segregationist," offered Ed-monds. Thus the debate was one of emotion, and all to the good. Edmonds rejected integration and wrote from the basis of his own feeling, "strong and deep." Instinct required honesty, a recognition that "we *feel* what it is we most ardently desire," and so "each one of us must be completely honest *with himself, in his most secret, innermost thoughts.*" In short, when segregationists argued that integration was "violently . . . unthinkable," they meant it literally: a prospect allergic to thought.[53]

Ending with *Brown* seems fitting. Unlike a good deal of recent work concerning the meaning of the *Brown* decision, which treats 1954 as a starting point (a tendency probably inherent to the concept of anniversaries, fiftieth or otherwise), I see *Brown v. Board of Education* less as a beginning and more as an end, not least because it was a sensory keynote for southern segregationists, a moment in which over two centuries of assumptions, stereotypes, and the mindless, unthinking behavior that protected and empowered them, came crashing into the present with magnifying-glass precision. Whether or not *Brown* initiated long-term change in sensory stereotypes is difficult to say, but one thing is clear: the decision did not make segregationists think. Feeling alone shaped their view of *Brown*. Instinct—and the long historical experience that produced it—enabled segregationists to ignore evidence and act on gut. In the years surrounding *Brown*, viscera became, more than ever, a necessary virtue.[54]

I leave the last words to three white southerners who took their stand over *Brown*. "The people of Alabama might appear calm," ventured Mrs. W. H. Duke of Gadsden, Alabama, in May 1954, "but on the inside they are seething with indignation at the ruling." A "Superintendent of our Sunday school," a man "strictly opposed to violence in any form," a "very mild mannered man" from Magnolia Terminal, Alabama, felt his pacifism evaporate in the face of "my children going to school, marrying, or having social activities with the negroes." Others just erupted: "If the people of all the Great Southern States band together and fuck this Yankee ruling then how can they invoke it," screamed "A Loyal Southerner" from Baltimore, Maryland (originally from Virginia), to the governor of Alabama. Although he claimed, "I have never had a taste for Violence and unlawful procedure," the *Brown* decision and all it stood for riled his very guts: "I don't care by what means or how we can fuck this republican Communist Command."[55]

In years to come, civil rights activists let such men and women lay bare their visceral fury to the world, their glowering faces, punching fists, and kicking feet raw, frightening testimony to their determination to protect their society. It was a wise strategy. Seeing segregationists spew their hatred with such ferocity on national television shocked many. The extent of segregationists' hatred and the strength of their emotion were unfathomable except to those caught in their own sensory history. And, in truth, even most segregationists never really understood why they reacted so strongly to *Brown*. Their senses had stolen their capacity for reasoned thinking on racial matters. It was an intellectual poverty with which many seemed wholly comfortable.

NOTES

INTRODUCTION

1 Havelock Ellis, *Studies in the Psychology of Sex*, vol. 1, pt. 3: *Sexual Selection in Man* (New York: Random House, 1942; orig., 1903), 82.

2 On nonvisual ways of understanding the past, see my essays "Making Sense of Social History," *Journal of Social History* 37 (Sept. 2003): 165–86; "Listening to the Heard Worlds of Antebellum America," *Journal of the Historical Society* 1 (June 2000): 63–97; "Echoes in Print: Method and Causation in Aural History," *Journal of the Historical Society* 2 (summer/fall 2002): 317–36. Studies concerned with "whiteness," as innovative as they are, still tend to "see" race. Note especially David R. Roediger, *The Wages of Whiteness: Race and the Making of the American Working Class* (New York: Verso, 1991); David R. Roediger, ed., *Black on White: Black Writers on What It Means to Be White* (New York: Schocken Books, 1998); the revealingly titled book by bell hooks, *Black Looks: Race and Representation* (Boston: South End Press, 1992); and chapter 5, "Looking Jewish, Seeing Jews," of Matthew Frye Jacobson's *Whiteness of a Different Color: European Immigrants and the Alchemy of Race* (Cambridge: Harvard University Press, 1998).

3 See Edward T. Hall, *The Hidden Dimension* (New York: Anchor, 1982), esp. 30. Essential to any understanding of the role of vision in modern thinking is Martin Jay, *Downcast Eyes: The Denigration of Vision in Twentieth-Century French Thought* (Berkeley: University of California Press, 1993).

4 Quotation from Jay, *Downcast Eyes*, 5 (on the cultural construction of vision and visuality and the difference between the two, see 8–9). As is increasingly clear, the senses are mediated culturally and socially, and how people use them is contingent on a wide variety of factors. Such insights are hardly new. Plato, Aristotle, Hegel, and Marx, among others, recognized the importance of the senses to human history and offered commentary on the relationship between the senses and their relevance to human political, economic, and social identity and development. On early treatments of the senses, see Anthony Synnott, "Puzzling over the Senses: From Plato to Marx," in *The Varieties of Sensory Experience: A Sourcebook in the Anthropology of the Senses*, ed. David Howes (Toronto: University of Toronto Press, 1991), 61–78. I hesitate to accept too readily or enthusiastically the claim that the senses of the past can (or even ought to) be recovered and "replicate[d]," as Peter Charles Hoffer has argued in his *Sensory Worlds in Early America* (Baltimore: Johns Hopkins

University Press, 2003), 2, 8. My principal worry with Hoffer's position is that he fails to distinguish between the production of, say, a sound or smell (something that could be replicated in the present) and its consumption (something that is hostage to the context in which it was produced). See my comments in "Making Sense of Social History," 178–79; and my "Introduction: Onward to Audible Pasts," in *Hearing History: A Reader*, ed. Mark M. Smith (Athens: University of Georgia Press, 2004), xiii.

■ 5 Historians who attend to race, racism, and racial identity from a nonvisualist stance (albeit very briefly in most instances), include Eric Lott, *Love and Theft: Blackface Minstrelsy and the American Working Class* (New York: Oxford University Press, 1993); Grace Elizabeth Hale, *Making Whiteness: The Culture of Segregation in the South, 1890–1940* (New York: Pantheon Books, 1998); and, particularly, Lisa Gitelman, *Scripts, Grooves, and Writing Machines: Representing Technology in the Edison Era* (Stanford: Stanford University Press, 1999), esp. 119–47. Note, too, Shane White and Graham White, " 'At intervals I was nearly stunned by the noise he made': Listening to African American Religious Sound in the Era of Slavery," *American Nineteenth Century History* 1 (spring 2000): 34–61. Recent work on the senses by historians of colonial America offers helpful remarks on seeing and hearing "race." See Hoffer, *Sensory Worlds*, esp. 133–59, and Richard Cullen Rath, *How Early America Sounded* (Ithaca, N.Y.: Cornell University Press, 2003), 105, 149, 179. The most rounded discussion of the sensory dimensions of race in early America remains Winthrop Jordan's *White over Black: American Attitudes toward the Negro, 1550–1812* (Chapel Hill: University of North Carolina Press, 1968), esp. 256–57, 459, 492, 501, 518. Historians of the senses are not always in agreement, although work exploring the tensions and disagreements is virtually nonexistent; see my "Introduction: Onward to Audible Pasts." Other essential studies include Alain Corbin, *Time, Desire and Horror: Towards a History of the Senses*, trans. Jean Birrell (Cambridge: Polity Press, 1995); Alain Corbin, *The Foul and the Fragrant: Odor and the French Social Imagination*, trans. Miriam L. Kochan (Cambridge, Mass.: Harvard University Press, 1986); Alain Corbin, *Village Bells: Sound and Meaning in the Nineteenth-Century French Countryside*, trans. Martin Thom (New York: Columbia University Press, 1998); R. Murray Schafer, *The Tuning of the World: Toward a Theory of Soundscape Design* (Philadelphia: University of Pennsylvania Press, 1980); Leigh Eric Schmidt, *Hearing Things: Religion, Illusion, and the American Enlightenment* (Cambridge, Mass.: Harvard University Press, 2000); Constance Classen, *Worlds of Sense: Exploring the Senses in History and across Cultures* (London: Routledge, 1993); David Howes, *Sensual Relations: Engaging the Senses in Culture and Social Theory* (Ann Arbor: University of Michigan Press, 2003); David Howes, ed., *Empire of the Senses: The Sensual Culture Reader* (New York: Berg, 2005); and the work reproduced in my *Hearing History*. Other helpful work: Steven Feld, *Sound and Sentiment: Birds, Weeping, Poetics, and Song* in *Kalui Expression* (Philadelphia: University of Pennsylvania Press, 1982); Walter J. Ong, "The Shifting Sensorium," in *The Varieties of Sensory Experience: A Sourcebook in the Anthropology of the Senses*, ed. David Howes (Toronto: University of Toronto Press, 1991), 29–30; David Howes, "Sensorial Anthropology," ibid., esp. 170–73; Robert Rivlin and Karen Gravelle, *Deciphering the Senses: The Expanding World of Human Perception* (New York: Simon and Schuster, 1985); Stephen Kern, "Olfactory Ontology and Scented Harmonies: On the History of Smell," *Journal of Popular Culture* 7 (spring 1974): 816–24; Stephen A. Tyler, "The Vision Quest in the West, or What the Mind's Eye Sees," *Journal of Anthropological Research* 40 (spring 1984), 23–189; Marshall McLuhan, *The Gutenberg Galaxy: The Making of Typographic Man* (Toronto: University of Toronto Press, 1962); Bruce R. Smith, *The Acoustic World of Early Modern England* (Chicago: University of Chicago Press, 1999). My use of "race" in this book echoes Joel Williamson's sentiments so closely that I might as well quote them: "What seem to be races, one might say, are actually clusters of traits. But even though blood itself did not carry character and culture, and, scientifically, races did not really exist, I will sometimes speak as if they did." Joel Williamson, *New People: Miscegenation and Mulattoes in the United States* (Baton Rouge: Louisiana State University Press, 1995; orig., 1980), xiii. I trust readers will appreciate that even though the terms "black," "white," and "race" are intellectually misleading, they nonetheless serve as useful (if ironic) shorthands in this study. Let me also stress, courtesy of Barbara J. Fields, that "race and racism belong to different families of social construction," the former a fiction, the latter real and abiding. See Fields, "Of Rogues and Geldings," *American Historical Review* 108 (Dec. 2003): 1400. Because this study so plainly treats "race" as an ideological and social construction, I have largely resisted the clumsy use of quotation marks around the word "race." One other point: the importance of the senses to the construction of racial identity was not lost on a previous generation of scholars. As Harvard psychologist Gordon Allport argued in his landmark 1954 study, *The Nature of Prejudice*, race is usually treated as a "visual category," something mediated and framed by the eye. But Allport made a compelling case for identifying other—nonvisual—ways in which race was socially constructed in an effort to expose the mythology of race and the irrational nature of racial prejudice. He did so by suggesting the link between sight and the other senses. "Where visibility does exist," maintained Allport, "it is almost always thought to be linked with deeper lying traits than is in fact the case." "Many white people try to enhance the 'visibility' of the Negro by claiming that he has a distinctive smell, as well as appearance." Such "sensory aversion," Allport suggested, was common, powerful, and learned. Prejudice increased if sensory stereotypes were repeated often enough ("one *hears* that Negroes . . . have a peculiar odor"). Because of its associative function, smell especially gave prejudice an emotional, irrational edge. Sensory stereotypes generally, reckoned Allport, were potent and once acquired "bring a shudder and lead us to move away or otherwise protect ourselves from the stimulus." Although Allport left lots of questions hanging, his work reminds us that not all theories of race and prejudice have been vision-bound. Gordon W. Allport, *The Nature of Prejudice* (Reading, Mass.: Addison-Wesley, 1954), 109, 132, 136, 137.

6 On seeing, balance, rationality, "modernity," and the Enlightenment, see my "Introduction: Onward to Audible Pasts"; my "Echoes in Print," esp. 329–30; Steven Connor, "The Modern Auditory I," in *Re-writing the Self: Histories from the Renaissance to the Present*, ed. Roy Porter (London: Routledge, 1997), esp. 203–5; Jay, *Downcast Eyes*, esp. 17, 83–91. On sensory hierarchies, the proximate senses, and premodernity, see Classen, *Worlds of Sense*, esp. 2–7. Talking about the senses can be emotionally and linguistically challenging. Smell in particular is powerful: the scent of something can waft into the unwary nose, triggering memories, pleasant and foul. As important as smell is, though, our vocabulary to express olfaction is very limited. Unlike vision, which has numerous words to describe what is seen, smell is only like something else, never a smell in and of itself. Indeed, most of the words used to describe smells are derived from the other senses. For example, "pungent" is a transposition from touch (Latin signifying "prickly"); "sweet" derives, obviously, from taste. See Dan McKenzie, *Aromatics and the Soul* (London: William Heinemann, 1923), 48–58 (on memory), 59–61 (on language). Smell has also been used to mark ethnicity. During the World Wars, German soldiers claimed they knew the whiff of the English, and the English said likewise about Germans. See James Vaughn Kohl and Robert T. Francoeur, *The Scent of Eros: Mysteries of Odor in Human Sexuality* (New York: Continuum, 1995), 160–61. A good deal of pseudoscientific nonsense concerning smell and racial identity has made its way into the literature. See ibid., 161–62. Appreciating the role of the senses in the creation of race gives further meaning to Thomas C. Holt's insight that "power can only be *realized* at the level of everyday practice, and it is dependent—ultimately and inherently—on the reproduction of the relations, idioms, and the world-view that are its means of action. In short, the everyday is where macro-level phenomena—politics, economics, ideologies—are lived." Thus the segregationist portrayal of smelly black laborers was at once a local, everyday act and one that served in important ways to justify economic exploitation and the ideology of segregation. In other words, Holt's remark that "it is precisely within the ordinary and everyday that racialization has been most effective, where it *makes* race," applies well to this study. Thomas C. Holt, "Marking: Race, Race-Making, and the Writing of History," *American Historical Review* 100 (Feb. 1995): 2, 7, 10, 14. See also his *The Problem of Race in the Twenty-first Century* (Cambridge, Mass.: Harvard University Press, 2002). Also on "everydayness," see Michel de Cer-

teau, *The Practice of Everyday Life*, trans. Steven Rendall (Berkeley: University of California Press, 1984); Robin Kelley, " 'We Are Not What We Seem': Rethinking Black Working-Class Opposition in the Jim Crow South," *Journal of American History* 80 (June 1993): 75–112. On race as a historical phenomenon, see Barbara Jeanne Fields, "Slavery, Race and Ideology in the United States of America," *New Left Review* 181 (1990): 95–118. Nell Irvin Painter has rightly remarked that whatever the critical contributions of postmodernism, there are abiding "blind spots in the vision of prominent poststructuralists such as Michel Foucault with regard to race and slavery, matters on which they are almost uniformly silent." See Painter, "Thinking about the Languages of Money and Race: A Response to Michael O'Malley, 'Specie and Species,' " *American Historical Review* 99 (Apr. 1994): 403; Painter, "French Theories in American Settings: Some Thoughts on Transferability," *Journal of Women's History* 1 (spring 1989): esp. 92–95. The point is also made by Paul Gilroy in *Against Race: Imagining Political Culture beyond the Color Line* (Cambridge, Mass.: Belknap Press of Harvard University Press, 2001), 44–45, 65. A similar argument might be made with regard to the history of the senses. While it is certainly true that historical writing on the history of the senses owes a good deal to European historians, it seems increasingly clear that work by the *Annales* School and social historians—most recently by Alain Corbin—and not poststructuralism has been at the root of the sensory history project. Yet there is a curious quiet in such work on the sensory history of race, a quiet that cannot be explained away by the terms offered by Painter. See my "Making Sense of Social History."

7 W. J. Cash, *The Mind of the South* (New York: Alfred A. Knopf, 1941), 428–29. It should go without saying that it was perfectly possible for southerners to have a vibrant intellectual culture on matters not relating to race. Cash's book has, of course, been roundly and rightly criticized, yet even in the most cutting critiques, there is a quiet respect for some of his basic insights. See, for example, Eugene D. Genovese, *The World the Slaveholders Made: Two Essays in Interpretation* (Middletown, Conn.: Wesleyan University Press, 1988), 137–45; Michael O'Brien, "A Private Passion: W. J. Cash," in *Rethinking the South: Essays in Intellectual History*, ed. Michael O'Brien (Baltimore: Johns Hopkins University Press, 1988), 179–89; and Nell Irvin Painter, *Southern History across the Color Line* (Chapel Hill: University of North Carolina Press, 2002), 177–98.

8 Edward Byron Reuter, *The Mulatto in the United States, Including a Study of the Role of Mixed-Blood Races throughout the World* (New York: New American Library, 1969; orig., Ph.D. diss., University of Chicago, 1918), 13.

9 John Dollard, *Caste and Class in a Southern Town* (New Haven, Conn.: Yale University Press, 1937), 472. On the similarities between racist arguments based on "culturalism" and biology, see George M. Fredrickson, *Racism: A Short History* (Princeton, N.J.: Princeton University Press, 2002), esp. 7–9.

10 On scholarly rejection of the monolithic, see Lauren F. Winner, "Doubtless Sincere: New Characters in the Civil Rights Cast," in *The Role of Ideas in the Civil Rights Movement*, ed. Ted Ownby (Jackson: University Press of Mississippi, 2002), esp. 157.

11 On these matters, as well as for Du Bois's suggestion, see Holt, "Marking," 18.

12 Gilroy, *Against Race*, quotations on 7, 8, 42. For his remarks on seeing race, its appearance, even its hypervisibility, and the "social optics" guiding how we see, read 11, 13, 21–23, 35–37, 40, 44–45; for a brief comment on seeing the toughness of black skin and its implications for the regulation of slave labor, 46; on the inadequacy of the naked eye to ascertain authenticity, 48; on the role of icon and sound in fascism and the relationship between the optic and aural in music, 155–64, 191. The instability of race that Gilroy notes on 218 was, in many respects, prefigured by segregation, even at its birth.

CHAPTER ONE

1 See, for instance, Martin Jay, *Downcast Eyes: The Denigration of Vision in Twentieth-Century French Thought* (Berkeley: University of California Press, 1993), 1–148; D. R. Woolf, "Speech, Text, and Time: The Sense of Hearing and the Sense of the Past in Renaissance England," *Albion* 18, no. 2 (1986): 159–93.

2 Winthrop Jordan, *White over Black: American Attitudes toward the Negro, 1550–1812* (Chapel Hill: University of North Carolina Press, 1968), 4–5. See also Joyce E. Chaplin, *Subject Matter: Technology, the Body, and Science on the Anglo-American Frontier, 1500–1676* (Cambridge, Mass.: Harvard University Press, 2001), esp. 140–41; Alden T. Vaughan and Virginia Mason Vaughan, "Before Othello: Elizabethan Representations of Sub-Saharan Africans," *William and Mary Quarterly*, 3rd ser., 54 (Jan. 1997): 19–44. Visual representations of southern slaves for the colonial and antebellum periods in paintings and drawings are less common than visualist representations of slaves in language. On the former, see Alex Bontemps, "Seeing Slavery: How Paintings Make Words Look Different," *Common-Place* 1, no. 4 (July 2001): no pagination, online at <http://www.common-place.org/vol-01/no-04/slavery/bontemps.shtml> (July 17, 2004).

3 While there is evidence that aurality played a role in the early construction of blackness, it seems clear that in pictorial representations, in written descriptions, and in the Elizabethan theater, contemporaries stressed how Africans looked, their color, their visual blackness. Note Vaughan and Vaughan, "Before Othello," 25 (on aurality), 19–44 (on visuality). On hierarchies of the senses, much has been written, but see, especially, Anthony Synnott, "Puzzling over the Senses: From Plato to Marx," in *The Varieties of Sensory Experience: A Sourcebook in the Anthropology of the Senses*, ed. David Howes (Toronto: University of Toronto Press, 1991), 61–78; and Constance Classen, *Worlds of Sense: Exploring the Senses in History and across Cultures* (London: Routledge, 1993).

4 On pre-Columbian encounters, see Joel Williamson, *New People: Miscegenation and Mulattoes in the United States* (Baton Rouge: Louisiana State University Press, 1995; orig., 1980), xiii.

5 Oliver Goldsmith, *An History of the Earth, and Animated Nature* (London: J. Nourse, 1774), 1:209, 214, 217, 218; Jordan, *White over Black*, 248.

6 Charles White, *An Account of the Regular Gradation in Man, and in Different Animals and Vegetables; and from the Former to the Latter* (London: C. Dilly, 1799), 80–81, 67, 81–82; Jordan, *White over Black*, 501.

7 To the Right Honorable the Lords Commissioners for Trade and Plantations, The Memorial of the Trustees for establishing the Colony of Georgia in America, June 19, 1752, p. 73, British Manuscript Project, CO5.373, vol. K, nos. 1–40, 1753 ("Worms"); J. F. D. Smyth, *A Tour in the United States of America: Containing an Account of the Present Situation of That Country* (Dublin: G. Perrin, 1784), 1: 23–24 ("offensive"); Philadelphia resident quoted in Carl Bridenbaugh, *Cities in Revolt: Urban Life in America, 1743–1776* (New York: Alfred A. Knopf, 1955), 285.

8 White, *Account of the Regular Gradation in Man*, 58–59; Bryan Edwards, *The History, Civil and Commercial, of the British Colonies in the West Indies*, vol. 2, bk. 4 (Philadelphia: J. Humphreys, 1805–6), 266; Goldsmith, *History of the Earth*, 1:212. See also Jordan, *White over Black*, 175. Lord Henry Home Kames, *Sketches of the History of Man: Considerably Improved in a Second Edition, in Four Volumes* (Edinburgh: W. Strahan and T. Cadell, 1778), 1:25. For a brief but devastating critique of Kames's muddy thinking, see Jordan, *White over Black*, 245.

9 Mark Catesby, *The Natural History of Carolina, Florida and the Bahama Islands* (London: Printed for C. Marsh, 1754), 2:viii.

10 Jordan, *White over Black*, 492; Edward Long, *The History of Jamaica; or, General Survey of the Antient [sic] and Modern State of That Island* (London: T. Lowndes, 1774; repr., London: Frank Cass, 1970), 2:352–53, 425–26.

11 Thomas Jefferson, *Notes on the State of Virginia*, ed. William Peden (Chapel Hill: University of North Carolina Press, 1955), 139, 140; Jordan, *White over Black*, 436–39.

12 Jordan, *White over Black*, 246–47; John Mitchell, "An Essay upon the Causes of the Different Colours of People in Different Climates," *Philosophical Transactions* 43 (1744): 107, 108, 124, 131, 133, 143–44, 148.

13 Jordan, *White over Black*, 517–520; Benjamin Rush, "Observations Intended to Favour a Supposition That the Black Color (as It Is Called) of the Negroes Is Derived from the Leprosy," *Transactions of the American Philosophical Society* 4 (1799): 290, 292.

14 Goldsmith, *History of the Earth*, 1:212; White, *Account of the Regular Gradation in Man*, 57, 71.

15 White, *Account of the Regular Gradation in Man*, 82. White was complicated insofar as he did not wish his findings to "be construed as to give the

smallest countenance to the pernicious practice of enslaving mankind." See Jordan, *White over Black*, esp. 499, 502. Note also Bruce Dain, *A Hideous Monster of the Mind: American Race Theory in the Early Republic* (Cambridge, Mass.: Harvard University Press, 2002), esp. 74–75. What of class? Evidence is scarce. To my knowledge, there is not a single tract, treatise, or essay published in colonial America that comes anywhere near attributing innate sensory differences to poor, lower-class whites. Although Mark Catesby in 1754 commented on "those Stinks or unsavory Smells that we meet with in the Dwellings of our Poor and Indolent," there was nothing to suggest that such scent was innate. Yes, some whites smelled to other whites, but the scent was always erasable. As an advertisement for the capture of two runaway indentured servants in the *Virginia Gazette* in 1775 put it: "To those used to the smell of servants just from a ship, they will be easily discovered, unless they have procured new clothes." Catesby, *Natural History*, 2:viii; *Virginia Gazette*, Williamsburg, Apr. 21, 1775.

16 Williamson, *New People*, 17. For evidence from Virginia, see the picture of a white man kissing a black woman in Bontemps, "Seeing Slavery." Bontemps argues that the kiss is "against her will." On the topic in general, see Kathleen M. Brown, *Good Wives, Nasty Wenches, and Anxious Patriarchs: Gender, Race, and Power in Early Virginia* (Chapel Hill: University of North Carolina Press, 1996), esp. 129–34, 187–211, 331–34, and the essays in *The Devil's Lane: Sex and Race in the Early South*, ed. Catherine Clinton and Michele Gillespie (New York: Oxford University Press, 1997). On smell, sex, and race, see John Dollard, *Caste and Class in a Southern Town* (New Haven, Conn.: Yale University Press, 1937), 144; on smell, race, repulsion, and allure, note the suggestive remarks offered in Michael Taussig, *Mimesis and Alterity: A Particular History of the Senses* (New York: Routledge, 1993), 66–68. On interracial "mixing," see, Williamson, *New People*, 7–8, 11. See also Kirsten Fischer, *Suspect Relations: Sex, Race, and Resistance in Colonial North Carolina* (Ithaca, N.Y.: Cornell University Press, 2002), esp. 160; Anthony S. Parent Jr., *Foul Means: The Formation of a Slave Society in Virginia, 1660–1740* (Chapel Hill: University of North Carolina Press, 2003), 106–34; Philip D. Morgan, *Slave Counterpoint: Black Culture in the Eighteenth-Century Chesapeake and Lowcountry* (Chapel Hill: University of North Carolina Press, 1998), esp. 14–18.

17 Williamson, *New People*, 13.

18 George F. Holmes, *The Southern Pictorial Third Reader: For Schools and Families* (New York: Richardson, [ca. 1866]), 150. On the association of smell with disease, see *The Class Book of Nature: Comprising Lessons on the Universe, the Three Kingdoms of Nature, and the Form and Structure of the Human Body: With Questions and Numerous Engravings*, ed. J. Frost (Hartford: Wm. Hamersley, 1850), 274–75. For sensory aspects of eighteenth- and nineteenth-century southern cities, see George C. Rogers Jr., *Charleston in the Age of the Pinckneys* (Columbia:

University of South Carolina Press, 1989), 76; Mark M. Smith, *Listening to Nineteenth-Century America* (Chapel Hill: University of North Carolina Press, 2001), 21, 31–32, 52–57.

19   *The Class Book of Nature*, 71, quotations, in order, on 73, 213, 214, 239–40, 277–78, 257.

20   On paternalism, see, most obviously, Eugene D. Genovese, *Roll, Jordan, Roll: The World the Slaves Made* (New York: Vintage, 1976). Genovese's paternalist paradigm has been challenged since its inception but still remains influential. For a reliable defense of Genovese's paternalist model—and for wise words on the ways in which critics have misunderstood the concept—see Peter Kolchin, "Eugene D. Genovese: Historian of Slavery," *Radical History Review* 88 (winter 2004): 52–67. On interracial sex, see Martha Hodes, *White Women, Black Men: Illicit Sex in the Nineteenth-Century South* (New Haven, Conn.: Yale University Press, 1997), and the relevant essays in her edited work, *Sex, Love, Race: Crossing Boundaries in North American History* (New York: New York University Press, 1999).

21   Richard N. Côté, *Mary's World: Love, War, and Family Ties in Nineteenth-Century Charleston* (Mount Pleasant, S.C.: Corinthian Books, 2002), 181–82, 184–85 (quotations, in order, on 182, 184). Frances Kemble said that her slaves' clothes "blended in fierce companionship" and that the colors "put one's very eyes out from a mile off." Quoted in Patricia K. Hunt, "Clothing as an Expression of History: The Dress of African-American Women in Georgia, 1880–1915," *Georgia Historical Quarterly* 76 (summer 1992): 464–65. Note, too, Shane White and Graham White, *Stylin': African American Expressive Culture from Its Beginnings to the Zoot Suit* (Ithaca, N.Y.: Cornell University Press, 1998), esp. 20–36.

22   William D. Valentine Diary, Nov. 4, 1837, vol. 2, Wilson Library, Southern Historical Collection, University of North Carolina at Chapel Hill, Chapel Hill, N.C.

23   D. R. Hundley, *Social Relations in Our Southern States* (New York: Henry B. Price, 1860; electronic ed., University of North Carolina, Chapel Hill, digitization project, 1999), 90–91; Fredrika Bremer, *The Homes of the New World; Impressions of America*, trans. M. Howitt (New York: Harper and Brothers, 1853), 444.

24   *The Story of a Slave: A Realistic Revelation of a Social Relation of Slave Times—Hitherto Unwritten—from the Pen of One Who Has Felt Both the Lash and the Caress of a Mistress* (Chicago: Wesley, Elmore and Benson, 1894; electronic ed., University of North Carolina, Chapel Hill, digitization project, 2001), 74.

25   Early assessments of broken implements, even by sympathetic, liberal observers, attributed the tendency to black incompetence. See John E. Cairnes, *The Slave Power: Its Character, Career, and Probable Designs* (Columbia: University of South Carolina Press, 2003; orig., 1863), 46. On tool breaking as resistance, see Raymond Bauer and Alice Bauer, "Day to Day Resistance to

Slavery," *Journal of Negro History* 27 (Oct. 1942): 401–7; Eugene D. Genovese, *The Political Economy of Slavery: Studies in the Economy and Society of the Slave South* (Middletown, Conn.: Wesleyan University Press, 1989; orig., 1964), 74. Quotations from James Redpath, *The Roving Editor; or, Talks with Slaves in the Southern States*, ed. John R. McKivigan (University Park: Pennsylvania State University, 1996), 119; interview of George Womble, *Born in Slavery: Slave Narratives from the Federal Writers' Project, 1936–1938*, Georgia narratives, vol. 4, pt. 4, 184, American Memory Collection, Library of Congress, Washington, D.C.

26 Interview of Auntie Thomas Jones, *Born in Slavery*, Texas narratives, vol. 16, pt. 2, 207.

27 Bill Arp, *From the Uncivil War to Date, 1861–1903* (Atlanta: Hudgins, 1903; electronic ed., University of North Carolina, Chapel Hill, digitization project, 1998), 354 ("meat," "bloody"), 355 ("thick lips"); James Robert Gilmore [Edmund Kirke, pseud.], *Down in Tennessee, and Back by Way of Richmond* (New York: Carleton, 1864), 191 ("gourd"); John Andrew Jackson, *The Experience of a Slave in South Carolina* (London: Passmore and Alabaster, 1862; electronic ed., University of North Carolina, Chapel Hill, digitization project, 1996), 30 ("Turkeys," "slave-driver").

28 The first two quotations are from *Story of a Slave*, 11, 13; the last two from R. W. N. N., Albemarle, "Negro Cabins," *Southern Planter* 16 (Apr. 1856): 121 (emphasis in original).

29 Arp, *From the Uncivil War to Date*, 187; interview of "Princess Quango Hennadonah Perceriah," *Born in Slavery*, vol. 11, pt. 1, 33; "A Few Thoughts on Slavery," *Southern Literary Messenger* 20 (Apr. 1854): 198.

30 *Story of a Slave*, 145, 11, 13. On female slave resistance to sexual advances, see Brenda E. Stevenson, "Gender Convention, Ideals, and Identity among Antebellum Virginia Slave Women," in *More Than Chattel: Black Women and Slavery in the Americas*, ed. David Barry Gaspar and Darlene Clark Hine (Bloomington: Indiana University Press, 1996), 169–90; Deborah Gray White, *Ar'n't I a Woman: Female Slaves in the Plantation South* (New York: W. W. Norton, 1985); Jacqueline Jones, *Labor of Love, Labor of Sorrow: Black Women, Work, and the Family from Slavery to Freedom* (New York: Basic Books, 1985), 11–43. On sexual improprieties among slaveholders and their exploitation of slave women, consult Elizabeth Fox-Genovese, *Within the Plantation Household: Black and White Women of the Old South* (Chapel Hill: University of North Carolina Press, 1988), 49, 189, 236–41, 325, 380.

31 *Story of a Slave*, 151, 152.

32 Jackson, *Experience of a Slave*, 30–31.

33 Elliot J. Gorn, " 'Gouge and Bite, Pull Hair and Scratch': The Social Significance of Fighting in the Southern Backcountry," *American Historical Review* 90 (1985): 18–43. D. R. Hundley hinted at a contempt for poor whites when he

suggested in 1860 that "Southern villages have a more wo-begone look, and smell stronger of mean whisky and hogs than the trim villages of New-England." Hundley, *Social Relations in Our Southern States*, 74.

34 Gilmore, *Down in Tennessee*, quotations, in order, on 104, 186, 184, 185, 193.

35 Hundley, *Social Relations in Our Southern States*, 69, 194–95. But not all tensions were between elite and poor; Hundley pointed to the pretension of what he termed the Cotton Snobs, vulgar aspirants who made up a class wholly different from the southern gentleman planter. While planters labored side by side with slaves, the Cotton Snob affected revulsion, "sneer[ing] at whatever he considers low" and "seek[ing] every opportunity to talk about 'my niggers',", a term, Hundley said, abhorred by a southern gentleman. Ibid., 170.

36 William J. Grayson, "Mackay's Travels in America—the Dual Form of Labor," *De Bow's Review* 28 (July 1860): 49, 59–60.

CHAPTER TWO

1 Joel Williamson, *New People: Miscegenation and Mulattoes in the United States* (Baton Rouge: Louisiana State University Press, 1995; orig., 1980), 56, 63.

2 Olaudah Equiano, *The Interesting Narrative of the Life of Olaudah Equiano; or, Gustavus Vassa, the African: Written by Himself* (London: Published by the Author, [1789]; electronic ed., University of North Carolina, Chapel Hill, digitization project, 2001), 1:25–26, 13–15. On the variety of African American responses to antebellum white ethnology, see Mia Bay, *The White Image in the Black Mind: African-American Ideas about White People, 1830–1925* (New York: Oxford University Press, 2000), esp. 38–74.

3 Equiano, *Interesting Narrative*, 71, 72, 75, 73, 78, 79. In this context, see also Elizabeth B. Clark, " 'The Sacred Rights of the Weak': Pain, Sympathy, and the Culture of Individual Rights in Antebellum America," *Journal of American History* 82 (Sept. 1995): 463–93.

4 *Born in Slavery: Slave Narratives from the Federal Writers' Project, 1936–1938*, Arkansas narratives, vol. 2, pt. 2, 245 (Evans); vol. 11, pt. 1, 249 (Debro); Georgia narratives, vol. 4, pt. 4, 32, American Memory Collection, Library of Congress, Washington, D.C. On sound, see Mark M. Smith, *Listening to Nineteenth-Century America* (Chapel Hill: University of North Carolina Press, 2001), esp. 67–91.

5 Charles Ball, *Fifty Years in Chains; or, The Life of an American Slave* (New York: H. Dayton, 1859; electronic ed., University of North Carolina, Chapel Hill, digitization project, 1997), 106; Samuel Ringgold Ward, *Autobiography of a Fugitive Negro: His Anti-Slavery Labours in the United States, Canada, and England* (London: John Snow, 1855; electronic ed., University of North Carolina, Chapel Hill, digitization project, 1999), 141.

6 *The Story of a Slave: A Realistic Revelation of a Social Relation of Slave Times—Hitherto*

Unwritten—from the Pen of One Who Has Felt Both the Lash and the Caress of a Mistress (Chicago: Wesley, Elmore and Benson, 1894; electronic ed., University of North Carolina, Chapel Hill, digitization project, 2001), 145.

7 Rev. William G. Hawkins, *Lunsford Lane; or, Another Helper from North Carolina* (Boston: Crosby and Nichols, 1863; electronic ed., University of North Carolina, Chapel Hill, digitization project, 2000), 21; Douglass quoted in John Dollard, *Caste and Class in a Southern Town* (New Haven, Conn.: Yale University Press, 1937), 317 n. 4.

8 Ward, *Autobiography of a Fugitive Negro*, 142; Ball, *Fifty Years in Chains*, 160, 163, 164. On sound and slave culture, see Lawrence Levine, *Black Culture and Black Consciousness: Afro-American Thought from Slavery to Freedom* (New York: Oxford University Press, 1977), esp. 80–82. Shouting, noise, and sound during religious services were important to the slaves because they demonstrated authenticity of conviction, acting as a prerequisite for salvation, as a release from the enforced quietude of aspects of plantation life, and served as a connection to the emotional and "tonal characteristics of African speech." See Shane White and Graham White, " 'At intervals I was nearly stunned by the noise he made': Listening to African American Religious Sound in the Era of Slavery," *American Nineteenth Century History* 1 (spring 2000): 51. On silence and smothered sound, Mark M. Smith, *Listening to Nineteenth-Century America*, 79–91.

9 Quotations and observations in John Hope Franklin and Loren Schweninger, *Runaway Slaves: Rebels on the Plantation* (New York: Oxford University Press, 1999), 214–15, 225. The light-skinned Ellen Craft escaped slavery in Georgia in 1848 by looking like, and passing as, a white man. See [William Craft], *Running a Thousand Miles for Freedom; or, The Escape of William and Ellen Craft from Slavery* (London: William Tweedie, 1860).

10 Robert Russa Moton, *What the Negro Thinks* (Garden City, N.Y.: Doubleday, Doran, 1929), 10–11; *Born in Slavery*, Georgia narratives, vol. 4, pt. 4, 185; Ball, *Fifty Years in Chains*, 223–24. On the link between freedom, taste, and food, see Sidney W. Mintz, *Tasting Food, Tasting Freedom: Excursions into Eating, Culture, and the Past* (Boston: Beacon Press, 1996), esp. 34–36.

11 Ball, *Fifty Years in Chains*, 234–36, 238.

12 Interview of Anna Pritchett, *Born in Slavery*, Indiana narratives, vol. 5, 143; William H. Heard, *From Slavery to the Bishopric in the A.M.E. Church: An Autobiography* (Philadelphia: A.M.E. Book Concern, 1928; electronic ed., University of North Carolina, Chapel Hill, digitization project, 2000), 27. Other quotations: on turpentine, see slave quoted in Mark M. Smith, *Listening to Nineteenth-Century America*, 230; on water, Allen Parker, *Recollections of Slavery Times* (Worcester, Mass.: Chas. W. Burbank, 1895; electronic ed., University of North Carolina, Chapel Hill, digitization project, 2000), 29, and Ward, *Auto-*

biography of a Fugitive Negro, 183; on pepper, James Watkins, *Narrative of the Life of James Watkins, Formerly a "Chattel" in Maryland, U.S.; Containing an Account of His Escape from Slavery* . . . (Bolton: Kenyon and Abbatt, 1852; electronic ed., University of North Carolina, Chapel Hill, digitization project, 2001), 21; on dung, J. D. Green, *Narrative of the Life of J. D. Green, a Runaway Slave, from Kentucky, Containing an Account of His Three Escapes, in 1839, 1846, 1848* (Huddersfield: Henry Fielding, 1864; electronic ed., University of North Carolina, Chapel Hill, digitization project, 2000), 25. Not all of these feints and distractions worked. Merely running through swamps in an effort to dampen scent with water was by no means a certain way to fool dogs. After all, masters often trained dogs to hunt runaways and conducted rehearsals for the day when the dog's senses would be put to the test. As one former North Carolina slave, born in 1826, explained: "The slave used in the training process would be compelled by the dog's trainer to resort to all the artifices that an escaping slave could use to throw a dog off the scent, such as climbing trees, walking in water, doubling on his own track, etc., in order that the dog might become thoroughly proficient in his business." Quotation from William Mallory, *Old Plantation Days* (Hamilton, Ont. [?]: s.n., 1902 [?]; electronic ed., University of North Carolina, Chapel Hill, digitization project, 1999), 9, 21–22. On the use of hounds, scent, and tracking runaways, see interview of Tom Randall, *Born in Slavery*, Maryland narratives, vol. 8, 58. For evidence that whites trained particular dogs to attack and track slaves by sight and scent, see Franklin and Schweninger, *Runaway Slaves*, 160–61.

13 John Andrew Jackson, *The Experience of a Slave in South Carolina* (London: Passmore and Alabaster, 1862; electronic ed., University of North Carolina, Chapel Hill, digitization project, 1996), 23. To say that antebellum African Americans tended to shy away from essentialist explanations of racial difference is not, emphatically, to also say that they harbored no prejudice toward whites or, indeed, other blacks. "Negroes are as tenacious of caste as other races," recalled one former slave whose mother, "no common negress," "no Guinea blood in her veins, no ashy Congo, but pure, proud Senegambia," despised "the common negro, the plebian herd." *Story of a Slave*, 5–6. Moreover, antebellum black intellectuals, as Mia Bay has shown, were not unknown to endorse ethnological thinking in self-defense. See her *White Image in the Black Mind*, 38–74. That much said, there is little evidence indeed suggesting African American slaves consistently applied essentialist sensory stereotypes to whites.

14 Jackson, *Experience of a Slave*, 29.

15 H. G. Adams, ed., *God's Image in Ebony: Being a Series of Biographical Sketches, Facts, Anecdotes, etc., Demonstrative of the Mental Powers and Intellectual Capacities of the Negro Race* (London: Partridge and Oakley, 1854; electronic ed., University

of North Carolina, Chapel Hill, digitization project, 1999), i, 11, 163, 164, 165. On abolitionists' humanitarian sensibilities and the senses, see Mark M. Smith, *Listening to Nineteenth-Century America*, 150–94.

16 Wendell Phillips, "Burial of John Brown," speech delivered Dec. 8, 1859, in *Speeches, Lectures, and Letters* (Boston: Lee and Shepard, 1872), 19. See also Clark, " 'The Sacred Rights of the Weak.' "

17 Johann Georg Heck, ed., *Iconographic Encyclopedia of Science, Literature, and Art*, trans. and ed. Spencer F. Baird (New York: D. Appleton, 1860), 129; Hermann Burmeister, *The Black Man: Comparative Anatomy and Psychology of the African Negro*, trans. Julius Friedlander and Robert Tomes (New York: William C. Bryant, 1853), 12. On northern racism and investments in whiteness, see, among others, George M. Fredrickson, *The Black Image in the White Mind: The Debate of Afro-American Character and Destiny, 1817–1914* (Middletown, Conn.: Wesleyan University Press, 1987; orig., 1971), 97–164, and David R. Roediger, *The Wages of Whiteness: Race and the Making of the American Working Class* (New York: Verso, 1991).

18 Peter Wallenstein, *Tell the Court I Love My Wife: Race, Marriage, and Law—an American History* (New York: Palgrave Macmillan, 2002), fig. 4; "Stealing—and giving odors," *Old Guard* 2 (Jan. 1864): n.p.; Wade quoted in Eugene D. Genovese, *Roll, Jordan, Roll: The World the Slaves Made* (New York: Vintage, 1976), 540. On black awareness of the strength of northern sensory racial stereotypes—especially with regard to olfaction—see "Selections," *Frederick Douglass' Paper*, Sept. 8, 1864.

19 Williamson, *New People*, 56, 14, 63. Whites in both the upper and the lower South, while happy to see mulatto offspring enslaved, "went into a rage against white blood mixed with black and being free," not least because the significant increase in numbers of "a class of persons visibly black but legally white" challenged a race-based slave system that could not, on any significant scale, be accommodated by appeals to "reputation" and character. Ibid., 65. In the 1850s, then, white southerners, threatened by the sheer scale of mixing, began to rely ever more on all of their senses in an effort to detect blackness and, by default, the status of slave or free. Williamson summarizes the shift in thinking thus: "If one looked closely, one could always detect [blackness]" in the nails, hands, and feet especially, which meant, of course, that "any black blood, no matter how remote, made one black, and endless mixture with pure whites would never erase that fact." Williamson, *New People*, 65. South Carolina slaveholders viewed free mulattoes with largesse and saw them as important in linking black slaves and free whites. This helps explain why South Carolinians "steadfastly refused to attempt a fractional definition of blackness for mulattoes." Blackness and whiteness for these people was not just a question of visibility but one of interior worth not always apparent to the naked eye. As Judge William Harper argued in 1835,

"We cannot say what admixture of negro blood will make a colored person," explaining that "the condition of the individual is not to be determined solely by distinct and visible mixture of negro blood, but by reputation" and behavior. While, according to Harper, "a slave cannot be a white man," his line of thinking, as articulated by Williamson, allowed "visible mulattoes . . . by behavior and reputation [to] be 'white,' " and mulattoes did marry into white families. This was, then, a rejection of the one-drop rule, and, curiously enough, the emphasis on the invisibility of race was to be used during segregation for precisely the opposite effect—to lump all nonwhites whose racial identity betrayed itself but not necessarily to the eye. Williamson, *New People*, 18, 19. On the role of hierarchies and dependencies in addition to race in southern society, see Elizabeth Fox-Genovese and Eugene D. Genovese, "The Divine Sanction of Social Order: Religious Foundations of the Southern Slaveholders' World View," *Journal of the American Academy of Religion* 55 (summer 1987): 211–34; Eugene D. Genovese, *The Slaveholders' Dilemma: Freedom and Progress in Southern Conservative Thought, 1820–1860* (Columbia: University of South Carolina Press, 1992); and Stephanie McCurry, *Masters of Small Worlds: Yeoman Households, Gender Relations, and the Political Culture of the Antebellum South Carolina Lowcountry* (New York: Oxford University Press, 1995). Note, too, Susan Gillman, " 'Sure Identifiers': Race, Science, and the Law in *Pudd'nhead Wilson*," in *Mark Twain's Pudd'nhead Wilson: Race, Conflict, and Culture*, ed. Susan Gillman and Forrest G. Robison, 86–104 (Durham: Duke University Press, 1990), 89.

20 Williamson, *New People*, 66–67, 69 (Bremer's observation), 70, 71. For additional evidence that some antebellum slaves certainly looked white and that northern travelers and foreign visitors, as well as free white southerners, often remarked on their presence, see Lawrence R. Tenzer, "White Slaves," online at <http://www.multiracial.com/readers/tenzer3.html> (Jan. 23, 2004).

21 My indebtedness here is obvious: see Williamson, *New People*, 73, quotation on 75. As slavery pushed westward, especially in the trans-Mississippi South, it also became whiter, and everywhere it seemed as though increasing worries about ever-whitening slaves were matched with an increasing racial consciousness and exclusiveness among whites. Williamson, *New People*, 24–25, 57–59. For a detailed discussion on race, slavery, and the variations in the proslavery position, see Fredrickson, *The Black Image in the White Mind*, 43–96.

22 Williamson's analysis is brilliant, entirely ahead of its time, but, I think, wrongheaded in one important respect: it, like more recent efforts, assumes that slaveholders relied solely on their eyes to ascertain racial identity. They did not. Williamson, *New People*, 24. See also Walter Johnson, "The Slave Trader, the White Slave, and the Politics of Racial Determination in the 1850s," *Journal of American History* 87 (June 2000): 13–38, and Ariela J. Gross,

"Litigating Whiteness: Trials of Racial Determination in the Nineteenth-Century South," *Yale Law Journal* 108 (Oct. 1998): 109–88. That reliance on seeing race alone can lead to historians' exaggerated claims concerning the instability of race is suggested by Matthew Frye Jacobson's analysis in *Whiteness of a Different Color: European Immigrants and the Alchemy of Race* (Cambridge, Mass.: Harvard University Press, 1998), chaps. 4, 5. For a sense of the variations in the intellectual quality of proslavery thinkers, see Fox-Genovese and Genovese, "The Divine Sanction of Social Order," 211–34, and Genovese, *The Slaveholders' Dilemma*.

23 Spartanburg District, Court of Magistrates and Freeholders, Trial Papers, Case 224, *State v. Elias*, June 11, 1859, South Carolina Department of Archives and History, Columbia, S.C.

24 George Fitzhugh, "The Conservative Principle; or, Social Evils and Their Remedies, Part II: The Slave Trade," *De Bow's Review* 22 (May 1857): 450; "The Message, the Constitution, and the Times," *De Bow's Review* 30 (Feb. 1861): 161; A. Woodward, *A Review of Uncle Tom's Cabin; or, An Essay on Slavery* (Cincinnati: Applegate, 1853), 20.

25 Josiah Priest, *Bible Defence of Slavery* (Glasgow, Ky.: W. S. Brown, 1852), 179–80.

26 Ibid., 228–29; Francis Lieber, ed., *Encyclopaedia Americana: A Popular Dictionary of Arts, Sciences, Literature, History, Politics and Biography, . . .* (Boston: Mussey, 1851), s.v. "fishes," 132.

27 Josiah C. Nott and George R. Gliddon, "On the Unity of the Human Race," *Southern Quarterly Review* 20 (Oct. 1854): 299. For thoughtful words on Nott, see Bruce Dain, *A Hideous Monster of the Mind: American Race Theory in the Early Republic* (Cambridge, Mass.: Harvard University Press, 2002), esp. 229–37.

28 Samuel A. Cartwright, "Diseases and Peculiarities of the Negro Race," *De Bow's Review* 11 (July 1851): 66, 67, 69.

29 Samuel A. Cartwright, "Diseases and Peculiarities of the Negro Race," *De Bow's Review* 11 (Oct.–Nov. 1851): 506, 508.

30 William H. Holcombe, "Characteristics and Capabilities of the Negro Race," *Southern Literary Messenger* 33 (Dec. 1861): 401, 402.

31 Ibid., 406.

32 Ibid., 402.

CHAPTER THREE

1 Frances Butler Leigh, *Ten Years on a Georgia Plantation since the War* (London: Richard Bentley and Son, 1883; electronic ed., University of North Carolina, Chapel Hill, digitization project, 1998), 20, 117, 113–14, 131–32, 117. On Leigh as a "staunch Confederate" and for an interpretation that differs in some respects from the one advanced here, see Clara Juncker, "Island Queen:

Frances Butler Leigh's *Ten Years on a Georgia Plantation since the War*," *American Studies in Scandinavia* 33, no. 2 (2001): 14. On the stench of rice fields, see Elizabeth Waties Allston Pringle [Patience Pennington, pseud.], *A Woman Rice Planter* (New York: Macmillan Company, 1914; electronic ed., University of North Carolina, Chapel Hill, digitization project, 1998), 3, 115. For other examples of freedpeople talking back to whites, see John William Graves, *Town and Country: Race Relations in an Urban-Rural Context, Arkansas, 1865–1905* (Fayetteville: University of Arkansas Press, 1990), 80–81. On the importance of creating an idealized past to the culture of southern segregation and on the role of white women in that process, see Grace Elizabeth Hale, *Making Whiteness: The Culture of Segregation in the South, 1890–1940* (New York: Pantheon Books, 1998), esp. 48–49, 92–97. For specific ways in which postbellum authors sensed the Old South, particularly their use of scents and repeated references to springtime air filled "with honeyed perfume," honeysuckle "perfuming the air," and the scent of roses in an effort to romanticize the past, see, for example, Thomas Nelson Page, *Social Life in Old Virginia before the War* (New York: Charles Scribner's Sons, 1897; electronic ed., University of North Carolina, Chapel Hill, digitization project, 1998), 8, 17, 18. Note, too, Bill Arp, *From the Uncivil War to Date, 1861–1903* (Atlanta: Hudgins, 1903; electronic ed., University of North Carolina, Chapel Hill, digitization project, 1998), 53.

2 C. Vann Woodward, *The Strange Career of Jim Crow*, 3rd rev. ed. (New York: Oxford University Press, 1974), 11–19, quotation on 12. See also Joel Williamson, *After Slavery: The Negro in South Carolina during Reconstruction, 1861–1877* (Chapel Hill: University of North Carolina Press, 1965), 274. None of this is to suggest, though, that segregation did not exist in the Old South. Plainly it did, but it was confined largely to the cities and tended to increase in the 1850s, at exactly the point when slavery was becoming whiter. Urban segregation in such instances was an effort to clarify who was free and who was slave precisely because color—and the visual means of registering it—was no longer a wholly reliable way to authenticate race. It was a process that would endure and become fully articulated after the Civil War. On segregation in the urban antebellum South, see Richard C. Wade, *Slavery in the Cities: The South, 1820–1860* (New York: Oxford University Press, 1964); Howard N. Rabinowitz, *Race Relations in the Urban South, 1865–1890* (New York: Oxford University Press, 1978); Ira Berlin, *Slaves without Masters: The Free Negro in the Antebellum South* (New York: Pantheon Books, 1974), esp. 326–30. On segregation in the antebellum North, see Leon F. Litwack, *North of Slavery: The Negro in the Free States, 1790–1860* (Chicago: University of Chicago Press, 1961).

3 See Hale, *Making Whiteness*, esp. 130; Neil R. McMillen, *Dark Journey: Black Mississippians in the Age of Jim Crow* (Urbana: University of Illinois Press, 1989),

23–25. On segregation and space, see, for example, David Delaney, *Race, Place, and the Law, 1836–1948* (Austin: University of Texas Press, 1998), esp. 98–100.

4 Woodward, *Strange Career*, 26, 31, 34–37, quotations on 42–43. Also see Edward L. Ayers, *The Promise of the New South: Life after Reconstruction* (New York: Oxford University Press, 1992), 33, 136; Graves, *Town and Country*, 31; Glenda Elizabeth Gilmore, *Gender and Jim Crow: The Political Culture of Reconstruction* (Chapel Hill: University of North Carolina Press, 1996), 21; Howard N. Rabinowitz, "From Exclusion to Segregation: Southern Race Relations, 1865–1890," *Journal of American History* 63 (Sept. 1976): 325–50.

5 Williamson, *After Slavery*, 275, 298; Rabinowitz, *Race Relations in the Urban South*, esp. 125–30, 330–34; John W. Cell, *The Highest Stage of White Supremacy: The Origins of Segregation in South Africa and the American South* (Cambridge: Cambridge University Press, 1982), esp. 133–35; McMillen, *Dark Journey*, 7; William Cohen, *At Freedom's Edge: Black Mobility and the Southern White Quest for Racial Control, 1861–1915* (Baton Rouge: Louisiana State University Press, 1991), 201–9.

6 Leon F. Litwack, *Been in the Storm So Long* (New York: Knopf, 1979), esp. 260–62; Cohen, At Freedom's Edge, 213–17.

7 Arp, *From the Uncivil War to Date*, 73. On bitterness, see Williamson, *After Slavery*, 275.

8 Richard N. Côté, *Mary's World: Love, War, and Family Ties in Nineteenth-Century Charleston* (Mount Pleasant, S.C.: Corinthian Books, 2002), 247, 248, 250, 259, 278.

9 Ibid., 279, 304, 326–27.

10 Edward King, *The Great South: A Record of Journeys . . .* (Hartford, Conn.: American Publishing Co., 1875), 443 ("numerous"); other quotations from "Education of the Freedmen," *De Bow's Review* 2 (July 1866): 95.

11 Lawyer quoted in Williamson, *After Slavery*, 288. For the quotation and evidence on "crowding," see ibid., 291–92; Ayers, *The Promise of the New South*, 139; editorial, *New Orleans Times*, May 7, 1867, in *The Thin Disguise: Turning Point in Negro History, Plessy v. Ferguson; a Documentary Presentation (1864–1896)*, ed. Otto Olsen (New York: Humanities Press, 1967), 34. For use of the word by Arp and Pringle, see nn. 7–8 above. On tenderness, see Williamson, *After Slavery*, 295–97. For examples of whites who rejected segregation on streetcars, see Graves, *Town and Country*, 224–25.

12 See Woodward, *Strange Career*, 6, 7; Graves, *Town and Country*, 131.

13 As Glenda Gilmore writes, white men who denounced white supremacy "simply did not have much influence on the racial climate and politics of the state from 1896 to 1920," and it is easy to exaggerate their influence before the 1890s too. Gilmore, *Gender and Jim Crow*, xix; Jane Dailey, *Before Jim Crow: The Politics of Race in Postemancipation Virginia* (Chapel Hill: University of North

Carolina Press, 2000); Graves, *Town and Country*, 78–79. Southern efforts to circumvent blacks' right to vote were hideously imaginative and effective while, for the most part, allowing for the political participation of whites of all classes. Beginning in 1871, some states (Georgia and, later, Texas, Virginia, and Florida) passed poll taxes in an effort to exclude blacks from the polls. A more effective ploy was race-specific property taxes (not least because poll taxes infringed on poor whites as well as blacks). Other practices included infamous "understanding" clauses in which blacks were "tested" on their understanding of state constitutions, redistricting, literacy tests, and secret (and confusing) ballots. Poor white men were included by way of grandfather clauses that permitted voting for those descended from men who had voted before 1867. Such measures seemed to work: the number of black voters dropped by 50 percent or more in some states between 1880 and 1888; by 1910, most southern states had effectively disenfranchised their black population. See Cohen, *At Freedom's Edge*, 204–8; Ayers, *The Promise of the New South*, 146–49, 288–90; Eric Foner, *Reconstruction: America's Unfinished Revolution, 1863–1877* (New York: Harper and Row, 1988), esp. 588–99, 604, 609.

14 Joseph H. Cartwright, *The Triumph of Jim Crow: Tennessee Race Relations in the 1880s* (Knoxville: University of Tennessee Press, 1976), esp. 18, 76–78, 105–7, 244; W. Lewis Burke and William C. Hine, "The South Carolina State College Law School: Its Roots, Creation, and Legacy," in *Matthew J. Perry: The Man, His Times, and His Legacy*, ed. W. Lewis Burke and Belinda F. Gergel (Columbia: University of South Carolina Press, 2004), esp. 17–18.

15 Woodward, *Strange Career*, esp. 54–59. Note, too, Thomas W. Hanchett, *Sorting Out the New South City: Race, Class, and Urban Development in Charlotte, 1875–1975* (Chapel Hill: University of North Carolina Press, 1998), 111–20, on the relationship between black political influence and the emergence of segregation in an urban environment.

16 Gilmore, *Gender and Jim Crow*, 3, 12–13.

17 See Cell, *Highest Stage*; Leon F. Litwack, *Trouble in Mind: Black Southerners in the Age of Jim Crow* (New York: Alfred A. Knopf, 1998), esp. 226–30. Segregation emerged because three principal forces that had acted to keep extreme racism in check all declined in their effectiveness. According to C. Vann Woodward, the three forces were northern liberalism, southern conservatism, and southern radicalism. Woodward, *Strange Career*, 69–71, 75, 76, 77–80, 81–82. For an argument that Woodward overstated the extent and intensity of the support the paternalists gave to black suffrage, see J. Morgan Kousser, *The Shaping of Southern Politics: Suffrage Restriction and the Establishment of the One-Party South, 1880–1910* (New Haven, Conn.: Yale University Press, 1974), esp. 275–78. On sectional reconciliation framed in part around a resurgent national racism, see Eric J. Sundquist, "Mark Twain and Homer Plessy," in *Mark

Twain's Pudd'nhead Wilson: Race, Conflict, and Culture, ed. Susan Gillman and Forrest G. Robison (Durham: Duke University Press, 1990), 49.

18 Woodward, *Strange Career*, 86–90, 93–94, 97. Note, too, Graves, *Town and Country*, 34; on Cable, see Hale, *Making Whiteness*, 44–46.

19 Thomas Dixon Jr., *The Leopard's Spots: A Romance of the White Man's Burden, 1865–1900* (New York: Doubleday, 1902; electronic ed., University of North Carolina, Chapel Hill, digitization project, 1998), 27, 29–30, 32, 63.

20 Ibid., 341.

21 Gilmore, *Gender and Jim Crow*, 68–69; Joel Williamson, *The Crucible of Race: Black-White Relations in the American South since Emancipation* (New York: Oxford University Press, 1984), 156–59; Thomas Dixon Jr., *The Sins of the Father: A Romance of the South* (New York: Appleton, 1912), 79–80, 123.

22 Thomas Dixon Jr., *The Clansman: An Historical Romance of the Ku Klux Klan* (New York: Doubleday, 1905; electronic ed., University of North Carolina, Chapel Hill, digitization project, 1997), 155, 208.

23 W. E. B. Du Bois, *The Autobiography of W. E. B. DuBois: A Soliloquy of Viewing My Life from the Last Decade of Its First Century* (New York: International Publishers, 1968), 121; on gender, race, and manhood, see Jacquelyn Dowd Hall, " 'You Must Remember This': Autobiography as Social Critique," in *Gender and the Southern Body Politic*, ed. Nancy Bercaw (Jackson: University Press of Mississippi, 2002), esp. 8–10; on black regression after slavery and the propensity to rape, see Philip Alexander Bruce, *The Plantation Negro as a Freeman: Observations on His Character, Condition, and Prospects in Virginia* (New York: G. P. Putnam's Sons, 1889).

24 See, for example, Ayers, *Promise of the New South*, 156–57, 159. As Joel Williamson has sagely remarked: "The Southern white did not always have a clear reason why racial 'mixing' (as they called it)" or, in fact, any kind of interracial association "in a given situation was wrong, why the color bar should be leveled in one place and not in another. Nevertheless, he had no difficulty in recognizing a breach of proprieties when he saw it." See Williamson, *After Slavery*, 277.

25 Quotations in Gilmore, *Gender and Jim Crow*, 84.

26 Grace Elizabeth Hale argues persuasively that although the spectacle of lynching especially transgressed the ideology of segregation, the practice also "denied that any space was black space." Hale, *Making Whiteness*, 229; Litwack, *Trouble in Mind*, 281, 285, 286, 287, 297. See also the fascinating (and complicating) discussion of the photography of lynching—and attendant visual tensions—offered in Shawn Michelle Smith, *Photography on the Color Line: W. E. B. Du Bois, Race, and Visual Culture* (Durham, N.C.: Duke University Press, 2004), 113–45. On the modernity of spectacle lynching, see Hale, *Making Whiteness*, 203, 206–7, but note also Jacquelyn Dowd Hall's argument that lynching was in tension with the South's modernizing tendencies. See

her *Revolt against Chivalry: Jesse Daniel Ames and the Women's Campaign against Lynching* (New York: Columbia University Press, 1974). On lynching in the context of social and economic forces, especially with regard to the increase of black populations, see W. Fitzhugh Brundage, *Lynching in the New South: Georgia and Virginia, 1880–1930* (Urbana: University of Illinois Press, 1993).

27 Ayers, *Promise of the New South*, 10, 140, 137.

28 Ibid., 10 ("velvet," "heavenly feel"), 137–38, 145, 152.

29 See ibid., 138.

30 Quotations from Graves, *Town and Country*, 151. Pear's soap was in southern stores in the 1880s. See Hale, *Making Whiteness*, 170.

31 New Orleans newspaper quoted by Ayers, *Promise of the New South*, 139. See also the thoughtful essay by Dolores Janiewski, "The Reign of Passion: White Supremacy and the Clash between Passionate and Progressive Emotional Styles in the New South," in *An Emotional History of the United States*, ed. Peter N. Stearns and Jan Lewis (New York: New York University Press, 1998), 126–49.

32 Barbara Y. Welke, "When All the Women Were White, and All the Blacks Were Men: Gender, Class, Race, and the Road to *Plessy*, 1855–1914," *Law and History Review* 13 (fall 1995): 295, 296–98. See also her *Recasting American Liberty: Gender, Race, Law, and the Railroad Revolution, 1865–1920* (New York: Cambridge University Press, 2001).

33 Welke, "When All the Women Were White," esp. 299. On Ida B. Wells's challenge to being relegated to a dirty smoker and her willingness to bite a white man's flesh to protest the assault on her senses, see Hale, *Making Whiteness*, 126–27.

34 *The Complete Writings of Charles Dudley Warner*, ed. Thomas R. Lounsbury, vol. 8 (Hartford, 1904), in Olsen, *Thin Disguise*, 43.

35 My discussion here relies on the fascinating and important work of JoAnne Brown, which explores "how invidious assumptions about race persisted in medical discourse even as the hereditarian understanding [of] tuberculosis was revised in light of germ theory." JoAnne Brown, "Purity and Danger in Color: Notes on Germ Theory and the Semantics of Segregation, 1895–1915," in *Heredity and Infection: The History of Disease Transmission*, ed. Jean-Paul Gaudillière and Ilana Löwy (London: Routledge, 2001), 101. Note, too, Charles A. Lofgren, *The Plessy Case: A Legal-Historical Interpretation* (New York: Oxford University Press, 1987), 107.

36 I am indebted to the insights offered by Tera W. Hunter in *To 'Joy My Freedom: Southern Black Women's Lives and Labors after the Civil War* (Cambridge, Mass.: Harvard University Press, 1997), 187–90, 195, all quotations on 196.

37 Quotation in Brown, "Purity and Danger in Color," 105. "Both white and black physicians agreed that TB rates among African Americans were too high, but they differed on both causes and remedies," argues Brown, explain-

ing: "Black physicians stressed the role of class, education, and environment . . . while many white doctors increasingly favored race, though not necessarily heredity." White doctors tended to see "blacks not only as a race of sick people, but as 'careless consumptives' and 'promiscuous spitters.'" Ibid., 107, 108.

38 Hunter, To 'Joy My Freedom, 197, 198, 204–6. As Brown further explains, "This understanding does not legitimate segregated drinking fountains . . . for the very racial distinctions that obtained in these [medical] debates failed to address the problem of contagion wholly within the 'innocent' white population, much less the dangers of contagion within the black population, or the dangers of contagion from whites to blacks." In fact, "it was the conviction of white supremacy in the dominant culture, and the higher value placed by whites on white health, that actually confounded the understanding and control of the disease in whites as well as blacks." Brown, "Purity and Danger in Color," 111–12, 116.

CHAPTER FOUR

1 On touch authenticating sight, see Martin Jay, Downcast Eyes: The Denigration of Vision in Twentieth-Century French Thought (Berkeley: University of California Press, 1993), 8, and note pages 26–32 for thoughtful remarks on the role of vision in classical thought. For work stressing the importance of senses other than vision, their subsequent denigration, and the emergence of vision as the sense of truth, balance, perspective, and focus, see Lucien Febvre, The Problem of Unbelief in the Sixteenth Century: The Religion of Rabelais, trans. Beatrice Gottlieb (Cambridge, Mass.: Harvard University Press, 1982), 423–42; Robert Mandrou, Introduction to Modern France, 1500–1640: An Essay in Historical Psychology, trans. R. E. Hallmark (New York: Holmes and Meier, 1976), 49–61. Pioneering though their insights are, Febvre and Mandrou state their cases on pretty thin evidence, and I share the reservations about positing a wholly visualist "modern" era against an antivisual premodern era noted by Jay, Downcast Eyes, 34–35, 41, and Leigh Eric Schmidt, Hearing Things: Religion, Illusion, and the American Enlightenment (Cambridge, Mass.: Harvard University Press, 2000), 18. That much said, there was, in the very broadest respect, a shift in sensory hierarchies, with sight becoming more important as a validator of experience, especially during the Enlightenment, sometimes to the detriment of the other senses, although, obviously, never to their utter exclusion. Put simply, Enlightenment thinking led to a greater reliance on seeing as the source of stability, perspective, and truth. See Marshall McLuhan, The Gutenberg Galaxy: The Making of Typographic Man (Toronto: University of Toronto Press, 1962); Norbert Elias, The Civilizing Process, trans. E. Jephcott (New York, 1973), 203–4; Mark M. Smith, "Making Sense of Social History," Journal of Social History 37 (Sept. 2003): 169–71.

2 As Kate Flint has shown, Victorians were "fascinated with the act of seeing, with the question of reliability—or otherwise—of the human eye, and with the problems of interpreting what they saw." The Romantic belief in the power of imagination and memory and its distortion of seeing in real time had a powerful legacy among Victorians, reaffirming the idea that the physical act of seeing was a subjective performance liable to distortion. Kate Flint, *The Victorians and the Visual Imagination* (Cambridge: Cambridge University Press, 2000), 1, 2, 3, 8–9, 23, 30–33, quotation on 5. Jonathan Crary offers a similar though more radical argument, pointing out that doubts about the eye and objectivity emerged in the early nineteenth century. See his *Techniques of the Observer: On Vision and Modernity in the Nineteenth Century* (Cambridge: MIT Press, 1990). Also relevant here is Gillian Beer, " 'Authentic Tidings of Invisible Things': Vision and the Invisible in the Later Nineteenth Century," in *Vision in Context: Historical and Contemporary Perspectives on Sight*, ed. Teresa Brennan and Martin Jay, 83–98 (New York: Routledge, 1996); and, generally, Karen Halttunen, *Confidence Men and Painted Women: A Study of Middle-Class Culture in Victorian America, 1830–1870* (New Haven, Conn.: Yale University Press, 1982).

3 According to Flint, "Identity came to be recognized as something which was not innate, but performative," requiring additional details to authenticate what the eye thought it was seeing. Quiet doubts about seeing, while never enough to radically diminish the importance and superiority of sight in relation to the other senses, nevertheless empowered and promoted the other senses. While sight was unsurpassed in being able "to study the vastness and minutiae of the natural world," the other senses played roles in either authenticating or problematizing what was seen. Flint, *Victorians and the Visual Imagination*, 7, 13, 15, 18, 26. See also John M. Picker, *Victorian Soundscapes* (New York: Oxford University Press, 2003), esp. 6–14. On other challenges to vision, particularly in European and American philosophy, see Jay, *Downcast Eyes*, 14 n. 41.

4 Michael O'Malley, "Specie and Species: Race and the Money Question in Nineteenth-Century America," *American Historical Review* 99 (Apr. 1994): esp. 369, 375.

5 Ibid., esp. 377, 382, 391 (Vickers quoted on 378). The proof was in the pudding of the 1890s, when African Americans, because of their growing economic success and their embrace of the liberal credo, began to show whites that race was increasingly irrelevant. Markets threatened to sideline racial identity, replacing it with occupation, profession, and class. In O'Malley's opinion, whites recognized the trends and reacted: "Facing the possibility of the market remaking the meaning of racial difference, Jim Crow laws fixed the nature of the difference between black and white, rendering it 'non-negotiable.' " Ibid., 394–95. It should also be noted that new Ameri-

can technologies forced those peddling the poison to recalibrate their arguments. The Copyright Act of 1909, argues Lisa Gitelman, "displaced the visuality of reading and acknowledged the problematic visuality of recorded performances." In other words, thanks to the phonograph, "you didn't have to look to read, and you couldn't see the stage." The phonograph "coincided with displacements of other kinds, most notably the displaced visuality of racial identity in contemporary America." Lisa Gitelman, *Scripts, Grooves, and Writing Machines: Representing Technology in the Edison Era* (Stanford: Stanford University Press, 1999), 17. Obviously, the phonograph was but one source of sound in the South. More common were actual performances that did not separate vision from sound. See, for example, the discussion of jazz in Edward L. Ayers, *The Promise of the New South: Life after Reconstruction* (New York: Oxford University Press, 1992), 380–85. Increasingly, though, disembodied sound would become important, particularly in the case of the radio. On the phonograph and disembodiment, see Dave Laing, "A Voice without a Face: Popular Music and the Phonograph in the 1890s," *Popular Music* 10, no. 1 (1991): 1–9.

6 This was part of a national trend. According to Gitelman, "Recorded sound destabilized the connections between hearing music and seeing it performed. . . . The most acute destabilization took place around the recorded coon song, since it was a complex, late-nineteenth-century survival of an already intricate and naggingly visual experience, the mid-century minstrel show." But recorded coon songs, incredibly popular by the 1890s, also helped essentialize race. Recorded sound meant "that the sound of white-constructed 'blackness' survived without the sight of minstrel blackface, as performers of coon songs could go without burnt cork." Indeed, according to Gitelman, recorded coon songs "seemed to assert that white-constructed 'blackness' was a matter of sound, not skin color," something white southerners could only nod to in agreement. The arrival and subsequent dissemination of the phonograph in the 1880s and 1890s, then, helped fix race aurally. Gitelman, *Scripts, Grooves, and Writing Machines*, 133, 134–36; Laing, "A Voice without a Face," 5 (on the dissemination of the phonograph), 6–7, 8 (on the tension between scopic and aural). Gitelman's discussion is subtle and notes that the sound of blackness was hardly monolithic, that even as listeners treated recorded coon songs as racialized performances, there remained "no single, uncomplicated sound for skin color." There was also the complication that white performers of coon songs (not unlike convincingly good white blackfaced antebellum minstrels) sounded black enough to fool many and elicited statements from record companies clarifying the racial identity of performers. See Eric Lott, *Love and Theft: Blackface Minstrelsy and the American Working Class* (New York: Oxford University Press, 1993).

7 Glenda Elizabeth Gilmore, *Gender and Jim Crow: The Political Culture of Reconstruction* (Chapel Hill: University of North Carolina Press, 1996), 62.

8 On this, see Joel Williamson, *New People: Miscegenation and Mulattoes in the United States* (Baton Rouge: Louisiana State University Press, 1995; orig., 1980), 108.

9 Williamson, *New People*, 103. Ascertaining how many people passed and when is, of course, extraordinarily difficult to do with any accuracy. Some types of passing could not be measured, of course, particularly the "occasional 'passing' of the light Negro to get a Pullman berth, a meal, a hotel room, or just for the hell of it. . . . It is agreed that this type of passing occurs," argued sociologist E. W. Eckard in the mid-1940s, "but there is no way to measure the amount." Estimates of just how many African Americans passed often took the form of skirmishes in sociological journals. They varied enormously and often lacked geographic specificity. At the high end—and based on a rather dubious reading of census data—Herbert Asbury offered that about 30,000 blacks passed annually in the 1930s and 1940s. Eckard offered a more sober estimate, putting the number at "probably less than 2,600 per year." John H. Burma thought fewer than two thousand people a year passed during 1930–1940. In 1952, *Ebony* magazine estimated that "more than five million white Negroes . . . have passed over completely into the white world in the last 20 years." Whatever the case, whites and blacks alike tended to exaggerate the numbers and frequency: whites because they were alarmist, blacks because they saw passing as indicative of oppression and because they considered "passing as fitting revenge upon white exclusiveness." E. W. Eckard, "How Many Negroes 'Pass'?" *American Journal of Sociology* 52 (May 1947): 498, 500; Herbert Asbury, "Who Is a Negro?" *Collier's*, Aug. 3, 1946; John H. Burma, "The Measurement of Negro 'Passing,'" *American Journal of Sociology* 52 (July 1946): 18–22; *Ebony*, Apr. 1952, 31. Exact numbers aside, just a handful of passers were often enough to persuade segregationists that they had to rely on more than just their eyes to verify racial identity. Ray Stannard Baker in his 1908 study, *Following the Colour Line*, observed: "I saw plenty of men and women who were unquestionably Negroes, Negroes in every physical characteristic, black of countenance with thick lips and kinky hair, but I also met men and women as white as I am, whose assertion that they were really Negroes I accepted in defiance of my own senses." By his "senses," Baker meant sight: "I have seen blue-eyed Negroes and gold-haired Negroes." Passing was not just a northern phenomenon: "I have met several people, passing everywhere for white, who, I knew, had Negro blood." If Baker found his senses rattled, southern whites did too: "Southern people, who take pride in their ability to distinguish the drop of dark blood in the white face, are themselves frequently deceived. Several times I have heard

police judges in the South ask concerning a man brought before them: 'Is this man coloured or white?' " Ray Stannard Baker, *Following the Colour Line: An Account of Negro Citizenship in the American Democracy* (New York: Young People's Missionary Movement of the United States and Canada, 1908), 151. Joel Williamson puts the problem facing southern whites at the turn of the century into appropriate perspective: "It is not too much to say that Southern whites in the early twentieth century became paranoid about invisible blackness." As blackness assumed an increasingly visual slipperiness, segregationists scrutinized newcomers to a community—were they black? white? passing?—in an effort to read even the faintest signs. Williamson, *New People*, 103.

10 See Ayers, *Promise of the New South*, 3–11, 24, 151–54. On urbanization, see Don H. Doyle, *New Men, New Cities, New South: Atlanta, Nashville, Charleston, Mobile, 1860–1890* (Chapel Hill: University of North Carolina Press, 1990). Ironies abounded, forming lived tautologies. Philip A. Bruce, a white Virginian, argued in 1900 that the effect of movement, of encountering strangers, was to relax what was an increasing prohibition against interracial sex in the postbellum South. "In the towns, where the white population, unlike that of the country, is so largely a floating one, and where the opportunities for a single act of intimacy between white men and negro women, entirely unacquainted with each other and passing at once out of each other's knowledge, are so numerous." Moreover, strangers themselves, especially racially ambiguous ones, were often a product of the very illicit relations white men had with black women in the anonymous safety of towns. And so the cycle would continue until liaisons were stamped out altogether. Bruce quoted in Ayers, *Promise of the New South*, 153.

11 Baker, *Following the Colour Line*, 33.

12 Ayers, *Promise of the New South*, 139. Potentially damaging mistakes were also made in small towns. In 1908 a white farm woman by the wondrous name of Magnolia LeGuin told of her twelve-year-old son's trip to Barnesville, Georgia. Her son—Askew LeGuin—got into a scrap with a black lad who asked "if he was a *white* boy." Magnolia's reaction revealed the twitchiness of being just a little off white in a segregated South, especially in a South where cities hid pasts and color: "I guess the negro said it with impudence, or at least Askew thought so, 'tho Askew is tolerably dark and there are *white* negroes in cities." Quoted in Grace Elizabeth Hale, *Making Whiteness: The Culture of Segregation in the South, 1890–1940* (New York: Pantheon Books, 1998), 183. Fear of eyes being fooled led to hypersensitivity among whites and some marvelously pathetic moments that exposed the segregationist fiction. According to the Atlanta *Georgian*, on Mar. 6, 1907, residents of Albany, Georgia, expelled from their town Peter Zeigler, who "had been here for a month and palmed himself off as a white man. He has been boarding with one of the best white families

in the city and has been associating with some of Albany's best people." Luck failed Zeigler, it seemed, when "a visiting lady recognized him as being a Negro who formerly lived in her city, and her assertion was investigated and found to be correct." But Zeigler re-whitened and returned to Albany "accompanied by a party composed of relatives and influential friends from his native state of South Carolina," who verified that he was, in fact, white. Quoted in Baker, *Following the Colour Line*, 152.

13 Ayers, *Promise of the New South*, 157.

14 Hale, *Making Whiteness*, 8, 9, 47, 155–57, 168–69. Also on clothes, see Patricia A. Turner, *Ceramic Uncles and Celluloid Mammies: Black Images and Their Influence on Culture* (New York: Anchor Books, 1994), 20. As B. L. Putnam Weale put it, black skin had an "unalterable odour which accompanies it." B. L. Putnam Weale, *The Conflict of Colour: The Threatened Upheaval throughout the World* (New York: Macmillan, 1910), 228. See also Sir Edwin Arnold, "Japonica," *Scribner's Magazine* 9 (Jan. 1891): 17; J. Studdy Leigh, "Somali Land, or the Eastern Horn of Africa," *Overland Monthly and Out West Magazine* 19 (June 1892): 652.

15 J. C. Peters, *The Science and Art, or the Principles and Practice of Medicine* (New York: William Raddle, n.d.), 1:4.

16 Keith Weldon Medley, *We as Freemen: Plessy v. Ferguson* (Gretna, La.: Pelican Publishing Company, 2003), 53–55, 131, 136–37, Martinet quotation on 133, *Crusader* quotation on 146. For the point that Tourgée deliberately selected Plessy because he was "nearly white," see also Otto Olsen, ed., *The Thin Disguise: Turning Point in Negro History, Plessy v. Ferguson; a Documentary Presentation (1864–1896)* (New York: Humanities Press, 1967), 12.

17 Louis A. Martinet to Albion W. Tourgée, Oct. 5, 1891 (Tourgée Papers, Chautauqua Historical Museum, New York), in Olsen, *Thin Disguise*, 56–57; Medley, *We as Freemen*, 50–57, 131–37. On the railroad's dislike of the expense of segregation, see Charles A. Lofgren, *The Plessy Case: A Legal-Historical Interpretation* (New York: Oxford University Press, 1987), 32. Some African Americans complained that the choice of the light-skinned Plessy pandered to "nearly white" African Americans, some of whom just wanted to "pass for white." Martinet dismissed such claims as "nonsense." See Mark Elliott, "Race, Color Blindness, and the Democratic Public: Albion W. Tourgée's Radical Principles in *Plessy v. Ferguson*," *Journal of Southern History* 77 (May 2001): 307–8. See also C. Vann Woodward, *American Counterpoint: Slavery and Racism in the North-South Dialogue* (Boston: Little, Brown, 1964), 212–33. Tourgée, Charles A. Lofgren argues in his detailed study of the case, "sought to narrow the issue to color; and by setting up the case around a light-complexioned negro, the arbitrariness of the classification would be accentuated." More than that, Tourgée played with an evolving mind-set that asserted the scientific, categorical essence of race while quietly doubting the strength of essentialist assumptions. As Eric J. Sundquist has shown, the *Plessy* case echoed larger

contemporary developments, particularly in literature (and especially in Mark
Twain's *Pudd'nhead Wilson*, published in 1894), which posited the genetic and
irreversible nature of race but also reflected a "color hallucination" that
defined color "not by optical laws but by tendentious genetic theories that
reached metaphysically into a lost ancestral world." Local reaction to the case
latched on to the way that Plessy problematized the visuality of race. For
example, the New Orleans *Times Democrat*—a paper sympathetic to the 1890
statute—argued a day after Plessy's arrest that "the question whether a dark
cuticle shall provide against its possessor's riding in the same railway coach
with Caucasians, is at last before the courts." Lofgren, *The Plessy Case*, 31;
Eric J. Sundquist, "Mark Twain and Homer Plessy," in *Mark Twain's Pudd'nhead
Wilson: Race, Conflict, and Culture*, ed. Susan Gillman and Forrest G. Robison
(Durham: Duke University Press, 1990), 47; *Times Democrat* quoted in Olsen,
Thin Disguise, 13.

18 Quotations in Medley, *We as Freemen*, 162. On Ferguson, see Elliott, "Race,
Color Blindness, and the Democratic Public," 308.

19 Preamble of Act No. 111, the Laws of Louisiana, July 10, 1890, in Olsen, *Thin
Disguise*, 54. In all, fourteen objections to the segregation statute were raised
by Plessy's legal team and argued by a number of his attorneys. See Olsen,
Thin Disguise, 14–16.

20 *Ex parte Homer A. Plessy*, 45 La. Ann. 80, Decision by Justice Charles E. Fenner,
Dec. 19, 1892, in Olsen, *Thin Disguise*, quotations on 73, 74. For context and
exquisite detail, see Lofgren, *The Plessy Case*, 42–60. Lofgren's summary of
Adams's claim regarding smell is on 41.

21 Assignment of Errors, *Ex parte Homer A. Plessy*, Jan. 5, 1893 (Supreme Court
Records, National Archives), in Olsen, *Thin Disguise*, 75–76 (note, too, page
69); Brief for Homer A. Plessy by Albion W. Tourgée, *File Copies of Briefs 1895*,
VIII (Oct. term, 1895), in Olsen, *Thin Disguise*, 80, 81, 83, 85, 90, 98. For an
intelligent discussion of the origins of the color-blind argument and the
contention that Tourgée's legal strategy in part "was to use the 'whiteness' of
Homer Plessy to probe the very logic of racial categories themselves," see
Elliott, "Race, Color Blindness, and the Democratic Public," esp. 321. Elliott
also makes the point that by trying to convince the Court of the arbitrariness
of racial classification, Tourgée "gambled" and offered an argument that was
likely to backfire simply because the Court could have invoked the "one-
drop" rule, maintaining that any fraction of "colored" blood was enough to
make one "colored." Elliott counters this, though, with the idea that Tourgée
worked his argument both ways and called "attention to the detrimental
social effects that public assessments of race might have for whites," for
example, being mistaken for black by a train conductor ill equipped to ascertain racial identity. See ibid., 322, 323.

22 *Plessy v. Ferguson*, 163 U.S. 537, decision by Justice Henry Billings Brown,

May 18, 1896, in Olsen, *Thin Disguise*, 109, 110, 112; Elliott, "Race, Color Blindness, and the Democratic Public," 325.

23 Williamson, *New People*, 96–97; Gilmore, *Gender and Jim Crow*, 67. See also the thoughtful remarks in Shawn Michelle Smith, *American Archives: Gender, Race, and Class in Visual Culture* (Princeton, N.J.: Princeton University Press, 1999), esp. 189–90. On mixed marriages and the evolution of the one-drop rule, see the still useful study by Charles S. Mangum Jr., *The Legal Status of the Negro* (Chapel Hill: University of North Carolina Press, 1940), esp. 1, 7 n. 38, 9–12. More recent work includes three fine studies: Peter Wallenstein, *Tell the Court I Love My Wife: Race, Marriage, and Law—an American History* (New York: Palgrave Macmillan, 2002); Randall Kennedy, *Interracial Intimacies: Sex, Marriage, Identity, and Adoption* (New York: Pantheon Books, 2003); Rachel F. Moran, *Interracial Intimacy: The Regulation of Race and Romance* (Chicago: University of Chicago Press, 2001). By way of potted history: Before the 1960s, the U.S. Supreme Court treated state miscegenation laws as constitutional, upholding them in *Pace v. Alabama* (1883) and reaffirming them in *Plessy v. Ferguson* (1896) and *Buchanan v. Warley* (1917). Questions regarding interracial marriage were left to local discretion, and, as such, there was tremendous variation in where and when interracial marriages were banned: some laws against interracial marriages were enacted as early as 1664 (Maryland), repealed as early as 1780 (Pennsylvania), "and elaborated as late as the 1930s, when California, Arizona, Maryland, and Utah all acted to bar men from the Philippines from marrying white women" (Wallenstein, *Tell the Court*, 3).

24 How (indeed, whether) the Chinese, Jewish, Greek, and other ethnic communities in the South were sensorily categorized by segregationists remains an open—and important—question, but one beyond the scope of this study. The topic should provide grist for several dissertations. Any consideration of these groups, sensate or otherwise, would do well to ponder the points raised by Peter Wallenstein in his book *Tell the Court* and in his essay "Reconstruction, Segregation, and Miscegenation: Interracial Marriage and the Law in the Lower South, 1865–1900," *American Nineteenth Century History* 6 (Mar. 2005): 55–73.

25 John Dollard, *Caste and Class in a Southern Town* (New Haven, Conn.: Yale University Press, 1937), 103, 2, 3. Morton Rubin—a northern student of southern race relations who spent 1947 in the South—echoed Dollard. See his *Plantation County* (Chapel Hill: University of North Carolina Press, 1951), 4. Note, as well, Hortense Powdermaker, *After Freedom: A Cultural Study in the Deep South* (New York: Viking, 1939), 11, 12, 16.

26 Dollard, *Caste and Class*, 298 ("fields"); Powdermaker, *After Freedom*, 47–48 ("door").

27 David L. Cohn, *Where I Was Born and Raised* (Boston: Houghton Mifflin, 1948), 280; Dollard, *Caste and Class*, 45–46; Robert E. Seymour Jr., *"Whites Only": A*

Pastor's Retrospective on Signs of the New South (Valley Forge, Penn.: Judson Press, 1991), 35. See also Rubin, Plantation County, 98.

28 Rosa Parks, with Jim Haskins, Rosa Parks: My Story (New York: Dial Books, 1992), 149–50; Seymour, "Whites Only," 36. Neither should blacks dress too well, lest they offend white eyes. See Hylan Lewis, Blackways of Kent (Chapel Hill: University of North Carolina Press, 1955), 54.

29 Dollard, Caste and Class, 29, 342–43.

30 Rubin, Plantation County, 90.

31 Cohn, Where I Was Born and Raised, 43, 47, 31, 360, 362; Rubin, Plantation County, 158. See also Seymour, "Whites Only," 17.

32 Powdermaker, After Freedom, 12; Howard W. Odum, "Social and Mental Traits of the Negro," Studies in History, Economics and Public Law 37, no. 3 (1910): 550.

33 Dollard, Caste and Class, 2, 3.

34 Powdermaker, After Freedom, 11, 13; Cook quoted in Ted Ownby, American Dreams in Mississippi: Consumers, Poverty, and Culture, 1830–1998 (Chapel Hill: University of North Carolina Press, 1999), 96.

35 Miss Hollace Ransdell, Report on the Scottsboro, Ala. Case, May 27, 1931, online at <http://www.law.umkc.edu/faculty/projects/FTrials/scottsboro/SB_HRrep. html> (Apr. 5, 2002). See also James Vaughn Kohl and Robert T. Francoeur, The Scent of Eros: Mysteries of Odor in Human Sexuality (New York: Continuum, 1995), 159.

36 Group for the Advancement of Psychiatry, Psychiatric Aspects of School Desegregation: Report No. 37 (n.p., 1957), 22; Dollard, Caste and Class, 353; Rubin, Plantation County, 95. See also Allison Davis, Burleigh B. Gardner, and Mary R. Gardner, Deep South: A Social Anthropological Study of Caste and Class (Chicago: University of Chicago Press, 1941), 77.

37 Robert Russa Moton, What the Negro Thinks (Garden City, N.Y.: Doubleday, Doran, 1929), 72, 81.

38 The "early unpublished experiment" is summarized in Otto Klineberg, Race Differences (New York: Harper and Brothers, 1935), 130–31; George K. Morlan, "An Experiment on the Identification of Body Odor," Journal of Genetic Psychology 77 (1950): 263–64.

39 Born in Slavery: Slave Narratives from the Federal Writers' Project, 1936–1938, Georgia narratives, vol. 4, pt. 3, 286; North Carolina narratives, vol. 11, pt. 1, 100, 102, American Memory Collection, Library of Congress, Washington, D.C. On using the "slave narratives" for insight into the 1930s, see Stephanie J. Shaw, "Using the WPA Ex-slave Narratives to Study the Impact of the Great Depression," Journal of Southern History 69 (Aug. 2003): 623–58. On the appalling living and working conditions experienced by black rural workers in the 1930s South, see Davis, Gardner, and Gardner, Deep South, esp. 387–90. On the black middle class and indoor plumbing, see Dollard, Caste and Class, 103. Note, too, Powdermaker, After Freedom, 131.

40 Klineberg, *Race Differences*, 129; Morlan, "An Experiment on the Identification of Body Odor," 259. See also the various works in *The Biblical and "Scientific" Defense of Slavery: Religion and "The Negro Problem,"* ed. John David Smith (New York: Garland Publishing, 1993).

41 Dollard, *Caste and Class*, 379. Dollard weighed in: "I can only give my own testimony on this point. . . . What I smell mostly among Negroes is perfume, although, to be sure, I have not made a special research on the subject. It may be that the perfume is an effort to avoid the odious stigma of being ill-smelling which Negroes know to be one of the beliefs of white people about them. While Negroes, especially sweating Negroes and manual laborers, do have a strong odor, I cannot detect a categorical difference between it and body odors of white people." If the claim held any truth, thought Dollard, it applied to lower-class blacks: "We may remember that most of the supporting evidence for this belief must be based on Negro cooks, maids, house-boys, field laborers, and other lower-class Negroes who do not have either adequate bathing habits or facilities, who do not have in the hot southern climate very adequate wardrobes, and who have little time for washing either themselves or their clothes." But "among middle-class Negroes I have not been able to detect any identifiable body odors at all." Ibid., 379.

42 Group for the Advancement of Psychiatry, *Psychiatric Aspects of School Desegregation*, 22.

43 Hubert A. Eaton, *Every Man Should Try* (Wilmington, N.C.: Bonaparte Press, 1984), 7.

44 Interview, anonymous, Sept. 29, 2001, Camden, S.C.; interview, Kip Carter, Sept. 29, 2001, near Lancaster, S.C.

45 Dollard, *Caste and Class*, 349, 44. See also Moton, *What the Negro Thinks*, 190.

46 Anne Moody, *Coming of Age in Mississippi* (New York: Doubleday, 1968), 150.

47 Rubin, *Plantation County*, 95; Powdermaker, *After Freedom*, 38. See also the attitudes of northerners examined in Daniel Katz and Kenneth Braly, "Racial Stereotypes of One Hundred College Students," *Journal of Abnormal and Social Psychology* 28 (1933–34): esp. 284. On Miss Essie, see Kibibi Voloria C. Mack, *Parlor Ladies and Ebony Drudges: African American Women, Class, and Work in a South Carolina Community* (Knoxville: University of Tennessee Press, 1999), 157, quotation on 158. The washing and ironing of white clothes by black maids suggested that black skin could be trusted with white cloth, that the smell would not rub off, and that the dexterity necessary for the job could be had from some blacks. Davis, Gardner, and Gardner, *Deep South*, 444.

48 Davis, Gardner, and Gardner, *Deep South*, 16. Grace Elizabeth Hale argues that shopkeepers often applied the rule to what she calls "unclean whites." While this was probably true, evidence suggests that this practice was not as commonly enforced as it was with blacks. See her *Making Whiteness: The Culture of Segregation in the South, 1890–1940* (New York: Pantheon Books, 1998), esp.

184, 185, 189, 191. John Dollard "asked the proprietor of a dress shop whether white and Negro women are allowed to try on the same dresses. He said that occasionally they do, but that in Southerntown they buy dresses in different price classes, so that this does not happen often." Dollard, *Caste and Class*, 352–53. On this practice, see also Moton, *What the Negro Thinks*, 179.

49 Baker, *Following the Colour Line*, 40; Moton, *What the Negro Thinks*, 181.

50 Powdermaker, *After Freedom*, 50; on white gas-station attendants, see Davis, Gardner, and Gardner, *Deep South*, 463.

51 On "caste etiquette" and handshakes, see Dollard, *Caste and Class*, 342; Baker, *Following the Colour Line*, 63 ("clasping"); Powdermaker, *After Freedom*, 48 ("colored mammy"). See also Seymour, *"Whites Only"*, 59.

52 Davis, Gardner, and Gardner, *Deep South*, 23, 45; Cleveland Sellers, with Robert Terrell, *The River of No Return: The Autobiography of a Black Militant and the Life and Death of SNCC* (Jackson: University Press of Mississippi, 1990), 13–14.

53 Davis, Gardner, and Gardner, *Deep South*, 46; on children, see 130. The information about Charlottesville students is from Robert Blake and Wayne Dennis, "The Development of Stereotypes concerning the Negro," *Journal of Abnormal and Social Psychology* 48 (1953): 527, 529, 530.

54 See Hale, *Making Whiteness*, 224, 229.

55 Davis, Gardner, and Gardner, *Deep South*, 16, 448, 449; Powdermaker, *After Freedom*, 47.

56 Dollard, *Caste and Class*, 352.

57 Hale, *Making Whiteness*, 173 ("flour"); Davis, Gardner, and Gardner, *Deep South*, 444 n. 12 ("pig tails"); Dorothy Dickins, *A Nutrition Investigation of Negro Tenants in the Yazoo Mississippi Delta*, Mississippi Agricultural Experiment Station, Bulletin 254 (A&M College, Miss., 1928), 29, 33, 34. See also Ownby, *American Dreams*, 96.

58 Dollard, *Caste and Class*, 369. See also the thoughtful treatment of this and others instances in James C. Cobb's fine study *The Most Southern Place on Earth: The Mississippi Delta and the Roots of Regional Identity* (New York: Oxford University Press, 1994), esp. 160–61.

59 Powdermaker, *After Freedom*, 24. See also Leon F. Litwack, *Trouble in Mind: Black Southerners in the Age of Jim Crow* (New York: Alfred A. Knopf, 1998), 329; Glenda Elizabeth Gilmore, *Gender and Jim Crow: The Political Culture of Reconstruction* (Chapel Hill: University of North Carolina Press, 1996), 112.

60 Davis, Gardner, and Gardner, *Deep South*, 16 ("nurses"); Moody, *Coming of Age in Mississippi*, 124, 148 ("maids"); Morlan, "An Experiment on the Identification of Body Odor," 257. On interracial liaisons between white men and black women, see Mrs. Taylor, n.p., to Gov. Stanley, Richmond, Va., May 24, 1954, Governor Thomas B. Stanley Executive Papers, Box 99—Segregation 1954, Library of Virginia, Richmond, Va.

61 Baker, *Following the Colour Line*, 167, 168; Davis, Gardner, and Gardner, *Deep South*, 19.

62 Baker, *Following the Colour Line*, 11. See also Davis, Gardner, and Gardner, *Deep South*, 404–9.

63 Moton, *What the Negro Thinks*, 92. Why did white men in Southerntown betray, so it seemed, the very essence of their own rules? Dollard thought he had a partial answer, but one that would always remain partial: "Possibly the factor of odor plays a role, since white people generally profess to be revolted by the body odors of Negroes. The association between odor and sexual attraction is an old and well-known one, and it may be that just those odors which are revolting when one is in a conventional mood may be exciting in the sexual mood. But on this score direct and detailed study of white informants will be indispensable, a study which has been impossible in this research." Dollard, *Caste and Class*, 144. The tension between lack of attraction and allure of a constructed black scent parallels Eric Lott's observation regarding antebellum minstrelsy, which represented both a fear of and a desire for African Americans, replete with sexual eroticism. The blacking of white faces allowed for the visual crossing of the color line—but in safety. See Eric Lott, *Love and Theft: Blackface Minstrelsy and the American Working Class* (New York: Oxford University Press, 1993).

64 Dollard, *Caste and Class*, 143. "One woman bitterly referred to her native South as 'the land of sunshine, segregation, and midnight cohabitation.'" But a white woman would refuse "to believe that her own husband or father would 'do such a thing.'" Powdermaker, *After Freedom*, 36–37.

65 Quotations in Hale, *Making Whiteness*, 97, 94, 196; see also 100–101, 105, 125. Note, too, Mack, *Parlor Maids and Ebony Drudges*, esp. 62–63.

66 Davis, Gardner, and Gardner, *Deep South*, 54; Dollard, *Caste and Class*, 95.

67 Dollard, *Caste and Class*, 220; Liston Pope, *Millhands and Preachers: A Study of Gastonia* (New Haven, Conn.: Yale University Press, 1942), 86, 90. On the aural similarities between poor white and black religion, see Powdermaker, *After Freedom*, 273.

68 Sybil V. Wilson Hutton, "Social Participation of Married Women in a South Carolina Mill Village" (M.A. thesis, University of Kentucky, 1948), 19, 48; John Kenneth Morland, *Millways of Kent* (Chapel Hill: University of North Carolina Press, 1958), ix, 13; Walter Edgar, *South Carolina: A History* (Columbia: University of South Carolina Press, 1998), 459 ("white equality"). See also the poetic description offered by Bryant Simon, *A Fabric of Defeat: The Politics of South Carolina Millhands, 1910–1948* (Chapel Hill: University of North Carolina Press, 1998), 1–2.

69 Morland, *Millways of Kent*, 175, 176, 200, 180; Dollard, *Caste and Class*, 472. That Dollard was describing a town about twenty-five miles from Greenville, Mississippi, is suggested in Cohn, *Where I Was Born and Raised*, 283.

70 Morland, *Millways of Kent*, 33, 34.

71 C. Vann Woodward, *The Strange Career of Jim Crow*, 3rd rev. ed. (New York: Oxford University Press, 1974), 107. I do not mean to paint a static picture. Class, race, gender, region—all worked to make Jim Crow change over time and place. Yet, in the end, race triumphed, even in regions with, say, a strong history of class consciousness. For example, white workers' class consciousness, so apparent in upcountry South Carolina during the 1930s, evaporated after World War II. As Bryant Simon explains: "Bruised by several rounds of battle with the state's economic elite and frightened by the organizing efforts of African Americans, millhands jettisoned the politics of class that had unified them during the New Deal in favor of the politics of white supremacy." Simon, *Fabric of Defeat*, 9. Variation and plurality is the point behind the very fine book by J. William Harris, *Deep Souths: Delta, Piedmont, and Sea Island Society in the Age of Segregation* (Baltimore: Johns Hopkins University Press, 2001), esp. chap. 5. Yet even Harris, who argues powerfully for multiple "Souths," ends up affirming the singular "Age of Segregation." On the demise of paternalism in Virginia, see J. Douglas Smith, *Managing White Supremacy: Race, Politics, and Citizenship in Jim Crow Virginia* (Chapel Hill: University of North Carolina Press, 2002).

72 See Davis, Gardner, and Gardner, *Deep South*, 466 (all quotations), 175 (on poor whites). "Both the attitudes of the Whites and the conditions under which the Negroes live impose a false homogeneity, overshadowing intragroup distinctions." Powdermaker, *After Freedom*, 359. See also Lewis, *Blackways of Kent*, 28, 195–96.

73 Pope, *Millhands and Preachers*, 69. See also the discussion of the difference between the work of "scrubbers" and "sweepers" in Jacquelyn Dowd Hall, James Leloudis, Robert Korstad, Mary Murphy, Lu Ann Jones, and Christopher B. Daly, *Like a Family: The Making of a Southern Cotton Mill World* (Chapel Hill: University of North Carolina Press, 1987), 317.

74 Davis, Gardner, and Gardner, *Deep South*, 425, 426, 427, 464.

75 Gayle Graham Yates, *Life and Death in a Small Southern Town: Memories of Shubuta, Mississippi* (Baton Rouge: Louisiana State University Press, 2004), 62.

CHAPTER FIVE

1 Quotations in Leon F. Litwack, *Trouble in Mind: Black Southerners in the Age of Jim Crow* (New York: Alfred A. Knopf, 1998), 36 ("look . . . de eye"), 41 ("their every move"); John Dollard, *Caste and Class in a Southern Town* (New Haven, Conn.: Yale University Press, 1937), 352 ("porches"), 165 ("too-ready suspicion"). Note also Rosa Parks, with Jim Haskins, *Rosa Parks: My Story* (New York: Dial Books, 1992), 51. On white men looking at black women, see Dollard, *Caste and Class*, 146, and Robert Russa Moton, *What the Negro Thinks* (Garden City, N.Y.: Doubleday, Doran, 1929), 34–35.

2   Allison Davis, Burleigh B. Gardner, and Mary R. Gardner, *Deep South: A Social Anthropological Study of Caste and Class* (Chicago: University of Chicago Press, 1941), 230 ("stress," "colored"), 232–33 (middle-class stereotypes); Hortense Powdermaker, *After Freedom: A Cultural Study in the Deep South* (New York: Viking, 1939), 70 ("loud"). Note, too, Grace Elizabeth Hale, *Making Whiteness: The Culture of Segregation in the South, 1890–1940* (New York: Pantheon Books, 1998), 22. On the importance of understanding the fundamental idea that a common experience of exploitation and denigration does not necessarily give rise to a common consciousness of exploitation or a common course of action among the exploited, see Thomas C. Holt, "Marking: Race, Race-Making, and the Writing of History," *American Historical Review* 100 (Feb. 1995): 13.

3   Quotations from Glenda Elizabeth Gilmore, *Gender and Jim Crow: The Political Culture of Reconstruction* (Chapel Hill: University of North Carolina Press, 1996), 75. On class divisions and markers within the African American community, see Kibibi Voloria C. Mack, *Parlor Ladies and Ebony Drudges: African American Women, Class, and Work in a South Carolina Community* (Knoxville: University of Tennessee Press, 1999).

4   Dollard, *Caste and Class*, 88, 89. See also Powdermaker, *After Freedom*, 356. On the importance of class distinctions within a particular black community, see the sobering case study by Brian Kelly, *Race, Class, and Power in the Alabama Coalfields, 1908–21* (Urbana: University of Illinois Press, 2001).

5   Dollard, *Caste and Class*, 246. See also the account of a mass meeting during the Montgomery Bus Boycott by Anna Holden, in *Daybreak of Freedom: The Montgomery Bus Boycott*, ed. Stewart Burns (Chapel Hill: University of North Carolina Press, 1997), 213. Cottonville's black upper class, argued Hortense Powdermaker, practiced a sedate form of worship. "The 'shouters' and revivalists, who make a display of violent feeling in their religion, are never among this class." Powdermaker, *After Freedom*, 66.

6   Quotations in John William Graves, *Town and Country: Race Relations in an Urban-Rural Context, Arkansas, 1865–1905* (Fayetteville: University of Arkansas Press, 1990), 154, 155. On Washington, see Peter A. Coclanis, "What Made Booker Wash(ington)? The Wizard of Tuskegee in Economic Context," in *Booker T. Washington and Black Progress: "Up from Slavery" 100 Years Later*, ed. W. Fitzhugh Brundage (Gainesville: University Press of Florida, 2003), esp. 82; Hale, *Making Whiteness*, 25–26, 167. Note, too, the ability of middle- and upper-class blacks to acquire indoor plumbing and bathrooms but the simultaneous inability for these markers—and the more pleasant scents that accompanied them—to impress white society. See Mack, *Parlor Maids and Ebony Drudges*, esp. 13. Generally, see Lawrence Otis Graham, *Our Kind of People: Inside America's Black Upper Class* (New York: HarperCollins, 1999).

7   Davis, Gardner, and Gardner, *Deep South*, 232, 233. See also E. Franklin Frazier, *Black Bourgeoisie* (Glencoe, Ill.: Free Press, 1957).

8 Group for the Advancement of Psychiatry, *Psychiatric Aspects of School Desegregation: Report No. 37* (n.p., 1957), 22; Dollard, *Caste and Class*, 68 ("whiteness").

9 Ray Stannard Baker, *Following the Colour Line: An Account of Negro Citizenship in the American Democracy* (New York: Young People's Missionary Movement of the United States and Canada, 1908), 158; Powdermaker, *After Freedom*, 179; Henry Louis Gates Jr., *Colored People: A Memoir* (New York: Alfred A. Knopf, 1996), 85; Dollard, *Caste and Class*, 91.

10 Dollard, *Caste and Class*, 256 ("accommodated"); interview, anonymous, Sept. 29, 2001, Camden, S.C. ("Pumpkin spice"); Powdermaker, *After Freedom*, 184 ("colored men"), 191 ("nigger").

11 Dollard, *Caste and Class*, 68, 69; *Ebony*, Nov. 1951, 50. For the larger context, see Shane White and Graham White, *Stylin': African American Expressive Culture from Its Beginnings to the Zoot Suit* (Ithaca, N.Y.: Cornell University Press, 1998), esp. 184–92.

12 Clifton L. Taulbert, *Once upon a Time When We Were Colored* (Tulsa: Council Oak Books, 1989), 17; Joel Williamson, *New People: Miscegenation and Mulattoes in the United States* (Baton Rouge: Louisiana State University Press, 1995; orig., 1980), 98 ("individual"); Morton Rubin, *Plantation County* (Chapel Hill: University of North Carolina Press, 1951), 89 ("pass for white"; "kinship"; "cultural difference"); Davis, Gardner, and Gardner, *Deep South*, 43 ("easily lose"). See also Graham, *Our Kind of People*, 376–89. On passing occurring in the South, see Allison Davis and John Dollard, *Children of Bondage: The Personality Development of Negro Youth in the Urban South* (Washington, D.C.: American Council on Education, 1940), 67, 127, 130, 135–37, 155, and the instances noted in J. Douglas Smith, *Managing White Supremacy: Race, Politics, and Citizenship in Jim Crow Virginia* (Chapel Hill: University of North Carolina Press, 2002), 72, 77, 80, 91.

13 Mamie Garvin Fields, with Karen Fields, *Lemon Swamp and Other Places: A Carolina Memoir* (New York: Free Press, 1983), 64; Williamson, *New People*, 101. Note, too, Graham, *Our Kind of People*, 388; Moton, *What the Negro Thinks*, 229. Ray Stannard Baker's 1908 observations show that white fears of black passing were real. The practice was extensive, and some satisfaction was derived from fooling white senses and making a mockery of segregationist thinking: "Once, in a gathering of mulattoes I heard the discussion turn to the stories of those who had 'gone over to white'—friends or acquaintances of those who were present. Few such cases are known to white people, but the Negroes know many of them," he offered. Continued Baker: "It developed from this conversation (and afterward I got the same impression many times) that there is a sort of conspiracy of silence to protect the Negro who 'crosses the line' and takes his place as a white man. Such cases even awaken glee among them, as though the Negro, thus, in some way, was getting even with the dominant white man." Baker, *Following the Colour Line*, 162–63.

14 Reba Lee [pseud.], as told to Mary Hastings Bradley, *I Passed for White* (New York: Longmans, Green, 1955), 2, 3, 30, 31, 150. For an assessment of this work and commentary on the dangers of passing, see "The Curse of Passing," *Tan Confessions* 5 (Dec. 1955): 50.

15 Nella Larsen, *Quicksand; and, Passing*, ed. Deborah E. McDowell (New Brunswick, N.J.: Rutgers University Press, 1986), 206, 203; Lee, *I Passed for White*, 33, 31, 32, 67, 117, 99, 159, 175. Nella Larsen was born in Chicago in 1893, the daughter of a black West Indian father and a Danish mother. *Passing* was published in 1929.

16 Hale, *Making Whiteness*, 38–41; Williamson, *New People*, 105; Taulbert, *Once upon a Time When We Were Colored*, 107; Parks, *Rosa Parks*, 16. See also Pete Daniel, *Lost Revolutions: The South in the 1950s* (Chapel Hill: University of North Carolina Press, 2000), 203.

17 Evidence from Johnson and the 1930s is in Hale, *Making Whiteness*, 195; quotation describing Leroy and Cecil comes from Cecil J. Williams in his wonderful book *Freedom and Justice: Four Decades of the Civil Rights Struggle as Seen by a Black Photographer of the Deep South* (Macon, Ga.: Mercer University Press, 1995), 21.

18 The article elaborated: "To demonstrate how Negroes can pass as white, the photographs of 16 persons—both Negro and white—are shown on page 32 as a test of the reader's ability to identify a person's race purely by his physical appearance." "Correct Answers" were given on page 36. Even if readers got the answers "right," they were reminded that race was a social construction malleable enough to fool vision. See "Thousands Live Jekyll-Hyde Existence to Hold White Jobs," *Ebony*, Mar. 1952, 32, 36. My request to Johnson Publishing Company, Inc.—which owns *Ebony*—to reprint these photographs was rejected on the grounds "that the photographs are too dated and that they lack necessary releases from the subjects to permit use outside of this company." Letter of Feb. 25, 2005, in author's possession.

19 "I Hated My Race!" *Tan Confessions* 2 (Sept. 1952): 17–19, 58–61; "I Wanted My Daughter to Pass," *Tan Confessions* 2 (Jan. 1952): 15–19, 55–56; "Son of Intermarriage," *Tan Confessions* 4 (June 1954): 17–18, 59–64; Sarah Vaughan, "Dark Girls Can Make It Too!" *Tan Confessions* 3 (Mar. 1953): 27–29, 46–48. *Ebony* and other "black" magazines were read in the South. *Ebony*, for example, had been sold since 1945 in Jackson, Mississippi. See *Ebony*, Feb. 1952, 12; Hylan Lewis, *Blackways of Kent* (Chapel Hill: University of North Carolina Press, 1955), 31.

20 Powdermaker, *After Freedom*, 368.

21 See, for example, Hale, *Making Whiteness*, 198–201; Herman Belz, *Emancipation and Equal Rights: Politics and Constitutionalism in the Civil War Era* (New York: W. W. Norton, 1978); Howard N. Rabinowitz, *Race Relations in the Urban South, 1865–1890* (New York: Oxford University Press, 1978).

22 Quotations and interpretation from Hale, *Making Whiteness*, 194, 195. In Orangeburg, South Carolina, in 1940, the black-owned Pendarvis Barber Shop "chose to serve only white customers," not least because the shop owner could command higher prices by serving whites. Mack, *Parlor Ladies and Ebony Drudges*, 7. Certain forms of touching white skin were acceptable, depending on time, context, and gender: black men could, for example, shave white men in barber shops in Atlanta in 1908 and continued what was a tradition of black barbers. See Baker, *Following the Colour Line*, 10. But by the late 1920s this tradition was challenged, and at least one large southern city prohibited "Negro barbers from serving white patrons." Quotation from Moton, *What the Negro Thinks*, 199.

23 Gilmore, *Gender and Jim Crow*, 87 ("bodies"); Powdermaker, *After Freedom*, 329 ("alike").

24 Introductory statement, *Tan Confessions* 1 (Nov. 1950): 1; Dr. Julian Lewis, "Body Odor," *Tan Confessions* 2 (Jan. 1951): 48, 70. For commentary on the use of perfumes, see *Tan Confessions* 6 (June 1956): 47; 5 (Apr. 1955): 44–45.

25 Wright in Litwack, *Trouble in Mind*, 27; Otto Klineberg, *Race Differences* (New York: Harper and Brothers, 1935), 129. Working- and lower-class blacks were more likely than middle- and upper-class blacks, at least in the 1940s and 1950s, to describe whites as unclean. Part of the explanation might simply be that as maids lower-class blacks got to see the interior—and often dirty—lives of whites. See Tilman C. Cothran, "Negro Conceptions of White People," *American Journal of Sociology* 56 (Mar. 1951): 460.

26 Hubert A. Eaton, *Every Man Should Try* (Wilmington, N.C.: Bonaparte Press, 1984), 15.

27 Gates, *Colored People*, 35–36. Note the discussion in Hale, *Making Whiteness*, 29–30. See too the environmental critique of tuberculosis offered by black leaders in Atlanta in the early 1900s; they correctly (and empirically) argued that tuberculosis affected poor whites as much as it affected poor blacks. Tera W. Hunter, *To 'Joy My Freedom: Southern Black Women's Lives and Labors after the Civil War* (Cambridge, Mass.: Harvard University Press, 1997), 206. See also the discussion offered in Mia Bay, *The White Image in the Black Mind: African-American Ideas about White People, 1830–1925* (New York: Oxford University Press, 2000), esp. 187–204.

28 The black critique is not unlike Karl Marx's materialist understanding of the sensory effects of workers' alienation under the capitalist mode of production: "Man is affirmed in the objective world not only in the act of thinking but with all his senses. . . . The *forming* of the five senses is a labor of the entire history of the world down to the present." Karl Marx, *Economic and Philosophic Manuscripts of 1844*, trans. Martin Milligan (Buffalo: Prometheus Books, 1988), 108–9.

29 Quotation from Robinson in Litwack, *Trouble in Mind*, 336; Fields, *Lemon*

Swamp, 23. Black sociologists at the beginning of the century also explained the odor of black houses in material terms, pointing especially to overcrowding and poverty. See W. E. Burghardt Du Bois, ed., *The Negro Family: Report of a Social Study Made Principally by the College Classes of 1909 and 1910 of Atlanta University, under the Patronage of the Trustees of the John F. Slater Fund; Together with the Proceedings of the 13th Annual Conference for the Study of the Negro Problems, held at Atlanta University on Tuesday, May the 26th, 1908* (Atlanta: Atlanta University Press, 1908), 53, 59–61, 135.

30 Anne Moody, *Coming of Age in Mississippi* (New York: Doubleday, 1968), 253–54; Taulbert, *Once upon a Time When We Were Colored*, 21–22, 49. Rosa Parks on picking cotton as a child: "I will never forget how the sun just burned into me. The hot sand burned our feet whether or not we had our old work shoes on." Parks, *Rosa Parks*, 35.

31 Quotations from Graves, *Town and Country*, 158–59.

32 Speeches of Representatives C. F. Brown and Victor Rochon, June 4, 1890, *Official Journal of the House of Representatives of the State of Louisiana, 1890*, in *The Thin Disguise: Turning Point in Negro History, Plessy v. Ferguson, a Documentary Presentation (1864–1896)*, ed. Otto Olsen (New York: Humanities Press, 1967), 51.

33 "All People 'Smell'!," *Union* (Ohio) 12, no. 49 (Dec. 14, 1918): 1. Note also Fields, *Lemon Swamp*, 85. Cleveland Sellers—a black civil rights activist in the 1960s and native of Denmark, South Carolina—made a similar point in an interview I conducted with him. "So, you would say, then," I asked, "that there was an olfactory dimension to the black community and the white community in the 1950s?" His answer: "Absolutely." Sellers argued that blacks had a distinctive smell. Segregationists, he pointed out, said that blacks had a "putrid kind of odor," while he stressed that blacks merely smelled "different." Why? "African Americans might use Royal Crown hair oil," he said: "So now you smell the oil on the hair." "They might use a certain kind of deodorant"; "there are distinct differences in the African American community"; and "there are certain colognes that are peculiar to the African American community." Interview, Cleveland Sellers, Sept. 25, 2001, Columbia, S.C.

34 Davis, Gardner, and Gardner, *Deep South*, 450.

35 Susan Tucker, *Telling Memories among Southern Women: Domestic Workers and Their Employers in the Segregated South* (Baton Rouge: Louisiana State University Press, 1988), 208, 209, 221. On the response of black maids, see Jacqueline Jones, *Labor of Love, Labor of Sorrow: Black Women, Work, and the Family from Slavery to the Present* (New York: Norton, 1985), esp. 288; Trudier Harris, *From Mammies to Militants: Domestics in Black American Literature* (Philadelphia: Temple University Press, 1982), 30–31.

36 "Relax and Be Yourself," *Ebony*, Nov. 1953, 106. "You Don't Want to be White," shouted an ad for Edward's skin "Formula 718," explaining, "but you do

want and long for a Beautiful, Clear Skin and Complexion." *Ebony*, Nov. 1951, 26. Advertisements in black magazines tended not to play to sensory stereotypes of race but, instead, catered to gender. Only "Jeris Antiseptic Hair Tonic" had a "clean-scented Masculine Fragrance" that "is not greasy to the touch." Women were invited to buy the perfume "Enslavement," touted unashamedly as a "Secret Power That Makes Men Obey You"—"the most powerful perfume you have ever used." *Ebony*, Mar. 1952, 9, 70. See also ibid., 60; *Ebony*, Aug. 1952, 72. For advertisements for "MUM cream deodorant" and "Clorets," both of which stressed their power to combat offensive smells regardless of race, see *Ebony*, Apr. 1952, 22, and *Ebony*, Aug. 1952, 22, respectively.

37 James Weldon Johnson, *Along This Way: The Autobiography of James Weldon Johnson* (New York: Viking Press, 1967; orig., 1933), 387.

CHAPTER SIX

1 Agatha [illegible], Norman, Okla., Apr. 4, 1956, to Governor Folsom, Governor James Elisha Folsom Administrative Files, SG 13913, Requisitions, Public Safety—Miscellaneous, Folder 21, Segregation April 1 1956–April 30 1956, Alabama Department of Archives and History, Montgomery, Ala. (ADAH). From what I could gather, Folsom did not reply.

2 Randolph McPherson, Norfolk, Va., to Gov. Thomas B. Stanley, Richmond, Va., Nov. 17, 1956, Governor Thomas B. Stanley Papers, Accession Number 25184, Box 90—General Correspondence, Racial, Library of Virginia, Richmond, Va. (LV).

3 I do not mean to suggest that the life of the mind was dead in the South. Work by a variety of scholars shows that that was patently not the case. But when it came to race, many white southerners, and Americans generally, suffered a wretched intellectual blind spot. The best example of simultaneous displays of intellectual brilliance and utter incapacity to deal thoughtfully with race is *I'll Take My Stand: The South and the Agrarian Tradition*, by *Twelve Southerners* (New York: Harper and Brothers, 1930), a point made recently by Paul V. Murphy in his *The Rebuke of History: The Southern Agrarians and American Conservative Thought* (Chapel Hill: University of North Carolina Press, 2001). I realize I am going against the grain of a good deal of excellent intellectual history here, but the emotional, visceral dimension to white segregationist reaction generally—one shaped very much by sensory stereotypes—is worth stressing in part to balance the recent emphasis on the intellectual content of the Civil Rights Movement, contemporary liberalism, and aspects of conservatism. See, for example, the very fine essay by David L. Chappell, "Niebuhrisms and Myrdaleries: The Intellectual Roots of the Civil Rights Movement Reconsidered," in *The Role of Ideas in the Civil Rights South*, ed. Ted Ownby (Jackson: University Press of Mississippi, 2002), 3–18. In the same volume (113–36), Richard H.

King offers a superb essay on the content, meaning, and variety of southern intellectual thought. See his "The Struggle against Equality: Conservative Intellectuals in the Civil Rights Era, 1954–1975." In fact, the whole of Ownby's fine collection explores intellectual aspects of the Civil Rights Movement. See also Richard H. King, *A Southern Renaissance: The Cultural Awakening of the American South, 1930–1955* (New York: Oxford University Press, 1980); Daniel J. Singal, *The War Within: From Victorian to Modernist Thought in the South, 1919–1945* (Chapel Hill: University of North Carolina Press, 1982).

4 The critical work at the time—and still important now—on white reaction to integrationist impulses was Gunnar Myrdal, with Richard Sterner and Arnold Rose, *An American Dilemma: The Negro Problem and Modern Democracy* (New York: Harper and Row, 1944). Important contributions on massive resistance include Numan V. Bartley, *The Rise of Massive Resistance: Race and Politics in the South during the 1950s* (Baton Rouge: Louisiana State University Press, 1969); Neil R. McMillen, *The Citizens' Council: Organized Resistance to the Second Reconstruction, 1954–1964* (Urbana: University of Illinois Press, 1971); I. A. Newby, *Challenge to the Court: Social Scientists and the Defense of Segregation, 1954–1966* (Baton Rouge: Louisiana State University Press, 1967). Note, too, Adam Fairclough, *Race and Democracy: The Civil Rights Struggle in Louisiana, 1915–1972* (Athens: University of Georgia Press, 1995).

5 The five-year-window argument is by John Egerton, *Speak Now against the Day: The Generation before the Civil Rights Movement in the South* (New York: Alfred A. Knopf, 1995), 9–11. For the New Deal, see the seminal work by Patricia Sullivan, *Days of Hope: Race and Democracy in the New Deal Era* (Chapel Hill: University of North Carolina Press, 1996). On labor, consult especially Timothy J. Minchin, *What Do We Need a Union For? The TWUA in the South, 1945–1955* (Chapel Hill: University of North Carolina Press, 1997); the important book on biracial unionism, labor, and the emergence of civil rights activism in Memphis by Michael K. Honey, *Southern Labor and Black Civil Rights: Organizing Memphis Workers* (Urbana: University of Illinois Press, 1993); Robert Korstad and Nelson Lichtenstein, "Opportunities Found and Lost: Labor, Radicals, and the Early Civil Rights Movement," *Journal of American History* 75 (1988): 786–811. See also the helpful discussions in Jacquelyn Dowd Hall, "Women Writers, the 'Southern Front,' and the Dialectical Imagination," *Journal of Southern History* 69 (Feb. 2003): 2–38; Grace Elizabeth Hale, *Making Whiteness: The Culture of Segregation in the South, 1890–1940* (New York: Pantheon Books, 1998), 255–58. For definitions of southern "liberals" and discussion of how they were hardly immune to racial prejudice, see David L. Chappell, *Inside Agitators: White Southerners in the Civil Rights Movement* (Baltimore: Johns Hopkins University Press, 1994), esp. 3–4. Note also John T. Kneebone, *Southern Liberal Journalists and the Issue of Race, 1920–1944* (Chapel Hill: University of North Carolina Press, 1985).

6 Morton Rubin, *Plantation County* (Chapel Hill: University of North Carolina Press, 1951), 92. Eddie George, editor of the *Geneva County News*, of Samson, Alabama, told Persons in Dec. 1953: "This newspaper is unalterably opposed to segregation of any form. It [desegregation] would not, in our opinion, be 'unthinkable.'" Eddie George to Persons, Dec. 28, 1953, Governor Seth Gordon Persons Papers, SG 12761, Administrative Files, Fiscal Year 1954—Newspaper Editors and Writers (Segregation), Folder 5, ADAH. See also L. J. Smith, Editor, *The Chickasaw News*, Chickasaw, Ala., to Persons, Dec. 19, 1953, ibid. The last quotation is from Mrs. Martin Waldron, Eden, Ala., to Persons, Jan. 17, 1954, Segregation Letters, Misc., Folder 16, ADAH.

7 C. Vann Woodward, *The Strange Career of Jim Crow* (New York: Oxford University Press, 1974), 136, 137, 138; Robert E. Seymour Jr., *"Whites Only": A Pastor's Retrospective on Signs of the New South* (Valley Forge, Penn.: Judson Press, 1991), 49. Johnie M. Lane of the U.S. Air Force recommended "a rigid plan to make equal facilities available in every community" and justified his argument on the basis of military experience: "It is a period when men from the South and all parts of the United States must eat, sleep, and fight together with no questions asked. . . . The service has brought together men from all walks of life, race, background, and has made great strides in teaching them to work, fight, and live with each other." Johnie M. Lane, USAF, Hq, 36th Ftr-Bmr Wg., APO 132, NY, NY, to Persons, 3 Feb. 1954, Persons Papers, SG 12761, Administrative Files, Fiscal Year 1954, Segregation Letters—Misc., Folder 15, ADAH. Many home-front rumors concerned sensory intimacy, including hand-holding between black men and white women, black maids' use of white bathtubs, and black violation of customs regarding eating; these are documented in Howard W. Odum, *Race and Rumors of Race: The American South in the Early Forties* (Baltimore: Johns Hopkins University Press, 1997; orig., 1943), 62–63, 69, 79, 93. For Odum, such stories were a product of white fear of the possible impact of World War II on southern society and were characterized chiefly by their "emotional" and illogical nature (96).

8 Mrs. Francis Walter, Spring Hill, Ala., to Persons, Dec. 23, 1953, Persons Papers, SG 12761, Administrative Files, Fiscal Year 1954—Segregation Letters, Misc., Folder 16, ADAH; W. P. Ingram, Birmingham, Ala., to Persons, Jan. 16, 1954, ibid., Folder 15. See also David L. Chappell, *A Stone of Hope: Prophetic Religion and the Death of Jim Crow* (Chapel Hill: University of North Carolina Press, 2004).

9 David F. Conrad, National Lutheran Council, Montgomery, Ala., to Persons, Dec. 29, 1953, Persons Papers, SG 12761, Administrative Files, Fiscal Year 1954—Segregation Letters, Misc., Folder 16, ADAH.

10 Geoffrey Birt, The Advertiser Company, Inc., Publishers of the Montgomery *Advertiser* [and] *Alabama Journal*, Montgomery, Ala., to Persons, Dec. 19, 1953, Persons Papers, SG 12761, Administrative Files, Fiscal Year 1954—Newspaper

Editors and Writers (Segregation), Folder 5, ADAH; "Just a Friend," Stonewall, Miss., to Folsom, 3-12-56, Folsom Administrative Files, Segregation, 1956–1957, SG 13916, Folder 7, Segregation, White Citizens' Council, 1956, ADAH. See also James E. Anton, Birmingham, Ala., to Persons, Jan. 10, 1954, Persons Papers, SG 12761, Administrative Files, Fiscal Year 1954—Segregation Letters, Misc., Folder 15, ADAH; James E. Forrest, Mobile, Ala., to Persons, Jan. 1, 1954, ibid., Folder 16.

11 [Virginia Durr] to Nathan David, Feb. 2, 1956, in *Daybreak of Freedom: The Montgomery Bus Boycott*, ed. Stewart Burns (Chapel Hill: University of North Carolina Press, 1997), 153.

12 Willie James Russell, Sylacauga, Ala., to "Dear Sir," May 11, 1954, Persons Papers, SG 12761, Administrative Files, Fiscal Year 1954—Segregation Letters, Misc., Folder 16, ADAH; Walter T. Lumpkin, Committee Chairman, Talladega Negro Teachers Association, 617 Coosa Street, Talladega, Ala., to Persons, March 15, 1954, appended is a copy of "The President of the Alabama State Teachers Association Speaks on School Segregation," by J. D. Thompson, President, an open letter to the press in Alabama, ibid., Folder 15. See also Rev. T. M. Howze, First Presbyterian Church, 1030 Georgia Ave., Etowah, Tenn., to Persons, Feb. 4, 1954, ibid. On black leaders as key to creating contexts and conversations in which white liberals could participate and as making good use of white support, see Chappell, *A Stone of Hope*.

13 "Greater Birmingham and It's [sic] Enormous Negro Market," by Jesse J. Lewis and Associates, Advertising . . . Public Relations, Birmingham, Ala. [1955], Folsom Administrative Files, Public Welfare, U-2—Race, SG 13874, Fiscal Year 1956, Folder 15, Race, November, 1955–, ADAH. On the importance of black consumerism generally, see Hale, *Making Whiteness*.

14 Copy of "Racial Prejudice, A Barrier to the Economic[,] Cultural, Educational and Spiritual Progress of the South," editorial by Chastine C. Mason, in the *Negro Voice* (Joliet, Ill.), Tues., Aug. 9, 1955, Folsom Administrative Files, Segregation, SG 13914, Oct. 1 1954–Mar. 31 1956, Folder 3, Segregation, 1955, ADAH; M. H. Christian, "Let My People Go," 34, 41, 57, 83, Folsom Administrative Files, Segregation, SG 13916, Folder 9, ADAH. See also the copy in Governor George B. Timmerman Papers, Box 10, Misc. F–Le, South Carolina Department of Archives and History, Columbia, S.C. (SCDAH).

15 [Illeg. name], New York, N.Y., to Folsom, Mar. 3, 1956, Folsom Administrative Files, SG 13913, FY 1959 [sic], Public Safety—Miscellaneous, Folder 14, Segregation, 1955–1956, ADAH; Kitty [illeg.], Buffalo, N.Y., to Folsom, Feb. 26, 1956, Folsom Administrative Files, SG 13915, Segregation, Folder 11, Segregation 1956, Bus Boycott.

16 On the intellectual limitations of white liberalism, see Chappell, *A Stone of Hope*; on the limited role of white liberals after *Brown*, consult Michael Klarman, "How *Brown* Changed Race Relations: The Backlash Thesis," *Journal of*

American History 81 (June 1994): 81–118; on the withering of cautious liberal support with regard to the race issue just after World War II, see Sullivan, *Days of Hope*, 224–70; on the political cost of remaining liberal on race in the early 1950s, see Morton Sosna, *In Search of the Silent South* (New York: Columbia University Press, 1977). For other explanations for the loss of liberal support (ranging from the argument that southern liberals were too radical on some matters to southern conservative exploitation of anti-Communism and segregation), see the insightful essay by Tony Badger, " 'Closet Moderates': Why White Liberals Failed, 1940–1970," in Ownby, *Role of Ideas in the Civil Rights South*, 91–93.

17 Rev. Thomas R. Thrasher, "Alabama's Bus Boycott," *The Reporter: The Magazine of Facts and Ideas* (New York, N.Y.), 16, in Folsom Administrative Files, SG 13915, Segregation, Folder 10, Segregation 1956, Bus Boycott, ADAH. On Thrasher's role, see J. Mills Thornton III, *Dividing Lines: Municipal Politics and the Struggle for Civil Rights in Montgomery, Birmingham, and Selma* (Tuscaloosa: University of Alabama Press, 2002), 36, 72, 98.

18 Melton A. McLaurin, *Separate Pasts: Growing Up White in the Segregated South* (Athens: University of Georgia Press, 1987), 25–26, 37, 38.

19 Ibid., 38–39, 31, 30.

20 Eugene B. Collton, Arlington, Va., to Stanley, July 8, 1954, Governor Thomas B. Stanley General Correspondence, Box 101, June 1954, Segregation, LV. See also Woodward, *Strange Career*, 146.

21 Mrs. T. J.[?] Baker, [Decatur, Ga.?], to "President Eisenhower," n.d., received July 18, 1955, Record Group 12: Georgia Department of Education, Subgroup 2: Office of the State Superintendent, Series 25: Correspondence of the State Superintendent with the General Public, Box 1: Alphabetical Correspondence Files, 1955, Folder Ba–Br, Georgia Archives, Atlanta, Ga. (GA); Ben Howard, Athens, Ala. to Folsom, 10-5-57, Folsom Administrative Files, SG 13908, Requisitions, Allotments—Soil Conservation Committee, Folder 10, Segregation Oct.–Nov. 1957, ADAH. For belief in God-ordained black inferiority in the 1930s, see Allison Davis, Burleigh B. Gardner, and Mary R. Gardner, *Deep South: A Social Anthropological Study of Caste and Class* (Chicago: University of Chicago Press, 1941), 16–17. The question of religion has attracted recent attention. For the quality of the integrationists' theology, see Chappell, *A Stone of Hope*. Whatever shortcomings apparent in such thinking, the point is that its intellectual and theological depth and content was far superior to the kind of visceral ranting often pushed by religiously inspired segregationists. On the importance of sexualized, Christian prosegregation theology, see Jane Dailey, "Sex, Segregation, and the Sacred after *Brown*," *Journal of American History* 91 (June 2004): 119–44.

22 "The Negro, The Ape," National Citizens Protective Association, St. Louis, Mo., J. D. Rowlett Collection, 1954–1972 and n.d., ac 1971-0299M, Folder 3:

White Sentinel, GA; E. V. Hill, Columbraba [?], Ala., to Persons, n.d., Persons Papers, SG 12761, Administrative Files, Fiscal Year 1954, Segregation Letters—Misc., Folder 15, ADAH.

23 Quoted in Burns, *Daybreak of Freedom*, 154. The kind of environmentalist argument associated with anthropologists such as Franz Boas had little purchase in the segregated South. Note Joel Williamson, *New People: Miscegenation and Mulattoes in the United States* (Baton Rouge: Louisiana State University Press, 1995; orig., 1980), 124. Black activism often produced a white backlash, among southern white workers especially. For the late 1930s, see Bryant Simon, *A Fabric of Defeat: The Politics of South Carolina Millhands, 1910–1948* (Chapel Hill: University of North Carolina Press, 1998), esp. 219–22.

24 Martha Holman, Evergreen, Ala., to Persons, Dec. 23, [1953], Persons Papers, SG 12761, Administrative Files, Fiscal Year 1954—Segregation Letters, Misc., Folder 16, ADAH.

25 Sheet, "Who Are the Race Mixers?" n.d., Folsom Administrative Files, SG 13913, Requisitions, Public Safety—Miscellaneous, Folder 21, Segregation April 1 1956–April 30 1956, ADAH. See also the indispensable discussion on the link between rhythm and blues, rock and roll, and white resistance to *Brown* in Brian Ward, *Just My Soul Responding: Rhythm and Blues, Black Consciousness, and Race Relations* (Berkeley: University of California Press, 1998), esp. 89–115.

26 *The Southerner: News of the Citizens' Council* (Birmingham, Ala.), Feb. 1956, 3, 5, 6, Folsom Administrative Files, SG 13913, FY 1959 [sic], Public Safety—Miscellaneous, Folder 14, Segregation, 1955–1956, ADAH. See, generally, McMillen, *Citizens' Council*.

27 "A Rebel Friend, John," Chateauroux, France, to Persons, n.d., letter received Jan. 11, 1954, Persons Papers, SG 12761, Administrative Files, Fiscal Year 1954—Segregation Letters, Misc., Folder 15, ADAH; Thomas M. Taylor, Korea, to Gov. Allan Shivers, July 11, 1954, Folder: "Federal Segregation 1954," Governor's Office, Call # 1977/81–182, Texas State Archives, Austin, Tx. (TSA). World War II veterans were often at the vanguard of racial violence and heavily involved in white resistance to integration. See James C. Cobb, "World War II and the Mind of the Modern South," in *Remaking Dixie: The Impact of World War II on the American South*, ed. Neil R. McMillen (Jackson: University Press of Mississippi, 1997), esp. 6–11.

28 A Citizen, Houston, Tx., to "Gov. of Ala.," n.d., Folsom Administrative Files, SG 13913, FY 1959 [sic], Public Safety—Miscellaneous, Folder 15, Segregation March 5, 1956, ADAH.

29 Mrs. John F. Watlington, Reidsville, N.C., to Gov. Umstead, Raleigh, N.C., June 1, 1954, Governor William B. Umstead Papers, Segregation Correspondence Files W (2), Box 58.3, North Carolina State Archives, Raleigh, N.C. (NCSA); Mrs. B. B. Tart, Newton Grove, N.C., to Umstead, Raleigh, N.C.,

June 21, 1954, Umstead Papers, Segregation Correspondence Files 1954-T, ibid.; Mrs. L. M. [Lella M.] Galvani, 2116 Pierce Ave., Nashville, Tenn., to Persons, Mar. 9, 1954, Persons Papers, SG 12761, Administrative Files, Fiscal Year 1954, Segregation Letters—Misc., Folder 15, ADAH (her emphasis); see also Mrs. L. E. Galvani, Nashville, Tenn., to Stanley, Mar. 9, 1954, Stanley Papers, Accession Number 25184, Box 90—General Correspondence, Racial, LV; McMillen, *Citizens' Council*, 162 ("inherent"). See also Anonymous, Fort Worth, Texas, to Shivers, June 20, 1955, Folder: "Anonymous Letters #2," Governor's Office, Call # 1977/81–68, TSA.

30 Carlos H. Allen, Santa Ana, Calif., to Folsom, Mar. 6, 1956, Folsom Administrative Files, SG 13913, Folder 18, Segregation March 6–March 15, 1956, ADAH; Mrs. Eulalia Mangels, San Jose, Calif., Apr. 28, 1956, to "The Governors, Attorney Generals, Judges, City Authorities, Bus Lines, White Citizens Council[s], Mayors and Police, and many others of all Southern States," Folsom Administrative Files, SG 13913, Requisitions, Public Safety—Miscellaneous, Folder 21, Segregation April 1 1956–April 30 1956, ADAH. On touch, trains, and disease, see also Mrs. Mattie Smith, Dallas, Texas, to Shivers, May 18, 1954, Folder: "Anonymous Letters #1 1954," Governor's Office, Call # 1977/81–178, TSA.

31 S. E. Shockley, n.p., to Governor Griffin, Mar. 19, 1955, Record Group 1: Georgia Governor's Office, Subgroup 1: Executive Office, Series: Subject Files, Box 311: M–Z, 1955, Correspondence, Folder S 1955, GA.

32 "The Negro, The Ape," National Citizens Protective Association, St. Louis, Mo., J. D. Rowlett Collection, 1954–1972 and n.d., ac 1971-0299M, Folder 3: *White Sentinel*, GA.

33 "Gentlemen," copy of letter appended to Mrs. John E. Schmidt, Jr., Valdosta, Ga., January 22, 1956, to Timmerman, Timmerman Papers, Box 5, Misc. Segregation File, SCDAH; "A Friend," Bainbridge, Ga., to Folsom, n.d., received June 30, 1955, Folsom Administrative Files, Segregation, SG 13914, Oct. 1 1954–Mar. 31 1956, Folder 1, Segregation, 1954–55, ADAH. See also Mrs. Taylor, n.p., to Stanley, Richmond, Va., May 24, 1954, Stanley Executive Papers, Box 99—Segregation 1954, LV.

34 V. R. Upton, Magnolia Terminal, Ala., to "Dear Senators," Sept. 25, 1957, Folsom Administrative File, Segregation, 1956–1957, SG 13916, Folder 7, Segregation, White Citizens' Council, 1956, ADAH; Anon., n.p., to "Dear Governor," n.d., received July 18, 1955, Folsom Administrative Files, Segregation, SG 13914, Oct. 1 1954–Mar. 31 1956, Folder 2, Segregation, 1955, ADAH; Kathie Rose Swoop, Farmville, Va., to Stanley, Richmond, Va., n.d. (responded to by Governor's Office June 7, 1954), Stanley General Correspondence, Box 100, June 1954, Segregation, LV. See also Mrs. Williams, Tyler, Tx., to Stanley, May 22, 1954, Stanley Executive Papers, Box 99—Segregation 1954, LV.

35 Mrs. Lokr, Stanover County, to Stanley, Richmond, Va., June 8, 1954, Stanley General Correspondence, Box 100, June 1954, Segregation, LV. See also
Charles Catlett, Hampton, Va., to Stanley, June 4, 1954, Stanley General Correspondence, Box 101, ibid.

36 Pamphlet, "Danger! Warning! Pro-Stalin Politicians and Alien-Minded Trai-
tors in Cooperation with Blind Sentimentalists Are Attempting to Force Negro Rule Negro-White Intermarriage Negro Invasion of White Schools. White
Man, Awaken!," n.p., n.d., Persons Papers, SG 12761, Administrative Files,
1953—Segregation in Public Schools, Folder 17, ADAH.

37 Jane Revill, Sumter, S.C., to Timmerman, Columbia, S.C., Nov. 29, 1955,
Timmerman Papers, Box 5, Misc. Segregation File, SCDAH; M. J. Howle,
Savannah, Ga., to Folsom, Mar. 4, 1956, Folsom Administrative Files, SG
13913, Public Safety—Miscellaneous, Folder 22, Segregation April 1 1956–
April 30 1956, ADAH.

38 Address of Representative James C. Davis Delivered to States' Rights Coun-
cil, of Georgia, Inc., November 28, 1956, at Atlanta, pp. 6, 8, Integration:
The Right Wing Response, 1956–1964, Record Group 48, Series 3, Folder:
Speeches, GA; The Augusta Courier, Dec. 8, 1958, p. 1, Integration: The Right
Wing Response, 1956–1964, Record Group 48, Series 3, Acc.# 68–187,
Folder: Newspapers—Augusta Courier, LV.

39 Charles Eli. Sexton, Arlington, Va., to Stanley, Richmond, Va., May 28, 1954,
Stanley General Correspondence, Box 100, June 1954, Segregation, LV. See
also The White Sentinel, Vol. V, No. 9, Sept. 1955, p. 1, J. D. Rowlett Collection,
1954–1972, ac 71–299, Box 1, Folder 3: White Sentinel, GA.

40 "Gentlemen," copy of letter appended to Mrs. John E. Schmidt, Jr., Valdosta,
Ga., January 22, 1956, to Timmerman, Timmerman Papers, Box 5, Misc.
Segregation File, SCDAH.

41 Arthur Stoney, poem, "White Trash," 1950, State Forestry Commission, State
Parks Division, Desegregation Files (s162024), SCDAH.

42 "The Kiss of Death," The White Sentinel (Ft. Lauderdale, Fla.), n.d., J. D. Rowlett Collection, 1954–1972 and n.d., ac 1971-0299M, Folder 2: Annotated
Handouts, GA.

43 "Youth Movements," National Citizens Protective Association, St. Louis,
Mo., Integration: The Right Wing Response, 1956–1964, ac 1968-0187M,
Folder: Broadsides, GA. On biracial and interracial labor unionism and civil
rights and Communism in the 1940s and 1950s, see, for example, Honey,
Southern Labor, 252–77; Sullivan, Days of Hope, 237–47.

44 J. L. Elliott, Elliott Jewelry, Mobile, Ala., to Persons, Feb. 27, 1954, Persons
Papers, SG 12761, Administrative Files, Fiscal Year 1954—Segregation Letters,
Misc., Folder 16, ADAH; Printed flyer from G. W. Hanna, National Citizens
Council, Birmingham, Ala., n.d., received Mar. 3, 1956, to Folsom, Folsom
Administrative Files, SG 13913, FY 1959 [sic], Public Safety—Miscellaneous,

Folder 15, Segregation March 5, 1956, ADAH; Interviews with Bus Drivers, by Anna Holden, in Burns, *Daybreak of Freedom*, 179; Anonymous, "A Christian Grandmother," Denison, Tx., to Shivers, July 21, 1955, Folder: "Anonymous Letters #1," Governor's Office, Call # 1977/81–68, TSA.

45 Quotation from pamphlet entitled "The Supreme Kangaroo Court Is in Plenary Session," Pamphlets, assorted posters by C. C. Poff, Folder: "Federal Segregation September 1956," Governor's Office, Call # 1977/81–87, TSA. On continued southern fears of passing, see Sally H. Clopton and Mrs. Harvie Archer Clopton, Richmond, Va., to Mr. W. S. Rhoads, Jr., Virginia Museum of Arts, Richmond, Va., Jan. 26, 1956, Stanley Papers, Accession Number 25184, Box 90—General Correspondence, Racial, LV; "Remarks on the racial segregation issue by Hugh G. Grant, former member of the State Department and U.S. Minister to Albania and Thailand," Persons Papers, SG 12761, Administrative Files, Fiscal Year 1954, Segregation Letters—Misc., Folder 14, ADAH.

46 Emitt Daniel, Phoenix, Ariz., to "The Honorable Governor of Alabama and to all Southern Governors," n.d., received Mar. 22, 1956, Folsom Administrative Files, Public Safety—Miscellaneous, FY 1959 [sic], SG 13913, Folder 20, Segregation, March 16–March 31, 1956, ADAH.

47 W. Miley Diredder Susana, Ala., to Folsom, n.d., received Mar. 10, 1956, Folsom Administrative Files, SG 13913, Folder 18, Segregation, March 6–March 15, 1956, ADAH.

48 Copy of letter from B. T. Matthews to Mr. George Sam Harrell, House of Representatives, Columbia, S.C., Apr. 29, 1957, in William D. Workman Papers, Box 19, Folder, "Integration/Civil Rights—Citizen Councils," South Caroliniana Library, University of South Carolina, Columbia, S.C.

49 Arnold M. Rose, "Community Factors Related to Desegregation," *American Journal of Orthopsychiatry* 26, no. 3 (1956): 447; E. Terry Prothro, "Ethnocentrism and Anti-Negro Attitudes in the Deep South," *Journal of Abnormal and Social Psychology* 47, no. 1 (1952): 108. Generally, see David W. Southern, *Gunnar Myrdal and Black-White Relations: The Use and Abuse of "An American Dilemma,"* 1944–1969 (Baton Rouge: Louisiana State University Press, 1987). In the unlikely event that southern whites doubted the validity of their arguments, they received confirmation from northerners, nonsoutherners, and displaced southerners. Some of these people were members of national organizations opposed to integration, such as the Citizens' Councils, which had a presence in "at least 30 states" by 1956. But lots of people opposed to *Brown* were not part of any formal organization, and for every northerner happy to challenge segregation, one endorsed it. In letters to southern governors, they offered their two cents' worth by telling what had happened there and, by implication, warning what would happen in the South. A correspondent from Youngstown, Ohio, told Virginia governor Thomas B. Stanley, "I sit on my front porch last week & saw a negro boy coming from the White South high

school there, with his arms around a White girl & her arms around him. . . .
That courtship started in school." James Gilmartin—self-styled "person of
pure Northern origin" and advocate of "conditioning" all Americans in the
rituals of segregation—wrote to South Carolina governor George B. Timmerman in 1956 expressing his resentment of the Supreme Court's decision
"to compel me to have bodily contact—it amounts to that under economic
pressure—with the negro or any other colored race." "I am not a Southerner
but a Mid-Westerner," Horace Hudson of Chicago told Alabama governor
Gordon Persons in January 1954. What had happened in Chicago, warned
Hudson, would surely follow in Alabama if integration of the schools were to
occur: "Imagine your own daughter or wife dancing with one of these blacks
or swimming at the same time in a swimming pool. Sir it is unthinkable. . . .
It has already happened to the North and it is surely coming to the South
unless something is *done* and done *quickly*." Unidentified, Youngstown, Oh.,
June 22, 1955, Stanley Executive Papers, Accession Number 25184, Box 20,
Executive Departments, Education, Schools, Manuals—Problems Education
—School Problem, 1955, LV; James Gilmartin, Baldwin, Mich., to Timmer-
man, Columbia, S.C., Jan. 25, 1956, Timmerman Papers, Box 5, Misc. Segre-
gation File, SCDAH; Horace Hudson, Chicago, Ill., to "Your Excellency," Jan.
14, 1954, Persons Papers, SG 12761, Administrative Files, Fiscal Year 1954—
Segregation Letters, Misc., Folder 15, ADAH. On the Citizens' Councils outside the South, see McMillen, *The Citizens' Council*, 138–55 (quotation on 138).
Southern governors would get similar letters or telegrams in later years, too.
George Wallace got thousands of telegrams from outside the South supporting his 1963 rant. See Dan T. Carter, *From George Wallace to Newt Gingrich: Race in
the Conservative Counterrevolution, 1963–1994* (Baton Rouge: Louisiana State
University Press, 1996), 6.

50 Gordon W. Allport, *The Nature of Prejudice* (Reading, Mass.: Addison-Wesley,
 1954), 13, 14, 21, 23, 55; F. C. Owen, Durham, N.C., to Umstead, Raleigh,
 N.C., June 4, 1954, Umstead Papers, Segregation Correspondence Files, Box
 58, NCSA.

51 (Mrs. W. T.) Ruth Barnett, Pine Level, Ala., to Persons, Jan. 4, 1953 [sic],
 Persons Papers, SG 12761, Administrative Files, Fiscal Year 1954—Segrega-
 tion Letters, Misc., Folder 15, ADAH; *The Augusta Courier*, Apr. 2, 1956, Folsom
 Administrative Files, SG 13913, Requisitions, Public Safety—Miscellaneous,
 Folder 21, Segregation April 1 1956–April 30 1956, ADAH.

52 E. W. Calhoun, Indianola, Miss., to "Dear Fellow American," Nov. 27, 1953,
 Persons Papers, SG 12761, Administrative Files, Fiscal Year 1954—Segregation Letters, Misc., Folder 15, ADAH; *The Southerner: News of the Citizens' Council* (Birmingham, Ala.), February, 1956, n.p., Folsom Administrative Files, SG
 13913, FY 1959 [sic], Public Safety—Miscellaneous, Folder 14, Segregation,
 1955–1956, ADAH.

53 Richard W. Edmonds, *Foundation for Segregation* (n.p., 1957), 12, 1, Folsom Administrative Files, SG 13913, Public Safety—Miscellaneous, Folder 22, Segregation April 1 1956–April 30 1956, ADAH; Herve Charest, Jr., Editor and Publisher, *The Tallassee Tribune*, Tallassee, Ala., to Persons, Dec. 23, 1953, Persons Papers, SG 12761, Administrative Files, Fiscal Year 1954—Newspaper Editors and Writers (Segregation), Folder 5, ADAH.

54 As Charles M. Payne has recently pointed out, *Brown* was a challenge to law, not an attack on the culture of racism. See his " 'The Whole United States Is Southern!': *Brown v. Board* and the Mystification of Race," *Journal of American History* 91 (June 2004): 83–91. On the proliferation of white supremacist "scientific" literature in the years after *Brown*, see McMillen, *Citizens' Council*, 163–82; Newby, *Challenge to the Court*. See also the "Round Table: *Brown v. Board of Education*, Fifty Years After," *Journal of American History* 91 (June 2004): 19–118; "Forum: Reflections on the Brown Decision after Fifty Years," *Journal of Southern History* 70 (May 2004): 293–350. Note, too, the argument that the principal impact of *Brown* was to mobilize *white* resistance, as offered by Michael J. Klarman, *From Jim Crow to Civil Rights: The Supreme Court and the Struggle for Racial Equality* (New York: Oxford University Press, 2004). For tentative remarks on the post-1960 United States, see Mark M. Smith, "Making Scents Make Sense: White Noses, Black Smell, and Desegregation," in *American Behavioral History: An Introduction*, ed. Peter N. Stearns (New York: New York University Press, 2005), 181–98.

55 Mrs. W. H. Duke, Gadsden, Ala., to Persons, May 22, 1954, Persons Papers, SG 12761, Administrative Files, 1953—Segregation in Public Schools, Folder 17, ADAH; V. R. Upton, Magnolia Terminal, Ala., to "Dear Senators," Sept. 25, 1957, Folsom Administrative Files, Segregation, 1956–1957, SG 13916, Folder 7, Segregation, White Citizens' Council, 1956, ADAH; "A Loyal Southerner," George V. Johnson, Baltimore, to Persons, n.d., Persons Papers, SG 12761, Administrative Files, 1953—Segregation in Public Schools, Folder 17, ADAH.

ACKNOWLEDGMENTS

Historians employed at the University of South Carolina are a lucky bunch. The place ripples with individual and collective knowledge, all dispensed with doses of impeccable goodwill and refreshing honesty. Such, happily, has been my fate. Thomas J. Brown, Dan Carter, Bobby Donaldson, Bob Herzstein, Val Littlefield, Paul MacKenzie, and Jack Sproat always offered an encouraging word or passed along interesting sources. Dan Littlefield read this manuscript with his scrupulous eye and persuaded and encouraged me. Pat Sullivan could not have been more helpful and supportive if she had tried, and the book benefited from her comments. Ron Atkinson was his usual helpful self, and I am extremely grateful for his guidance. Paul E. Johnson again read my work and offered wise words. I am fortunate to have Pat Maney as a chairman. Not only did he do everything he could to help the book's completion, but he also read the manuscript, offering judicious and thoughtful comments along the way. It is nice to have a fabulous writer as a friend and critic. Mine is Janette Turner Hospital. Her warm comments and enthusiasm for the project continue to mean a great deal. A very special thanks to my colleague and friend Walter Edgar, who read my effort twice, editorialized many times, shared evidence, and counseled me with an infectious sincerity.

Many people kindly listened to me natter on (and on) about this book. They include Joyce Braun, Kevin Dawson, Kathryn Fenner, Trenton Hizer, Rhett Jackson, Judge Matthew Perry, and Sarah Skwire; I thank them for their patience and for sharing their knowledge. I am also grateful to my graduate students, who often alerted me to likely sources. Aaron Marrs, Rebecca Shrum, Eric Plaag, David Prior, Mike Reynolds, Jay Richardson, and Kathy Hilliard (whose research was simply exceptional) are wonderful scholars in their own right and probably teach me more than I educate them. I also thank Rhett Adams—an undergraduate student who taught his teacher—and Tina Manley, for her talented eye and for her listening ear. Thanks, too, to Robert Ellis for a fine index.

I had the privilege of interviewing several individuals for this book, some of whom wish to remain anonymous. I am grateful to them all for agreeing to talk with me about a difficult topic. My thanks to Kip Carter for helping me understand the complexities of southern life—he was helpful and hospitable in the extreme—and to my friend and colleague Cleveland Sellers. Cleveland taught me a great deal. I remain grateful for a detailed conversation with the Reverend David H. Cole concerning his experience in Montgomery, Alabama, in 1955–56. Cecil J.

Williams was extraordinarily helpful and generous when it came to sharing his photographs.

On the research front, my sincere thanks to Kevin Allen, Norwood Andrews, and Cheryl Wells for their excellent work and to Marna Hostetler of the University of South Carolina's Thomas Cooper Library for her detective work. Particular thanks go to the wonderful people at the Alabama Department of Archives and History in Montgomery and the Georgia Archives in Atlanta.

During the course of researching and writing this book, I've received fabulous support from my department, my university (particular thanks to Gordon Baylis and Harris Pastides in this regard), and a group of first-rate scholars who kindly agreed to read my manuscript. Pete Banner-Haley read carefully and gave really helpful advice. David L. Chappell offered an intelligent, witty, and immensely helpful critique of the manuscript; I am very grateful for his enthusiasm for the project and his counsel. I am also indebted to Jim Cobb, who, in the midst of doing a million other things, paused to read the manuscript, offered wonderful advice, saved me from distortions, and prodded me to think carefully about what I was trying to say. Peter Coclanis must be tired of reading my efforts by now. If he is, he has not let on. His comments are as crisp, helpful, penetrating, and weighty now as they were when I first had the privilege of his judgment more than a decade ago. Stanley Crouch is always busy, but he made time to read my manuscript and offer me some wickedly good advice about the history of U.S. race relations generally and the role of the senses in particular. Paul Gilroy's support for the project was especially important to me. His work has guided a good deal of my thinking on race over the years, and his willingness to read the manuscript and offer encouragement and support—to reassure me that there is worth in this venture—meant a great deal. Grace Elizabeth Hale has been nothing short of a gem. She read my work with extraordinary care and offered me ferociously intelligent insights. Because I wanted a sharp mind with sociological training, I asked Peggy Hargis to give the manuscript the once-over. Peggy knows a great deal about the senses, as well as about sociology and psychology, and her kind remarks on my work were appreciated. Jackie Jones took time to scrutinize the book and the study is better for it. Jackie's ability to see pictures big and small was immensely helpful, and I thank her for her wonderful comments. Peter Wallenstein—busy man that he is—was characteristically thoughtful, helpful, and generous with his time. He read the script with terrific care and helped me clarify at crucial junctures. He has my thanks.

Geri Thoma was central to this book's inception, and I cannot thank her enough for her support. Charles Grench is a remarkable editor with a frighteningly deep store of knowledge. Chuck read the study with sensitive eyes, and I remain deeply grateful for his help. Other people at the University of North Carolina Press also deserve thanks, including Amanda McMillan, who read part of the manuscript; Paul Betz, who did the copyediting; and Kate Torrey, the director of the Press, who came up with the book's title.

I twice presented snippets of this study. The first was before the History Department at the University of Florida in Gainesville. I benefited from excellent questions. I was pleased to meet Brian Ward on that occasion and even more chuffed when he agreed to read the book manuscript. I thank him for his thoughtful comments, encouragement, and generosity. The second presentation was in the form of the Susan H. Cone Family Distinguished Lecture hosted by the History Department of the University of Wyoming. I spoke in Laramie in September 2004, learned a lot from some excellent comments, and reveled in the department's wonderful hospitality.

Have I always made the best of the advice I have courted? Probably not. But I have thought very carefully about what the people who have read this manuscript have said. If I have not always made the best of good counsel, then, plainly, I alone am responsible.

I dedicate this book to four individuals who have, at one point or another, introduced me to new worlds. Tony Kushner of the University of Southampton sparked my interest in "race" years ago. A patient man with a quiet passion and high expectations, Tony always insisted on careful thinking and deep research. I have spent my career trying to live up to his standards, and he influenced me more than he probably realizes. My interest in southern history began when I read Eugene Genovese's *Roll, Jordan, Roll* as an undergraduate student. I still grapple with that book, but I am now privileged to know its author. Over the years, Gene has read a good deal of what I have written, including the present book. His critiques are as thorough, thoughtful, insightful, and unfailingly helpful as any scholar could wish for. For his part, Robert M. Weir introduced me to the University of South Carolina. That introduction ended up changing much more than I could imagine at the time. More than that, though, Rob also introduced me to the supreme importance of imaginative historical inquiry. I remain in his debt. This book is also for Bennett Smith. His introduction was the simplest and most poignant of all. Toward the end of the writing of this book, he chuckled his way into my life. I am thrilled you are here, son.

My final thanks go to Catherine and Sophie for their willingness to let me work on this project and for making my world the sensory delight that it is.

INDEX

Adams, Lionel, 74
African Americans, 3, 30, 36, 72;
  alleged aural acuity of, 23, 43–46;
  alleged odor of, 12–16, 18–19, 24,
  27–28, 30, 36–38, 40–42, 46, 50,
  54, 60, 62, 71, 74, 83, 96–101, 108,
  113, 116–29, 171 (n. 41), 173 (n. 63);
  alleged sexual promiscuity of, 80,
  91, 97, 98, 115, 124, 126; alleged
  visual acuity of, 13, 43–46; compared with animals, 11, 15, 16, 19,
  20, 22, 32–33, 42, 50, 71, 79, 90,
  124, 127, 129; free blacks, 19–20,
  49, 51–54, 107; and self-hatred, 106;
  and voter registration, 117
Africans, 11, 12
Alabama, 24, 116, 117; Council on
  Human Relations, 121
Allen, Carlos H., 127
Allport, Gordon, 137
American Revolution, 19
Aristotle, 11–12
Arkansas, 32, 61; and separate-coach
  bill, 110–11
Athens, Ala., 124
Atlanta, Ga., 65, 69–70, 90, 130
Augusta, Ga., 81
Aurality, 1, 2, 3, 21, 33; and bells, 79;
  and lynching, 59; and serenity, 79;
  and silence, 33; and sounding
  black, 25, 34, 40–41, 50, 79, 97,
  101–3, 152 (n. 8), 164 (n. 6); and
  sounding white, 25–26; sound-
  scapes, 79; as subversive tool, 33–
  34, 48

Baker, Ray Stannard, 69, 90–91
Baker, Robert, 11
Ball, Charles, 32–35
Ball, William Watts, 104
Barnett, Ruth, 137–38
Bates, Ruby, 80
Bell, Laura, 81
Birmingham, Ala., 118, 120, 138–39
Birt, Geoffrey, 119
Black Codes, 51
Blackness, 2, 5, 8, 11, 12, 16, 20, 21,
  42, 43, 44, 61, 65; as essentialist
  construction, 29, 37, 46, 62, 67–68,
  109, 124, 127, 146 (n. 3), 153 (n. 13);
  in twentieth century, 82, 89
Booker, Joseph A., 98–99
Bremer, Fredrika, 22, 39
Brodie, George, 59–60
Brookgreen Gardens (S.C.), 136
Brown, C. F., 112
Brown, Henry Billings, 75
Brown, John, 37
Brown v. Board of Education of Topeka, 3,
  114, 115–39, 190 (n. 54)
Burmeister, Hermann, 38

Cable, George Washington, 56
Carter, Kip, 84
Cartwright, Samuel A., 43–44, 46
Cash, W. J., 4
Catesby, Mark, 14
Catlett, Nannie, 59
Charleston, S.C., 21, 52–53, 110
Charlotte, N.C., 97
Charlottesville, Va., 87

Chesapeake (Va.), 19
Christian, Malcolm Henry, 120
Christianity, 22, 43, 44, 92, 118, 124
Christian Nationalist Crusade, 130
Church, 1, 98
Civil Rights Act of 1875, 55
Civil Rights Movement, 9, 77, 116, 135
Civil War, 6, 20, 48, 49, 55, 56, 58, 68, 97
Clark, Rosetta, 41
Class, 7–8, 92–94, 97–101, 132, 151 (n. 35); and black middle class, 82, 175 (nn. 5, 6); and poor whites, 25–26, 147–48 (n. 15); and working-class activism, 58
Cohn, David L., 77, 79
Columbus, Christopher, 12
Columbus, Miss., 80
Commission on Inter-racial Cooperation, 117
Conrad, David F., 118
Cook, Cecil, 80
Crowding, 54, 59, 62, 116, 126, 130
Cuba, 22
Currie, J. H., 90

Dabney, Wendell Phillips, 112
Daniel, Emitt, 136
David, Nathan, 119
Davis, Allison, 99
Davis, James C., 130–31
Debro, Sarah, 32
Democrats, 38, 111
Desdunes, Daniel, 73
Disease, 63–65, 122, 126, 128; leprosy, 18, 44; tuberculosis, 63–64, 161 (nn. 35, 37); venereal, 64–65
Dixon, Thomas, Jr., 56–58
Dollard, John, 76–77, 78, 79, 80, 82–84, 86, 87, 89, 93, 96, 98, 101
Douglass, Frederick, 33
Du Bois, W. E. B., 9, 59

Duke, Mrs. W. H., 139
Durham, N.C., 137
Durr, Virginia, 119

Eades, Sam, 78
Eaton, Hubert, 83–84, 108
Ebony, 101, 106, 113
Edison, Thomas Alva, 59
Edmonds, Richard W., 138
Edwards, Bryan, 14
Ellis, Havelock, 2
Emancipation, 58
Emotion: anger, 77, 84, 124; in opposition to logic, 2, 4, 47, 56, 115, 137–39
Enlightenment, Age of, 2, 3, 12, 67, 69
Equiano, Olaudah, 30, 32
Ethnology, 41, 43
Evans, Millie, 32
Evergreen, Ala., 125

Federal Writers' Project, 81
Fenner, Charles E., 73
Ferguson, John H., 66, 73
Fields, Mamie Garvin, 102, 110
Fitzhugh, George, 40, 41, 42
Florida, 51, 124, 127, 132
Floyd, Bart, 86
Folsom, James A., Sr., 115, 119, 120, 121, 124, 126, 127, 130, 136
Fort McClellan, Ala., 125
Fort Smith, Ark., 98
Fuller, James Robert, Jr., 122

Galvani, Lella M., 126
Gardner, Burleigh B., 99
Gardner, Mary R., 99
Gates, Henry Louis, Jr., 109
Gender, 9, 62–63
Georgia, 13, 22, 32, 48, 64, 104, 116, 127, 131
Gilmore, James, 26

Gilroy, Paul, 9–10
Glen Allan, Miss., 104
Gliddon, George R., 43
Goldsmith, Oliver, 12–13, 14, 18, 20
Grayson, William J., 27–28, 32
Great Depression, 32, 81, 86, 95
Greenville, Miss., 110
Greenwood, S.C., 78
Griffin, Marvin, 127
Gullendin family, 23

Hammond, James Henry, 40
Haptic. See Touching
Harlan, John Marshall, 67
Heck, Johann Georg, 38
Hoffman, Linda, 109
Holcombe, William H., 44, 46, 47
Holman, Martha, 125
Holmes, George F., 20
Home, Henry. See Lord Kames
Hose, Sam, 60
Howard, Ben, 124
Hundley, D. R., 26–27

Illinois, 120
Immigration, 58
Ingram, W. P., 118

Jackson, John Andrew, 25, 36
Jefferson, Thomas, 16, 43
Jim Crow, 49, 51, 69, 72, 94, 107, 130,
    174 (n. 71)
Johnson, Charles, 104, 107
Johnson, James Weldon, 113
Johnson, Margaret, 81

Kemble, Fanny, 48
King, Edward, 53
Kissing, 19, 133–32
Klineberg, Otto, 82
Knoxville, Tenn., 109
Ku Klux Klan, 86

Labor: domestic, 63–65, 84–85, 89,
    91, 112, 118; industrial, 110; profes-
    sional, 97, 99, 106–7; unskilled, 95
Larsen, Nella, 103
Lee, Reba, 102–3
Leigh, Francis Butler, 48–49
Leigh, James Wentworth, 48
Lewis, Jesse J., 119
Lewis, Julian, 108
Liberals, 117–23, 131
Lieber, Francis, 32
Lincoln, Abraham, 38
Little Rock, Ark., 62
Long, Edward, 14–15, 42
Lord Kames, 14
Louisiana, 22, 63, 66, 137; and Sepa-
    rate Car Act of 1890, 73–74, 112
Lucas, John Gray, 111–12
Lynchburg, Va., 44, 53
Lynching, 58–60, 70–71, 87

Mackay, Charles, 27, 32
Marriage, interracial, 75, 169 (n. 23)
Martinet, Louis A., 72
Maryland, 19, 22, 68
Massachusetts, 73
Matthews, B. T., 136
McLaurin, Melton, 122–23
McPherson, Randolph, 115
Mengels, Eulalia, 127
Meridian, Miss., 90
Miles, William Porcher, 54
Miscegenation. See Sex, interracial
Mississippi, 51, 60, 79, 80, 84, 87, 95,
    138; and Anti-Miscegenation
    Leagues, 90
Mitchell, John, 16, 17
Mobile, Ala., 135
Modernity, 69, 77, 79
Montgomery, Ala., bus boycott, 77–
    78, 119, 121, 124
Moody, Anne, 84, 110

Morlan, George K., 81, 82, 89
Morland, John Kenneth, 93
Moton, Robert, 81, 91

Nashville, Tenn., 70, 126
National Association for the Advancement of Colored People, 117
National Citizens Protective Association, 132
National Lutheran Council, 118
Native Americans: and alleged smell of, 14
New Deal, 117
Newman, Ga., 60
New Orleans, La., 27, 43, 62, 72–73
Newspapers, 62; *Crusader*, 72; Fort Smith *Times*, 61; *New York Evening Post*, 38;
Newton, Isaac, 16
Norfolk, Va., 115
North Carolina, 32, 54, 55, 59, 72, 116; and Native Americans, 14
Northern, William J., 64
Nott, Josiah C., 43, 44

Ocularcentrism. *See* Seeing: privileging of
Odum, Howard, 79
Ohio, 38
Oklahoma, 115, 130
Olfaction. *See* Smelling
One-drop rule, 7, 40, 75, 101
Orangeburg, S.C., 55
Owen, F. C., 137

Parks, Rosa, 78, 104
Passing, 7, 26, 34, 40, 69, 70, 76, 96–106, 165–66 (n. 9), 176 (n. 13), 177 (n. 18)
Penn, W. F., 69
Persons, Gordon, 117, 118, 119, 124, 125, 126, 129, 135, 138

Petersburg, Va., 53
Philadelphia, Pa., 14
Phillips, Wendell, 37
Physicians, 44, 69
Pine Bluff, Ark., 62
Plantations, 22, 24
Plessy, Homer, 66–76
Plessy v. Ferguson, 65, 66–76, 104
Pope, Liston, 92, 94
Populism, 56
Powdermaker, Hortense, 77, 80, 86, 87, 89, 100, 106
Priest, Josiah, 42–43
Pringle, John Julius, 53
Pringle, Mary, 21–22, 52–53
Pringle, Rebecca, 21
Pringle, William Bull, 21
Prothro, E. Terry, 137
Proslavery. *See* Slavery, defense of

Race, 1, 2, 142–43 (n. 5); instability of, 5, 60, 155 (n. 21), 163 (n. 5); mixed-race people, 5, 7, 9, 19, 34, 39, 40, 137; and sensorial intimacy, 50–51. *See also* Marriage, interracial; One-drop rule; Passing; Sex, interracial
Reconstruction, 51, 54, 55, 68, 72–73, 130
Reidsville, N.C., 126
Republicans, 27, 38, 51, 55, 84
Revill, Jane, 130
Rice, 53
Robinson, James, 109–10
Rochon, Victor, 112
Rose, Arnold M., 137
Rubin, Morton, 79, 80, 101, 117
Rush, Benjamin, 17–18, 44
Russell, Willie James, 119

Savannah, Ga., 130
Schmidt, Mrs. John E., 128
Schools: and desegregation, 83

Scottsboro, Ala., 80

Seeing, 1, 2, 33, 35, 40, 42, 76, 144 (n. 6); as detector of race, 61, 96, 102, 106, 146 (n. 12); privileging of, 2–3, 7, 11, 34, 67, 75, 141 (n. 2); as transgressive act, 78

Segregation, 1, 2, 3, 4, 8, 49, 157 (n. 2); defense of, 6, 20, 158–59 (n. 13), 180–81 (n. 3), 188–89 (n. 49); de jure, 55

Sellers, Cleveland, 86, 179 (n. 33)

Senses, 1, 3, 4, 5, 9, 11–12, 21, 40; of blacks, 22, 25, 33, 43, 46–47, 50, 62, 107, 109; cultural functioning of, 20, 29, 98; of nonsoutherners, 27; of whites, 35, 48–49, 57, 76, 95, 101, 103, 116, 123, 139. *See also* Aurality; Emotion; Seeing; Smelling; Tasting; Touching

Separate but equal doctrine, 55, 61, 73

Seward, William, 27

Sex, interracial, 19, 21, 24, 37–39, 50–51, 58–59, 64–65, 68, 77, 82, 90, 99, 148 (n. 16), 154–55 (n. 19), 166 (n. 10)

Seymour, Robert E., Jr., 77

Shivers, Allan, 126

Slavery, 1, 3, 4, 8, 18, 30, 56, 81; and abolition, 21, 37, 39, 59; and "crisis" of 1850s, 29, 39–47; defense of, 6, 40–47; and Middle Passage, 31; and paternalism, 5, 6, 12, 21, 24, 29, 41, 44, 49, 56, 149 (n. 20); and sensory evasion, 34–35; resistance to, 12, 23, 29–30, 34, 39

Smelling, 1, 2, 3, 17, 25, 35; in antebellum period, 5, 11–12; in colonial period, 4, 11; and fragrance, 80–83; in twentieth century, 6, 123. *See also* African Americans: alleged odor of; Whiteness: alleged odor of

Smith, J. H., 99

Smith, Lillian, 92

Smith, Mary, 81

Smyth, J. F. D., 13

South Carolina, 19, 22, 24, 27, 36, 42, 84, 86, 104, 116; and Native Americans, 14

Southern Literary Messenger, 24, 44

Space: black, 50; private, 62; public, 77; white, 50, 61, 85, 130

Spartanburg District, S.C., 41

Spring Hill, Ala., 118

Stanley, Thomas B., 115, 126

Stonewall, Miss., 119

Stoney, Arthur, 131

Sullivan, Ed, 125

Sulton, Leroy "Bunt," 104–6

Sumter, S.C., 130

Swoop, Kathie Rose, 128

Tan Confessions, 106, 108

Tart, Mrs. B. B., 126

Tasting, 1, 3, 21, 23, 41, 42, 43, 50, 123; in antebellum period, 5; in colonial period, 4, 19; and other senses, 88. *See also* Kissing

Taulbert, Clifton, 104, 110

Taylor, Thomas M., 126

Tennessee, 55

Texas, 51, 87, 116, 126

Textile mills, 92–94

Thrasher, Thomas R., 121–22

Touching, 1, 3, 18, 19, 24–25, 50, 130; in antebellum period, 5, 11–12, 23; and black skin, 36, 37, 38, 40–41, 44, 84, 95, 110, 162 (n. 1); in colonial period, 4, 11; and segregation, 86, 123; as white privilege, 60. *See also* Kissing

Tourgée, Albion W., 66, 72–73, 74, 76, 168 (n. 21)

Transportation, 55, 130; via balloons, 68; via railways, 51, 60–63, 66–76,

84, 94, 104, 127, 167 (n. 17); via
streetcars, 77, 81, 91, 102, 110
Truman, Harry S., 117–18

Umstead, William B., 126
U.S. Armed Services, 117–18, 125, 182
(n. 7)
U.S. Congress, 127
U.S. Constitution, 67; Fifteenth
Amendment of, 58; Fourteenth
Amendment of, 55, 58, 66, 75
U.S. Supreme Court, 55, 119, 127, 128;
and *Plessy v. Ferguson*, 66–76
University of South Carolina, 55

Valdosta, Ga., 128
Valentine, William D., 22
Vickers, George, 68
Virginia, 20, 54, 64, 75, 112, 116
Vision. *See* Seeing

Wade, Benjamin, 38–39
Wade, N.C., 121

Waldon, Mrs. Martin, 117
Walker, James C., 72–74
Walter, Mrs. Francis, 118
Ward, Samuel Ringgold, 32
Waring, Waties, 131
Warner, Charles Dudley, 63
Washington, Booker T., 99
Washington, D.C., 39, 119, 130
White, Charles, 13–15, 18, 20
Whiteness, 5, 7, 8, 12, 29, 59, 74, 100,
171–72 (n. 48); alleged odor of, 100,
108, 109; as normative, 46, 94; and
the senses, 30, 32
Williams, Cecil J., 104–6
Wilmington, Mrs. John F., 126
Winnsboro, S.C., 54
Winston-Salem, N.C., 83
Womble, George, 34
World War II, 78, 117
Wright, Richard, 97, 108–9

Yates, Gayle Graham, 95